The Fatal Woman

The Fatal Woman:

Sources of Male Anxiety in American *Film Noir,* 1941–1991

James F. Maxfield

Madison • Teaneck
Fairleigh Dickinson University Press
London: Associated University Presses

Associated University Presses
440 Forsgate Drive
Cranbury, NJ 08512

Associated University Presses
16 Barter Street
London WC1A 2AH, England

Associated University Presses
P.O. Box 338, Port Credit
Mississauga, Ontario
Canada L5G 4L8

The paper used in this publication meets the requirements
of the American National Standard for Permanence of Paper
for Printed Library Materials Z39.48-1984.

Library of Congress Cataloging-in-Publication Data

Maxfield, James F., 1936–
    The fatal woman : sources of male anxiety in American film noir,
1941–1991 / James F. Maxfield.
        p.   cm.
    Includes bibliographical references and index.
    ISBN 0-8386-3662-4 (alk. paper)
    1. Femmes fatales in motion pictures.   2. Film noir—United
States—History and criticism.   I. Title.
PN1995.9.F44M38   1996
791.43'652042—dc20   95-42165
                                                                                          CIP

Contents

Introduction

In my title I have preferred the English phrase "fatal woman" to the more commonly used French phrase *femme fatale*. In normal usage, I believe that a *femme fatale* is typically conceived of as an extremely attractive woman who deliberately tries to lead men to their destruction; she is composed of equal parts of seductive beauty and malice. While certainly many of the leading female characters in the films I have chosen to discuss do qualify as *femmes fatales*, others are more ambiguous or conflicted in their intentions. Evelyn Mulwray in *Chinatown* is almost entirely a victim of her monstrous father Noah Cross, but her ultimate victimization has a devastating effect on the male protagonist of the film Jake Gittes. Judy/Madeleine in Hitchcock's *Vertigo* is used as a tool by Elster in an intricate plot to murder his wife; the destructive effect she has on the hero of the film, Scottie Ferguson, is not something she wills. In allowing Scottie to make her over in the latter part of the movie, Judy seems to be trying to undo the harm she did to him earlier. Yet her attempt at redress culminates only in her own death and the probable psychological destruction of Scottie. Without intending to be *femmes fatales*, Evelyn and Judy nevertheless qualify as a "fatal women" in my terminology because of the extremely destructive effects they have on the male protagonists.

Lilly in *The Grifters* acts as a classic *femme fatale* toward the end of the film when she behaves seductively toward her own son Roy and winds up killing him (whether inadvertently or intentionally is uncertain). But this behavior contrasts sharply with her earlier treatment of Roy when she saved his life by paying for his hospitalization and advised him to abandon his dangerous career as "grifter." While these actions perhaps don't make her any less of a *femme fatale* at the end of the film, they complicate the audience's response to her. She is not the simply evil (perhaps psychopathic) *femme fatale* of 1940s *noir* films, as embodied for instance by Brigid O'Shaughnessy (*Maltese Falcon*), Phyllis Dietrichson (*Double Indemnity*), Helen Grayle (*Murder, My Sweet*). The 1940s films sought to evoke simple responses from their audiences; the films from the '60s and after seek far more complex responses. But in all of them the common linking factor is the threat which a woman (or love object) poses to the life, welfare, or psychological well-being of a male protagonist.

Although my title refers to the "Fatal Woman" as a standard character in American films over a fifty-year period, the full title is intended to suggest that the true theme of these movies could be regarded as "male anxiety over emotional vulnerability." Mary Ann Doane well delineates the psychological significance of the dangerous female character in such films:

> The femme fatale is an articulation of fears surrounding the loss of stability and centrality of the self, the "I," the ego. These anxieties appear quite explicitly in the process of her representation as castration anxiety. . . . The power accorded to the femme fatale is a function of fears linked to the notions of uncontrollable drives, the fading of subjectivity, and the loss of conscious agency. . . . But the femme fatale is situated as evil and is frequently punished or killed. Her textual eradication involves a desperate reassertion of control on the part of the threatened male subject.[1]

The desperate reassertion of male control is particularly apparent in the endings of films like *Double Indemnity* and *Out of the Past* and throughout nearly all of *Point Blank*. (Scottie toward the end of *Vertigo* attempts to reassert control but conspicuously fails to do so.) In all of the films the threat of loss of male control is a major issue. And manhood is chiefly defined in terms of dominance—dominance not only over the seductive female (who threatens to sap the male will) but over competing males as well.

The first and last films studied herein offer extremely opposed treatments of these issues, but confirm the centrality of the theme of male domination (and of the violence of the male response to threats to that dominance). *The Maltese Falcon* (1941) is a largely faithful adaptation of one of the central examples of the genre of "hard boiled" detective fiction. As Frank Krutnik puts it, the "hard-boiled" detective defines himself through proving "his masculine professionalism by outwitting his criminal adversaries, and often by triumphing over the dangers presented by the feminine—not just women in themselves but also any non-'tough' potentiality of his own identity as a man."[2] In the film we see Humphrey Bogart as Sam Spade not only outwitting his criminal adversaries but treating certain of their less 'manly' representatives (Joel Cairo and Wilmer) with maximum brutality. By turning Brigid O'Shaughnessy over to the police as the murderer of his partner, Spade not only resists the threat of female manipulation, he also resists the temptation to be ruled by tender (feminine) emotions rather than strict masculine professionalism. Only the tension apparent in Bogart's delivery of Spade's final lines to Brigid indicates that the character had any real difficulty in resisting the threat of the feminine in this film. Krutnik exaggerates only slightly in saying that "Spade's overcoming of the lure of sexual pleasure is made very easy, for, unlike the heroes of [later *films noirs*], he is never in any real danger of being overwhelmed by his desire for the erotic woman."[3] Although, as I will indicate in my later discussion of the film, Spade's will toward domination is actually quite neurotic, the principle of male dominance is upheld more directly, more positively (other films sustain the principle negatively by displaying the terrible things that happen when a man yields his dominance) in *The Maltese Falcon* than in any other of the films studied herein.

Thelma & Louise (1991) the final film studied, would seem at first to be the opposite of *Maltese Falcon,* in that it is dominated by two strong female characters instead of by a single (virtually) omnipotent male. But even though *Thelma & Louise* presents the feminine perspective far more positively than any of the other of the films in this book, in the end it too upholds the principle of male dominance, on a social if not individual scale. At the end of the film Thelma and Louise choose to die by driving their car off the rim of a canyon rather than turning themselves in to the law enforcement officials who have surrounded them. This decision could be (and has been by a number of critics of the film) taken as a final act of defiance toward the patriarchal culture that has formerly controlled their lives and destinies. But killing themselves is scarcely an effective protest against the patriarchy; rather it is an admission that from the male-dominated legal system they can expect no sympathy for—no acknowledgment of the justice of—Louise's shooting of the would-be rapist of her best friend. Unlike other films in which the *femme fatale* must be killed by the male protagonist to reassert his endangered supremacy, *Thelma & Louise* presents us with two women who kill themselves—implicitly acknowledging their inability to offer effective resistance to patriarchal authority.

The patriarchy is represented in different ways in the films under study in this book, but it is almost invariably present. Humphrey Bogart in the roles of Sam Spade and Philip Marlowe offers the only instances of male protagonists who seem self-sufficient—who are in a sense their own father figures. Most of the other films contain an older male character who represents paternal authority, often of a repressive, exploitative, even brutal nature. Noah Cross in *Chinatown,* the rapist of his own daughter and the murderer of her husband (a sort of surrogate son to him), is the most extreme instance of ruthless, oppressive patriarchal authority, but similar examples can be found in several other films: Fairfax in *Point Blank,* Don Corrado in *Prizzi's Honor,* Giovanni in *Mean Streets,* Bobo in *The Grifters.* (Gutman in *The Maltese Falcon* and Eddie Mars in *The Big Sleep* almost fit into the same category except that the films' protagonists never acknowledge their authority.) Although *Blue Velvet* would seem to offer an at least neutral father figure in Jeffrey's own father and a positive paternal model in Detective Williams, I agree with Laura Mulvey that by far the most vivid father figure of the film is Frank Booth, "the primal father": "Frank is both the sadistic father of the primal scene, and a fearfully erotic father whose homosexual aggression threatens the hero/child with sexual passivity and death."[4] Although Keyes would seem to be a benevolent father figure to Walter Neff in *Double Indemnity*, the faint homosexual undercurrent in his relationship with the younger man perhaps helps to explain why Walter sets himself in opposition to the older man's values. Whit Sterling in *Out of the Past* and Elster in *Vertigo* are about the same ages as the films' protagonists, but their control over and destructive manipulation of Jeff Markham and Scottie Ferguson lend them the status of evil fathers, who moreover control the women who are the objects of their 'sons' oedipal desires. There is one film in which the primary authority acknowledged by the protagonist would seem to be matriarchal. Cody Jarrett in *White Heat* does everything for the sake of his "Ma," but the values she has inculcated into her son are those of her deceased gangster husband so she can hardly be said to represent a purely feminine perspective.

In many of the films the fatal woman is dangerous to the hero precisely because, in order to possess her, he must defy the patriarchy. This conflict with authority is most obvious in the two films with mafia backgrounds. In the end, in a classic conflict between love and duty, Charley Partanna in *Prizzi's Honor* is ordered to kill his own wife Irene by Don Corrado. In a less severe conflict of interest, Charlie in *Mean Streets* is ordered to stay away from his epileptic girlfriend Teresa by his uncle (and local mafia chief) Giovanni. In order to possess the women they desire, Walter in *Double Indemnity* and Jeff in *Out of the Past* must both defy their employers. Scottie's attraction to the false Madeleine is also a betrayal of Elster, who had merely hired the detective to follow the woman and report on her activities. To possess Evelyn Mulwray, Jake Gittes must set himself in opposition to the wealthiest and most powerful man in Los Angeles, Noah Cross (who, according to Evelyn even "owns" the police).

In all of the films, though, the internal conflicts of the male protagonists are ultimately more important than external conflicts with other characters—even with the fatal woman. As Doane argues, the dangerous woman is merely an embodiment of male fears of loss of control, of will, of identity. Both the private detectives and the mafioso adhere to distinctly male codes of honor and to an ideal of masculine toughness. Attraction to a woman threatens one's ability to adhere to the code; it calls forth tender, yielding emotions that undermine toughness. In all of the films the male protagonists seem to have a sense of what their culture expects of them as men, and allowing themselves to be led or manipulated into acting contrary to those expectations is necessarily perceived by them as a significant weakness: it is a violation of what they expect themselves to be, which expectation is based on their understanding of what their culture expects them to be.

The conflict within all the male protagonists is between the desire to adhere to the male code—to the masculine ideal of toughness—and the impulse to give oneself up emotionally, usually for sexual gratification. The "fatal woman" is fatal chiefly to the man's sense of what he is or should be. More than the woman herself, the real threat to the male protagonists is emotional dependency. We see this most obviously in *Point Blank.* Although the hero of the film Walker is betrayed by his wife, this betrayal is less significant than that by his best friend Mal, who almost literally seduced Walker into taking part against his better judgment in an armed heist. Mal's shooting of him immediately after the robbery merely extends Walker's loss of control over his life and destiny that began when he agreed to participate in the crime. Most of the remainder of the film could be interpreted as Walker's dream or fantasy of reasserting his manhood by ruthlessly dominating all those who previously (directly or indirectly) exerted control over him. The rather cryptic ending of the film (in which Walker simply disappears into the shadows of Alcatraz prison where he was shot at the beginning of the film) may simply indicate Walker's recognition of the impossibility of his dream of total control over himself and others. What Walker may realize is what the viewer should realize from any of the films studied in this volume: the male ideal of self-sufficiency is not only impossible to achieve but in many ways self-destructive. The real message of the "fatal woman" films may be that the women are merely catalysts; in the end it is the men who are destructive to themselves.

1

La Belle Dame Sans Merci and the Neurotic Knight: Characterization in The Maltese Falcon

JOHN Huston's extremely successful and enduring adaptation of Dashiell Hammett's *The Maltese Falcon* established a mythic pattern that has been reused with variations since shortly after that film's release and up until the present time. Huston's was actually the third film version of the *Falcon* (the others had been directed by Roy del Ruth in 1931 and by William Dieterle in 1936), but in its visual style and the performances of its cast it proved to be the perfect and indelible incarnation of Hammett's novel—so much so that I for one find it impossible to reread *The Maltese Falcon* and visualize instead of Humphrey Bogart the Sam Spade the author described: "a blond Satan" with a "body like a bear's." Two myths are central to Hammett's book and hence to Huston's film. One is the myth of the Maltese Falcon itself, about which I will say more later in the essay; the other—the one which has had far stronger influence—might be termed the myth of The Tarnished Knight and *La Belle Dame Sans Merci*.

In the medieval legend—as it is adapted, for instance, in Keats's poem—a knight is deflected from his quest by a beautiful woman who lures him to moral and physical destruction. In the Hollywood film genre that has become known as *film noir* the female antagonists quite frequently play the same role in relation to the male protagonists. Whether the male succumbs to this temptation, resists it, or succumbs and then resists largely determines his fate—whether he perishes or not only survives but triumphs. In many *noir* films the hero is a private detective; his quest is for the truth behind mysterious circumstances and for justice. In the 1940s films based on Raymond Chandler's novels (*Murder, My Sweet* and *The Big Sleep*), the detective hero is almost literally an urban knight who has little difficulty resisting the temptations posed by the *femme fatale* in his successful quest for truth and justice; but in the 1947 *Out of the Past* the detective protagonist is seduced by the *femme fatale* and, although he later strives to break free of her influence, is ultimately doomed by his initial fall. At first glance Sam

Spade would seem to belong with the Chandler protagonists as a detective who successfully resists the lure of the evil woman in his pursuit of truth and justice (an impression reinforced by the fact that Humphrey Bogart also played the role of Philip Marlowe in Howard Hawks's *The Big Sleep*); but Hammett's protagonist is far more problematic than Chandler's, and the object of his quest is more difficult to define. Spade insists that Brigid O'Shaughnessy be "sent over" for the murder of his partner Miles Archer; however, a concern for justice is not necessarily his prime motivation for this action. In general, Spade's "quest" is not one sanctioned even by social standards, let alone by religion; it is instead highly personal, egocentric, even neurotic.

Some critics have viewed Sam Spade as a man of honor. Stanley J. Solomon terms *The Maltese Falcon* "a narrative of moral redemption,"[1] redemption which Spade achieves when he turns Brigid over to the authorities:

> The affirmation of his code requires the sacrifice of personal ambition, that is, his love for a woman. Were he to put aside his code at this particular moment of great temptation and choose her, he would really be abandoning his integrity . . . , thus becoming as corrupt as the villains. . . . [2]

In his later book *Beyond Formula* Solomon calls Spade "the most intense preoccupied moralist in all cinema."[3] Thomas Schatz similarly holds that Spade's "hardboiled exterior hides a vulnerable moralist and a man of uncompromising integrity."[4] Moreover, Schatz declares that Spade's adherence to "an outdated value system . . . continually places him at the mercy of manipulative women and cynical greedy villains."[5] Spade is led astray by Brigid's manipulations but finally recognizes her deceptiveness:

> Brigid is the archetypal hardboiled heroine: beautiful, apparently helpless and victimized, drawing the detective into the intrigue and then exploiting his particular talents—and his naive romanticism—in her perverse quest for wealth and power. Spade, after he has become Brigid's lover, realizes that he is simply another of her victims, and none of her entreaties is effective at the end of the film.[6]

The sentimental moralist hiding behind a gruff, hard-boiled exterior—this would be a good description of Chandler's Philip Marlowe, or of Bogart's Rick in *Casablanca*; but it is scarcely applicable to the Sam Spade of either Hammett's novel or Huston's film.

In his Preface to the 1934 Modern Library reprint of *The Maltese Falcon*, Hammett said that Spade was "a dream man" in that he represented what most private detectives would have wished to be: "a hard and shifty fellow, able to take care of himself in any situation, able to get the best of anybody he comes in contact with, whether criminal, innocent bystander or client."[7] Hammett's Spade is no "vulnerable moralist,"[8] motivated by his "hatred of evil";[9] he is a man whose whole life is ruled by an intense competitiveness, which makes it just as important to him to win out over the police—his nominal allies in the war against crime—as over the criminals. He is a prototype of Karen Horney's "arrogant-vindictive" neurotic, who in response to being treated harshly in childhood "has a need to retaliate for all injuries and to prove his superiority to all rivals. . . . He trusts no one, avoids emotional involvement, and seeks to exploit others in order to enhance his own feelings of mastery."[10] Spade triumphs in Hammett's novel and in doing so reinforces his idealized self-image of invulnerability, but his secretary Effie Perine makes a prediction (repeated nearly verbatim in the film) that is likely to prove true sometime: "You always think you know what you're doing, but you're too slick for your own good, and someday you're going to find it out."[11] Huston's script and direction and Bogart's portrayal of Sam Spade rather surprisingly leave the character's personality much as Hammett had developed it in the novel, with little attempt to blunt the sharp edges or reveal a soft inner core beneath the steely surface.

Spade in the film as in the book is never "at the mercy of manipulative women," although he does still have problems with his feelings toward one woman—Brigid—whose manipulations he has seen through from the beginning of the film. Spade's wary gaze toward "Miss Wonderly" (Mary Astor) in the opening scene of the movie prepares us for his declaration the second time he meets her (now calling herself Brigid O'Shaughnessy) that he "didn't exactly believe [her] story."[12] In the same scene he responds to Brigid's plea for his help with the comment, "You won't need much of anybody's help. You're good. It's chiefly your eyes, I think, and that throb you get in your voice when you say things like 'Be generous, Mr. Spade.'" Certainly, if Spade chooses to "help" Brigid, it is for reasons of his own and not because he naively accepts her lies as truth.

In fact, if one pays close attention to Spade's reaction to Miles's death toward the beginning of the film, it becomes apparent that he knows or at least strongly suspects from the outset that Brigid has shot his partner. After police detective Tom Polhaus has briefly told Spade about the circumstances of the murder, he asks if Spade wants to take a closer look at the body. Spade says, "No, you've seen everything I could." The reply indicates his total lack of sentimental attachment to his partner, but it also shows that Spade has already learned enough to know what sort of person must have shot Miles. His partner has been shot from close range right in the heart (in the actual presentation of the shooting in the film the pistol seems to be pointed somewhat lower); Polhaus adds to his initial description that Miles's "gun was still tucked away on his hip. . . . His overcoat was buttoned." This additional information merely con-firms what Spade already knows: that Miles couldn't have been shot by Floyd Thursby, a man the detective would have been far more wary of because "Miss Wonderly" had characterized him as "dangerous." As Spade tells Brigid toward the end of the film:

> Miles . . . had too many years of experience as a detective to be caught like that by a man he was shadowing up a blind alley with his gun in his hip and his overcoat buttoned. But he would have gone up there with you, angel. . . . And then you could have stood as close to him as you liked in the dark. And put a hole through him with a gun you got from Thursby that evening.

Although both Brigid and the viewer (initially) are likely to be surprised by Spade's interpretation of the events, it is clear that he must have formulated it long before he reveals it to us. Probably he was reasonably certain Brigid had to be the killer when he tried to call her at her hotel just after he talked to Tom Polhaus at the scene of the murder. When Brigid contacts Spade the following day, she thinks she is using him to protect her from Gutman et al.; but actually Spade is stringing her along to get at the underlying reasons why the murders of Miles and Thursby have occurred. Although Brigid believes she is manipulating Spade, he is actually manipulating her.

The movie's Samuel Spade, like the book's, is a hard man. He seems at times more directly motivated by greed and sadism than by a disinter-ested concern for truth and justice. Money is certainly one of the things that makes Spade's world go round. When "Miss Wonderly" initially retains the services of Spade and Archer, Spade simply stares coldly when she hands over a bill and asks, "Will that be enough?" Then he breaks into smiles when she adds additional money. On the following day, when Brigid reveals her true identity and pleads for Spade's help, he denies her request until she turns over to him the only money she has—$500—although he does give back an unspecified but undoubtedly small portion of that cash before parting from her. When Joel Cairo (Peter Lorre) offering Spade a retainer, asks, "Er, you will take, say, one hundred dollars?"—the detective replies, "No. I will take, say, two hundred dollars." And Spade bargains continually with Gutman (Sydney Greenstreet) over how much money he (Spade) should be paid for plac-ing the Falcon in the fat man's hands. Even when the Falcon turns out to be a fake, Spade wants to retain his $10,000 finder's fee on the grounds that: "I held up my end. You got your dingus. It's your hard luck not mine, it wasn't what you wanted." And he keeps $1000 for his "time and expenses" when Gutman pulls a pistol to reinforce his request for the return of the envelope of money.

It could of course be argued that Spade's apparent greed is merely a pose—a performance designed to convince Gutman, Cairo, and Brigid of his essential dishonesty so that they will not realize he intends to bring them to justice for their crimes. At the end he tells Brigid, "Don't be too sure I'm as crooked as I'm supposed to be." But the reasons he gives for why he might feign dishonesty scarcely clear him of a charge of avarice: "That sort of reputation might be good business—*bringing high-priced jobs* and making it easier to deal with the enemy . . ." (italics added). Solomon claims that Spade's turning Gutman's thousand dollar bill over to the police at the end of the film "is a token of moral affirmation",[13] but it is hardly that. It is merely the price Spade is willing to pay in order to triumph over the policeman Dundy who had punched him in the jaw earlier in the film. After he hands Tom Polhaus the "thousand dollar bill I was supposed to be bribed with," Spade glances over toward Dundy and asks, "What's the matter with your little playmate? He looks broken-hearted. I bet when he heard Gutman's story, he thought he had me." Giving back this fee enables Spade to gloat over the discomfiture of an enemy; it is certainly not a case of his wanting nothing to do with filthy lucre deriving from immoral sources. There is no indication that Spade ever considers returning the "retainers" he had more or less extorted from Brigid and Cairo.

It is important to Spade to achieve dominance over almost everyone he comes in contact with (Effie Perine and Tom Polhaus are partial exceptions, but only because they already acknowledge his authority). Even before he exposes her as a murderess, Spade rarely lets slip an opportunity to let Brigid know he sees through her lies and manipulations. In his first meeting with Joel Cairo, Spade disarms him with one hand, then smiles triumphantly at him for several seconds before quite deliberately knocking him out. (Throughout the scene Spade keeps a lighted cigarette steady between his lips.) Later when Spade breaks up a fight between Brigid and Joel, he slaps the man again. Joel declares indignantly, "This is the second time that you laid hands on me!" Spade replies, "When you're slapped you'll take it and like it"—and promptly and viciously slaps Joel again on both sides of his face. Spade is also consistently sadistic toward Gutman's "gunsel" Wilmer (Elisha Cook, Jr.). He assaults Wilmer verbally ("The cheaper the crook, the gaudier the patter, huh?"), disarms him just before they enter Gutman's hotel suite ("This'll put you in solid with your boss."), and proposes him as the "fall guy" for the murders of Thursby and Jacoby (killings Wilmer has actually carried out under Gutman's orders). Finally he knocks Wilmer out while the boy's arms are being held by Cairo and Gutman.

Spade doesn't succeed in gaining the same degree of mastery over the suave Gutman, who indeed scores heavily against the detective by drugging his drink and later arranging to have Brigid send him off on a wild goose chase to Burlingame. But Spade himself scores by feigning violent indignation when Gutman won't tell him about the "black bird" in their first interview, by talking the fat man out of torturing him to force him to reveal where the falcon is hidden, by getting Gutman to explain the circumstances surrounding the murders of Thursby and Jacoby, by exposing his adversary's palming of the thousand dollar bill from the envelope, and finally by collecting his thousand dollars for "time and expenses" while a gun is pointed at him. In the end Gutman is forced to pay tribute to Spade:" . . . you're a man of nice judgment and many resources." But their ongoing verbal duel would basically end in a draw except for the final advantage Spade gains by turning Gutman over to the police.

Because of the drive for dominance he demonstrates with other characters, one might take the view that in his final conversation with Brigid, Spade is merely toying sadistically with the woman. Certainly it is unlikely that Spade really means it when he says that he will be "waiting for" Brigid when she gets "out of Tehachapi in twenty years"; and he seems similarly mocking when adds, "If they hang you, I'll always remember you." Julie Kirgo strongly doubts Solomon's view that Spade makes a genuine "sacrifice" in renouncing "his love for" Brigid; she takes the view that no such love exists on the part of either of these characters: "Ostensibly, we should feel sympathy for Spade, forced to make a painful decision between justice and love. But it all rings false as there have been no intimations of anything like love between Spade and Brigid, who are two manipulators par excellence."[14]

I have already indicated my agreement with Kirgo's characterization of Sam and Brigid as "manipulators," but the question remains for me whether manipulators are necessarily incapable of love. The answer of course depends upon the definition of "love": if it includes a willingness to sacrifice one's own desires and interests for the sake of the beloved, then it truly seems doubtful that either of the characters is capable of love in this sense. But if love is defined simply as an intense sexual attraction, it definitely seems to exist on Spade's part and perhaps on Brigid's as well. And Spade unquestionably is giving up something part of him craves when he decides Brigid must take the fall.

From a moral perspective Brigid, of course, is totally unworthy of a man's love, no matter how the word might be defined. She is the prototype of the evil heroines of film noir: "[t]he dark lady, the spider woman, the evil seductress who tempts man and brings about his destruction."[15] Her murder of Miles Archer was a totally ruthless act. Not only had

Miles done nothing to harm her, but neither apparently had Floyd Thursby the man she sought to pin the killing on. At one point she implies to Spade that Thursby had betrayed her; she says a man of Thursby's "sort could have helped me, if he'd been loyal." But Gutman later says that Thursby "was quite determinedly loyal to Miss O'Shaughnessy"—so much so that he refused to make any kind of deal with the fat man, who then ordered Wilmer to shoot him. Brigid's only possible motive for framing Thursby, therefore, was to eliminate from the picture someone who would have insisted on sharing the proceeds to be raised from the falcon. When Brigid is off in Spade's kitchen filling the classic female role of making coffee, Gutman gives the detective a bit of friendly advice: "I dare say you're going to give her some money, but if you don't give her as much as she thinks she ought to have, my word of advice is, be careful." Spade glances toward the kitchen, then asks Gutman, "Dangerous?" The fat man's reply is "Very." While Gutman might just as well have supplied the same kind of warning about himself, it is significant that Brigid is regarded as dangerous even by those who are dangerous themselves.

Spade, to be sure, is also rather dangerous. This quality is repeatedly acknowledged by Brigid through the adjectives she applies to him: "wild" and "unpredictable." Toward the end he tells Brigid, "You never played square with me for half an hour at a stretch since I've known yuh!" But she could easily say the same to him (and more or less does when she complains, "You've been playing with me; just pretending you cared, to trap me like this"). Spade is attracted to Brigid not only because she is a beautiful woman but also because she is a dark mirror image of himself. She too doesn't want anyone to get the better of her. She will employ the most effective devices at her disposal to seek money and control over others. With most males her most powerful tool is her sexual attractiveness, but with the homosexual Joel Cairo she strikes blows with both her hands and a pistol barrel. The scene in which Brigid starts to rough up Cairo and then Spade finishes the job indicates just how similar the detective and the murderess are in their basic impulses.

In killing Miles, Brigid has also done something that Spade wanted to have done. He clearly didn't like Miles, as evidenced by his response to Tom Polhaus's question: "Miles had his faults . . . , but I guess he must o' had some good points too, huh?" Spade's answer as he walks away is a not even lukewarm "I guess so." The day immediately after his partner's death Spade asks Effie to "have Miles' desk moved out of the office" and his name taken off the doors and windows. His affair with Miles's wife Iva is not so much an additional reason why he would desire his partner's death (he clearly shows no interest in linking his life to this woman) as another indication of how much he disliked the man.

The affair must have primarily been a way of getting back at or triumphing over Miles, even if he never found out about it. In removing Miles from the scene, Brigid has basically done Samuel Spade a favor and perhaps enacted one of his own desires.

If this is so, why should he deem it necessary to turn her over to the police? At one point when he is forcing her to confess, Spade exclaims, "We're both of us sitting under the gallows!" But this statement is only comprehensible as an expression of Spade's guilt for having desired his partner's death. Neither Spade nor Brigid is at the moment in danger of being suspected of Miles's murder by the police, who already have a "fall guy" for that killing in the person of Floyd Thursby, who can't even defend himself. The apprehension of Wilmer and Gutman for the murders of Thursby and Jacoby could have cleared the slate for the authorities.

Admittedly the question I asked at the beginning of the preceding paragraph is one that is not likely to occur to most viewers of *The Maltese Falcon*. In American detective films we expect the police or the private eye to bring the murderer to justice in one way or another (prison or death). If Spade had let Brigid go, the shock to the audience would have been so great as to limit the film's box office success. (And of course in 1941 the Hays Office would never have permitted an ending in which a criminal escaped punishment—just as it did not permit Huston to make clear, as Hammett had, that Brigid spent the night in bed with Spade after the set-to with Cairo and the police.) The *Falcon* is a highly unusual film in that Spade has to give reasons to Brigid to explain why he must turn her over to the police instead of simply assuming this is the only proper and natural thing to do. The cumulative effect of the reasons Spade gives should demonstrate to a thoughtful viewer of the film that the detective's decision is not fundamentally governed by conventional ethics. The reasons he gives to Brigid can be grouped into three basic categories: the professional, the pragmatic, and the psychological.

Solomon declares that Spade's "chief reason"[16] for turning Brigid over is indicated by his statement, "When a man's partner's killed, he's supposed to do something about it." The statement in itself is interesting in that Spade has replaced a concern for universal ethics (murder is a crime that must be punished) with a declaration of professional ethics (a private detective is expected to avenge the death of a partner). His concern for the welfare of other people seemingly extends only to other members of his profession:" . . . when one of your organization gets killed, it's bad business to let the killer get away with it; bad all around; bad for every detective everywhere." (The phrase "bad business" is also ambiguous in that it could refer to the financial interests of the organization: would people want to employ an agency that couldn't even protect its own operatives?) In reality, of course, Spade's ethical concerns seem to be broader than he admits since he has arranged for the police to arrest Gutman and Wilmer for their murders of the non-detectives Thursby and Jacoby, but here he is trying to convince Brigid (and perhaps himself) that his professional honor requires him to ensure that she is arrested and tried for Miles's murder.

Brigid is not impressed by these arguments: "You can't expect me to think that these things you're saying are sufficient reasons for sending me to the. . . ." Spade, therefore, switches to more pragmatic grounds when he says, "I've no earthly reason to think I can trust you. . . . Since I've got something on you, I couldn't be sure that you wouldn't put a hole in me some day." This at least is an argument she can understand better than his concern for professional ethics. But is either one of these arguments the primary reason why Spade has to turn Brigid over to the police? I think not.

A far stronger motivation is revealed in two declarations that Spade makes to Brigid, one before and one after his enumeration of professional and practical reasons. He first tells Brigid succinctly, "I won't play the sap for you!" Later he elaborates on the idea as follows: "I won't [let you go free] because all of me wants to, regardless of consequences, and because you've counted on that with me, the same as you counted on that with all the others." The chief reason Spade must turn Brigid in is that he fears she will dominate him by means of her sexual desirability—that she will reduce him to the same level as Thursby, Jacoby, and Miles, who all played the sap for her. She implies that if Spade really loved her, he wouldn't consider turning her in to the police; but for Spade it is precisely because he loves her—or at least desires her so fervently that he *wants* to help her escape punishment—that he must turn her in. It is not Brigid herself who threatens Spade so much as it his "love" for her. This love makes him vulnerable; it threatens the dominance he strives to achieve in each and every one of his personal relationships. Spade must make sure that Brigid takes "the fall" because if she doesn't, he will experience a fall from dominant self-sufficiency to submissive dependency.

Perhaps more clearly than later films *The Maltese Falcon* reveals what the mythic figure of the *femme noire* represents. In America, as in most countries of the world, the predominance of power—social, political, economic—resides with men. The *femme noire*, then, is the archetype of the subversive female. In the absence of social, political, or economic means of control she strives to rule men through their emotions. Men typically will do things for women they desire sexually. The great fear which this film and nearly all of *film noir* expresses is that men can be led by female seduction to act so contrary to their self interests that they allow themselves to be destroyed.

In *The Maltese Falcon* Kasper Gutman and Brigid O'Shaughnessy basically desire the same thing: the legendary Maltese Falcon and the enormous wealth that can be gained from possession of it. A well-to-do man, Gutman can hire people to assist him in his quest for the falcon; he can even order Wilmer to kill others who obstruct the quest. A comparatively poor woman, Brigid must use her seductive wiles to acquire a well-armed protector in the person of Floyd Thursby. Then, when she comes to perceive Thursby not as her protector but as an unwelcome potential sharer of the proceeds to be raised from the Falcon, she uses her charms (plus one of Thursby's pistols) on Miles Archer as an indirect means of ridding herself of her partner. The unexpected appearance of Cairo and Gutman makes her turn to Spade as a replacement for Thursby. When the detective complains to her, "Haven't you tried to buy my loyalty with money and nothing else?"—Brigid simply asks, "What else is there I can buy you with?" As she must have expected, Spade answers the question by kissing her. Sexual allure is Brigid's currency.

In the end Spade refuses to be brought. Is he truly the knight who cannot be deflected from his quest by *la belle dame san merci?* Actually it would seem there is no genuine knight figure in the film, although Gutman is a parody knight. It is Gutman who has the strongest sense of a quest within the film, the Falcon being for him the secular equivalent of the Holy Grail. After his initial disappointment upon discovering that the falcon in his hands is merely lead beneath its black enamel coating, Gutman is quite content to set off once more for Istanbul to "spend another year on the quest." One actually gets the impression that it is the pursuit of the Falcon that has given Gutman's life meaning, and disenchantment would quickly set in if he truly did obtain the jewel-encrusted gold statuette, no matter how much money he might gain from its sale. The movie version of the *Falcon* leaves Gutman still a potentially happy man in that he will be able to continue to dream of the Falcon in prison. (Hammett was less generous to the fat man, allowing Wilmer to shoot him before the police could get to them.)

Lawrence Benaquist tries to make a comparison between the Falcon and Brigid O'Shaughnessy: ". . . they are both objects of a quest, objects which ultimately display nothing of value."[17] But Brigid is actually not in any sense an object of Spade's quest. Frank Krutnik is correct in stating that Spade "is never in any real danger of being overwhelmed by his desire for the erotic woman. Brigid never poses any real threat to his rationality, his control or his phallic self-containment."[18] As I have argued above, Spade seems to realize from very early in the film that Brigid has shot his partner. While he may be strongly enough attracted to her to go to bed with her (a scene the viewer has to imagine taking place off screen in the film), in the book he got up early the next morning and went off to search her apartment (a scene that may have originally been in the movie—as it was in Roy del Ruth's 1931 version— because the day after the wrangle with Cairo and the police Brigid rushes into Spade's office to tell him, "Somebody's been in my apartment! It's all upside down."). Spade definitely does desire Brigid, but he is resolute in refusing to invest any transcendent value in her.

If Spade does have a quest, it is not for Brigid or the Falcon (although it, like Brigid, does tempt him: his eyes light up with eagerness when Gutman is unwrapping the bird) or even justice; it is simply for dominance over all the men and women with whom he comes in contact. Although most critics of *The Maltese Falcon* film seem to have ignored the fact, Bogart's portrayal of Spade displays quite clearly the neurotic compulsiveness of the character. Virginia Wright Wexman has cited numerous examples of the "obsessive gestures, protective of the self, hostile toward others" that Bogart employs in the film.[19] Although Spade triumphs in the movie, his is the triumph of an essentially disturbed man.

In one of the rare lines that Huston added to Hammett's original dialogue, Spade responds to Tom Polhaus's question about the falcon— "What is it?"—with the phrase, "The, er, stuff that dreams are made of." These dreams, needless to say, are not a positive influence on the characters of the film. Spade's own dreams of dominance and self-sufficiency are—unlike those of Brigid, Gutman, and Cairo—largely fulfilled. But when at the end of the film Spade stands holding the Falcon and staring at Brigid as she is about to descend in the elevator with the policeman (the despair of her expression intensified by the shadow of the elevator grill that passes directly through one of her eyes), his own expression shows the loss he feels. In order to maintain his dream of dominance he has had to suppress the emotions that would make him vulnerable to the manipulations of others, but in stifling such emotions Spade has had to deny a significant portion of his own being (which he himself refers to as "all of me" when he speaks of the part of him that desires Brigid). When Spade descends the stairs clutching the falcon, he could be carrying the symbol of his own cold, hard, heavy, and ultimately valueless dream.

2

Something Loose in the Heart:
Wilder's *Double Indemnity*

IF Huston's *The Maltese Falcon* (1941) established the basic plot motifs of *film noir*—the evil seductress, the tempted hero, an atmosphere of pervasive evil—*Double Indemnity* and *Murder, My Sweet* (both 1944) provided models for the visual style of the genre: expressionist lighting (dark shadows, sometimes with strongly contrasting highlighted areas), many night scenes, confined settings, tight close-ups, high angle shots which diminish the stature of the characters. Huston's film employs such techniques far more selectively, with a majority of its scenes being brightly and evenly lit—an appropriate analogue to Hammett's simple, highly objective prose style. A pervasive distortion of normal camera angles can be found in the preponderance of below eye-level shots, which may create the subconscious impression in the viewer that the characters in the film are larger than life—perhaps legendary like the story of the Falcon itself. For the most part, though, Huston's camera techniques do not pass moral judgments, whereas in *Double Indemnity* and *Murder, My Sweet* the physically dark, high angle shots of the films' openings clearly signal a descent into evil; and dark shadows and night scenes are similarly suggestive throughout.

Huston's film as a whole also refrains from judging its protagonist— the reason why one critic can see Spade as "a vulnerable moralist and a man of uncompromising integrity"[1] and another claims that he is "petty" and "sadistic . . . only a few steps away from the psychopathic."[2] *Double Indemnity* and *Murder, My Sweet*, on the other hand, are unambiguous in their verdicts on the protagonists: Walter Neff (Fred MacMurray) recognizes evil when he sees it, but still succumbs to it; Philip Marlowe (Dick Powell) has to work harder to achieve his perception of evil, but when he does has no trouble rejecting it The two films thus represent the extremes of *film noir*: the *noir* that ends in the total darkness of death for the fallen protagonist and the *noir* that ends in the restoration of light through the hero's triumph over the forces of darkness. (Actually the hero of *Murder, My Sweet* is literally left in the

26

dark—since he is temporarily blinded at the end of the film—but all the sources of evil have been eliminated.)

Unlike *The Maltese Falcon*, which stuck quite close to the original plot and dialogue of Hammett's novel, the film *Double Indemnity* deviates considerably from its source, the short novel of the same name by James M. Cain. The scriptwriters, the director Billy Wilder and novelist Raymond Chandler, considerably expanded the role of Barton Keyes, the claims investigator; changed the character of Phyllis from a mentally unstable, death-obsessed woman in Cain's novel ("'I think of myself as Death, sometimes. In a scarlet shroud, floating through the night. I'm so beautiful, then. And sad.'"[3]) to a cold-hearted manipulative bitch; totally altered the conclusion of the story, and were responsible for much of the racy, idiomatic dialogue. The consequence of the changes *in toto* is to convert Cain's story of a man doomed by his involvement with an insane woman to that of a man largely destroyed by his own psychological obsessions.

Double Indemnity opens with a car driving erratically on the night streets of Los Angeles: the car passes through a red light and barely avoids colliding with a newspaper truck. The physical action suggests moral implications. The car presumably has brakes, but the driver doesn't bother to use them. In the same manner Walter Neff knows that Phyllis Dietrichson (Barbara Stanwyck) is evil and that murder is a heinous act, but he puts up only minimal resistance to her idea that her husband be insured without his knowledge so that he can be killed for the policy's benefits. As Neff says, "I fought it [the idea of murder], only I guess I didn't fight it hard enough." Indeed, he soon goes beyond Phyllis's original proposition and concocts a scheme wherein her husband will seem to meet his accidental death on a train, thereby invoking the policy's double indemnity clause and requiring it to pay $100,000 instead of $50,000. Neff has more than one reason for involving himself in this plot, but certainly a strong motive is his sexual attraction to Phyllis, which she humorously describes with a driving metaphor in their first meeting. After he makes a mild verbal pass, the following exchange takes place:

> *Phyllis.* There's a speed limit in this state, Mr. Neff. Forty-five miles an hour.
> *Neff.* How fast was I going, officer?
> *Phyllis.* I'd say around ninety.

This dialogue adds another level of meaning to Neff's wild driving in the opening sequence of the film: it is simply an extension of the recklessness manifested in the earlier scene with Phyllis.

A remark by the elevator operator when he is taking Neff up to his office in the Pacific Building also has application to Walter's moral character. The operator says that he couldn't be insured because "They said I had something loose in my heart." Walter also has something loose in his heart: he has emotions that he has been unable to control, emotions that have indeed dominated him and driven him inexorably to his doom.

When Neff starts telling his story into the dictaphone, he tells Keyes, "I suppose you'll call this a confession when you hear it. Well, I don't like the word 'confession.' I just want to set you right about something you couldn't see. . . ." But Neff is also telling his story to himself, perhaps trying to understand how he could have committed the crimes he has. If the latter is truly the case, both Walter and the viewer probably fall somewhere short of full comprehension. As Walter initially explains it, his motives for committing murder were simple: "I killed Dietrich-son. . . . I killed him for money—and a woman. I didn't get the money, and I didn't get the woman." But Walter should have known from the beginning that he couldn't truly "get the woman" because he could only gain her if she freely gave herself to him—an action obviously foreign to the nature of an inveterate manipulator like Phyllis. With his expert, insider knowledge of the insurance business, Neff probably did think he had at least a good chance of deceiving the Pacific All-Risk Company and getting it to pay off the double indemnity policy. But what did Walter want the money for? Curiously absent from the film are any plans or fantasies on Walter's part about how he will spend his share of the proceeds from the faked accidental death. Walter does want to get the better of—or at least *test*—his company and its ace claims investigator Barton Keyes (Edward G. Robinson), but it is unlikely that his deepest, underlying motivation is either the woman or the money.

Walter Neff's flashback begins with three major scenes: two with Phyllis in her house and, sandwiched in between, one with Keyes in his office. The scene with Keyes at first seems intended merely to introduce the third major character in the film, but in reality it provides an unconscious motivation for decisions that Neff makes shortly thereafter. When Neff enters Keyes's office, the older man is chewing out Sam Gorlopis (described in Wilder and Chandler's script as "a big, dumb bruiser"[4]), accusing him of having set fire to his own truck in order to collect the insurance money. Keyes so completely intimidates Gorlopis that by the end of the interview the burly truck driver is reduced to the mental state of a small child. The final bit of dialogue between the two characters goes like this:

Keyes. What's the matter, Gorlopis? Don't know how to open the door? Just put your hand on the knob, turn it to the left, now pull it toward you—

[*Gorlopis smiles childishly as he pulls open the door.*]
Keyes. That's the boy.
Gorlopis. Thank you, Mr. Keyes.

This scene that Neff has witnessed has both a short-term, then longer-term effect on him.

When he next visits Phyllis Dietrichson at her house, he reacts indignantly when he realizes that she wants to take out an accident policy on her husband without his knowledge:

> *Neff.* What did you think I was, anyway? A guy that walks into a good-looking dame's front parlor and says "Good afternoon, I sell accident insurance on husbands. You got one that's been around too long? One you'd like to turn into a little hard cash? Just give me a smile and I'll help you collect." Boy, what a dope you must think I am!

But what offends Neff almost as much as her apparent low opinion of his intelligence is that Phyllis's scheme to defraud Pacific All-Risk Insurance is no more sophisticated than Gorlopis's. When in the following scene at his apartment she mentions a means by which her husband might seem to die accidentally (of carbon monoxide poisoning in the garage), Neff tells her,

> We've got a guy in our office named Keyes. For him a set-up like that would be just like a slice of rare roast beef. In three minutes he'd know it wasn't an accident. In ten minutes you'd be sitting under the hot lights. In a half hour you'd be signing your name to a confession.

In other words, Walter imagines Phyllis standing up to Keyes no better than Gorlopis had. But slowly bubbling up to the surface of his mind is the thought that he, "Walter Neff, insurance agent," could stand up to Keyes—could commit murder, make it look like an accident, allow Phyllis to collect $100,000 (which she would then split with him), and *not be caught.* He would not allow Keyes to reduce him to the level of a child, as had been the case with Gorlopis. He would be man enough to hold his own against Keyes's "little man" (the claims man's detective intuition).

Billy Wilder, the director and co-author of the film, has described its basic subject matter this way: "The idea was to write a love story between the two men and a sexual involvement with the woman. . . ."[5] He indicates that the emotional center of the film is the relationship between Walter Neff and Barton Keyes. Although the film devotes more time to the relationship between Walter and Phyllis, it is secondary to that between the two men. It could be argued that Walter helps Phyllis free herself from a burdensome relationship with an older man in an attempt to resolve his own relationship with an older man, Keyes. As Claire Johnston asserts, the Oedipus Complex is at "the centre of the enigma" of this film.[6] Phyllis stands for the desired mother, Dietrichson for the father as object of the son's jealous aggression, Keyes for the father as authority figure and potential punisher of the son's transgression.

If the Oedipal aspect of the film is ignored, the plot line of *Double Indemnity* is singularly lacking in complexity (although not necessarily uninteresting). Barbara Stanwyck's Phyllis Dietrichson is an extremely obvious *femme fatale,* possessing none of the deceptive innocence or vulnerability of Mary Astor's Brigid O'Shaughnessy. She flirts brazenly with Walter when they first meet, is totally unsubtle at their second meeting about introducing the idea of insuring her husband without his knowledge, and pursues the idea with equal obviousness when she comes uninvited to Neff's apartment. While Walter kills her husband, she stares unflinchingly ahead and continues to drive straight down the street. Nor does she manifest any apparent remorse after the murder (as Walter says, she displays "no nerves, not a tear, not even a blink of the eyes"). She could very well have the title "Evil Woman" engraved on her anklet; in any case, the label is apparent in nearly all of her behavior, and Walter Neff is able to read it quite early in the film.

Walter himself seems to suffer little from the kind of internal conflict that Sam Spade reveals toward the end of *The Maltese Falcon.* Part of Spade is intensely attracted to Brigid, but his professionalism and egoism enable him to resist her lure. In keeping with the first word of its title, Wilder's film splits Spade into two characters, each embodying one side of the conflict. Although he can perceive Phyllis's evil nature as clearly as any viewer of the film, Neff still wants her—apparently from the first moment he sees the gold anklet on her bare leg—and he is willing to commit murder in the attempt to gain her. The man dominated by his professionalism is Keyes, who has apparently sacrificed everything to his investigative instinct ("the little man"), including the woman he wanted to marry (until he investigated her and found she was—in Walter's phrase—"a tramp from a long line of tramps"). The contrast between Neff and Keyes would at first glance seem to be nearly absolute: the man who sacrifices his professional instincts and honor to his emotional desires and the man who does exactly the opposite. But underneath both are driven by emotions they seem to be only dimly recognizing by the end of the film.

Neff's attraction to Phyllis should be puzzling to any viewer who stops to think about it. Their banter in the opening scene at her house gives clear signals of sexual attraction on both of their parts, but it is the kind of conversation that takes place in a bar before a one-night stand. Why should Walter take Phyllis any more seriously than he would such a pick-up? She reveals an unexpected side to her personality in the second meeting with him, but her obvious desire to murder her husband for insurance money should drive any normal man away from her permanently not just temporarily as it does Walter. In her third scene with Walter, after she comes to his apartment, Phyllis does for the first time open up emotionally, but only to the extent of openly revealing her hatred of her husband. This scene is divided in two by a dissolve away from the couple sitting together on Neff's couch to Walter dictating his story in his office before returning to the couple on the couch. The viewer may assume, as Claire Johnston appears to,[7] that Walter and Phyllis have had sexual intercourse while the camera was back at the office, but Neff's voice-over specifically states, ". . . we just sat there. . . ." No conclusive evidence is presented in the film that Walter and Phyllis ever experience literal sexual consummation together.

What attracts Walter to Phyllis? When he refers to his attraction, he doesn't speak of such sexual attributes as breasts, legs, buttocks, face, or hair—instead he focuses on one small fetishistic detail: ". . . I kept thinking about Phyllis Dietrichson, and the way that anklet of hers cut into her leg." Why does the anklet so obsess him? For one thing it is a "gold" anklet.[8] Part of the promise of Phyllis Dietrichson is the promise of wealth: the $50,000 Walter hopes to clear from murdering her husband. But he is also lured by the way the anklet apparently "cuts into" her flesh. The anklet additionally seems to be a symbol of bondage and pain. Initially it may suggest to Walter the flattering thought of Phyllis as his sex slave, but it must quickly become apparent that in any intimate relationship between them he will be as painfully bound to her as she to him. Both sadism and masochism play a part in Neff's obsession with this woman.

When Lola, Dietrichson's daughter, reveals to Neff that Phyllis murdered Dietrichson's first wife before marrying him, the news probably comes as more of surprise to Walter than to most viewers; for by then Phyllis has clearly demonstrated her ruthless nature in her totally remorseless reaction to her husband's murder. Lola later tells Neff that her former boyfriend Nino Zachette is "at [Phyllis's] house, night after night"—a fact confirmed by Keyes's confidential report, which Walter listens to on the claims man's dictaphone machine. Neff draws the logical conclusion: that Phyllis is vamping Nino to get him to kill her accomplice in the murder of her husband. He at that points plots to kill Phyllis and pin the murder on Nino, who is Keyes's prime suspect as Phyllis's accessory. But by killing Phyllis, Neff is giving up both of the things for which he said he committed the crime: the woman and the money (Phyllis can't collect the insurance if dead).

Neff thinks he is giving up these things in a last desperate attempt to save his own skin, but an examination of his behavior in the final scene with Phyllis reveals even that is not true. He makes his intention to kill Phyllis blatantly obvious to her when he responds to her threat to "talk" and thereby reveal his part in the murder by telling her,

> Sometimes people are where they can't talk. Under six feet of dirt, maybe. And if it was you, they'd charge that up to Zachette, wouldn't they? . . . Sure they would. And that's just what's going to happen, Baby.

He then turns his back on her, giving her ample opportunity to pull her gun and shoot him in the back. When the shot merely wounds him in the shoulder, he takes a couple of steps toward her and asks. "What's the matter? You can do better than that, can't you, Baby? Better try it again. Maybe if I came a little closer?" Only after giving her one chance after another to end his life, does Walter take the pistol from Phyllis and kill her with it in their final embrace. His behavior in this scene is less that of a man trying to save himself than of a man seeking his own doom.

Indeed Walter's whole participation with Phyllis in the murder of her husband seems ultimately to be for him merely a convoluted method of committing suicide. He is seeking death to escape from emotions he not only can't come to terms with, but isn't even willing to recognize. These emotions can be better understood by examining Keyes who is the source of them. Although he probably doesn't consciously recognize the fact (and the authors of the script may not have either), Keyes has a deep homosexual attachment to Walter Neff. Keyes's feelings are symbolically revealed in the motif of his requiring Walter to light his cigars for him. While Freud did say that sometimes a cigar is just a cigar, in the context of this film it is quite plausible to regard Keyes's cigars as phallic symbols.[9] Keyes's dependency on Neff to strike the matches to light his cigars— to enable him to derive the satisfaction of being able to smoke them— reveals his subconscious desire to have the younger man satisfy him sexually. When Walter points out to Keyes that he could easily obtain his own matches ("They give you matches when you buy your cigars, you know. All you have to do is ask for them"), the older man's reply also lends itself to symbolic interpretation. Keyes says, "Don't like them. They always explode in my pocket." Keyes is afraid of his desires, afraid they might burst out uncontrollably and burn him badly. He prefers to express them in a sublimated manner: he wouldn't seek direct sexual gratification from Walter, but he can require the younger man to light his cigars and satisfy his oral cravings in that manner.

Keyes's feelings toward Walter are also expressed in behavior that is not quite so symbolic. Keyes wants Neff to work with him in the claims division. Moreover, he wants Walter to make a financial sacrifice in order to do so: "How would you like a fifty dollar cut in salary?" Keyes offers only two forms of incentive to Walter to take such a cut. One is a direct appeal to Walter's sympathy for him: "Too much stuff piling up on my desk. Too much pressure on my nerves. I spend half the night walking up and down in my bed." He wants Walter to care enough for him to ease his burden. When Walter is unresponsive to this appeal ("Why pick on me? . . . I'm a salesman."), Keyes heaps praise on the claims job—which of course is also praise for himself as a long-term holder of the position: "The job . . . takes brains and integrity. It takes . . . guts. . . . To me a claims man is a surgeon, . . . a doctor and a bloodhound and a cop and a judge and a jury and a father-confessor, all in one." Walter's rejection of the job offer, therefore, implies a refusal to be impressed by Keyes as well as a lack of a sympathy for his plight; and in both respects the refusal must be deeply disappointing to the older man. This disappointment he tries to mask with a sneer: ". . . I thought you were a shade less dumb than the rest of the outfit. . . . You're not smarter, Walter. You're just a little taller."

In the same scene Keyes's feelings for Walter come through in another way. Neff receives a telephone call from Phyllis, which Keyes answers before passing the phone to the younger man. Neff tries to get Keyes out of the office so that he can have a private conversation, but the older man refuses to leave. To hide Phyllis's identity, Neff calls her "Margie." When Walter hangs up, Keyes makes a disdainful comment about her: "Margie. I bet she drinks from the bottle." He then asks, "Why don't you settle down and get married, Walter?" But the younger man (knowing Keyes is not making a serious suggestion) replies by asking, "Why don't you, for instance?" Keyes's answer—his story about his engagement and the unpleasant things he found out about his fiancée when he investigated her background—clearly indicates his attitude toward women: they're not to be trusted, not a single one of them. It also leads one to believe that he only posed the question to Walter to find out if he was seriously interested in "Margie" and to introduce his own story as a warning against significant commitments to members of the opposite sex.

In the investigation of Dietrichson's death, Keyes's feelings for Walter prevent him from seriously considering his co-worker as Phyllis Dietrichson's accessory in the murder. These emotions he at least faintly acknowledges in his response to Neff's comment toward the end of the film: ". . . the guy you were looking for was too close. Right across the desk from you." Keyes adds, "Closer than that, Walter." The guilty man he was looking for was not merely across the desk but within his heart. Walter Neff becomes involved with Phyllis Dietrichson and the plot to murder her husband for the insurance money chiefly as a means of struggling against his feelings for Keyes. Not only is the thought of a homosexual relationship with the older man completely unacceptable to Walter, but he also wishes to resist the quasi-paternal dominance of Keyes. It may seem strange to the viewer that Neff turns down Keyes's offer of the job of assistant in the claims department, since it would seem to be to an advantage for him to be involved in any potential investigation of the death of Dietrichson; but his instincts against the job are stronger than any practical advantages it might have for him. As Keyes's assistant he would have to spend far too much time with the older man and would be subject constantly to his overbearing ego. By linking himself with Phyllis and the murder plot, Neff is declaring his heterosexuality and setting himself directly against everything Keyes stands for professionally.

But Walter seems to have chosen forms of rebellion that he knows unconsciously to be doomed to failure. From the outset he realizes that Phyllis is deceptive, manipulative, and ruthless—hardly the sort of woman with whom a man could expect to establish a long-term relationship. In killing Dietrichson, Neff is merely destroying one symbol of patriarchal authority to give another (personally more important to him) the opportunity to punish him for his transgression. Walter thinks that in murdering Phyllis's husband and fixing it to look like an accidental death he is merely succumbing to a long standing temptation to beat the system he operates under—like a croupier rigging the roulette wheel. But he is really trying to break free of Keyes by committing an action the older man will find intolerable and thus categorically reject him for. In other words, he commits his crime with the unconscious intention of being caught for it by Keyes.

If my argument is at all sound, it follows that Walter is not truly pleased but disappointed to discover that Keyes trusts him so completely that he can't conceive of him as Phyllis's accomplice and therefore casts Nino Zachette in the role. After listening to Keyes's report of these conclusions on the dictaphone, Neff formulates a plan that is consciously intended to produce one set of results, but unconsciously quite another. Walter consciously aims to kill Phyllis and frame Nino for the crime; unconsciously he is presenting Phyllis the opportunity to kill him and thus mete out the punishment Keyes has failed to provide. Why else would he make it crystal clear to her that he intended to kill her—and then turn his back on her?

Neff does kill Phyllis after she has been unable to take a second shot at him and has yielded her gun up to him, but this killing is not the ruthlessly pragmatic action he had consciously intended it to be. Shooting Phyllis as he embraces her is the logical consummation of their love affair. It always had more to do with death than sex. Phyllis does not deny Walter's charge that she only became involved with him because "[he knew] a little something about insurance." She wanted to use Walter to kill her husband and make money on the death, but he went along with her because he thought he could kill off his emotional dependency upon Keyes along with her husband. His shooting of her merely pronounces the ultimate futility of both of their desires.

Neff's shooting of Phyllis, however, is also an act that has a moral component to it. If Walter does not kill Phyllis, she will go on to manipulate and destroy other people. She has already been trying to manipulate Nino into killing her stepdaughter Lola. After Walter calls her "rotten," Phyllis countercharges, "We're both rotten." Then when he claims she's "just a little more rotten" and uses her scheme to get "Zachette to take care of Lola" as evidence, she asks rhetorically, "Is what you've cooked up for tonight any better?" His original scheme wasn't, but his actual behavior when he then meets Zachette outside the house is much better: he tells the young man that Phyllis has been lying to him and sends him off to reconcile with Lola. At this moment his disinterested concern for the welfare of two other people unequivocally differentiates him from Phyllis.

There is, however, a measure of symbolic self-interest in Neff's treatment of Zachette. As one of Phyllis's pawns, the younger man is a sort of double of Neff, who sends him away from Phyllis and her destructive influence (which potentially lives on after she is dead in the lies she has told about Lola). Neff is perhaps giving Zachette the sort of chance he wishes he could have availed himself of: to find the antidote to destructive obsessions in the arms of a good woman. In Cain's novel Walter is in love with Lola and hopes to marry her after killing Phyllis and framing Zachette[10]; in the film his attraction to the innocent younger woman is not made so explicit, but having a relationship with a woman like her would obviously have been a healthier way to break free from Keyes than following the lead of Phyllis. Neff, therefore, is giving Zachette the chance he has forfeited himself through his involvement with Phyllis.

For many viewers the strong, assertive, ruthless Phyllis probably appears to be the dominant character of the film. But as much as she is using Neff to achieve her cruel goals, he is using her in an attempt to resolve serious psychological conflicts. Phyllis's willingness to commit murder might also have psychological roots, but the film shows no interest in her psychology. It merely portrays her as a sociopath and omits the obsession with death that motivated the character in Cain's novel. Because sociopaths do exist, Phyllis is not an unconvincing character— until she undergoes a totally unmotivated character change just before the end of the film. After she allows Walter to "[take] the gun out of her unresisting hand,"[11] she says,

> I never loved you, Walter. Not you or anybody else. I'm rotten to the heart. I used you, just as you said. That's all you ever meant to me—until a minute ago, when I couldn't fire that second shot. I never thought that could happen to me.

Unfortunately, nothing in the film gives the viewer any reason to think it could happen to her either. At the moment when Barbara Stanwyck's formerly hard, mask-like face softens and tears glint in her eyes, Ruth Prigozy would have us believe that Phyllis "has recognized her own buried life"[12]—presumably a capacity for love that she has stifled. Perhaps. But on the other hand, Phyllis's last minute conversion (which doesn't dissuade Walter from killing her) may have merely been intended to deflect charges of misogyny against the film and more importantly to give Neff enough time to tell his story to Keyes over the dictaphone (which he couldn't have done if she'd fired additional shots to finish him off).

Cain's novel ends with Walter preparing to commit suicide with Phyllis; the film ends with Keyes lighting Walter's cigarette. This difference clearly indicates where the interests of the two works lie. Wilder and Chandler are primarily concerned with the relationship between Walter Neff and Barton Keyes. This is, as Wilder says, the "love story" of the film—a love that Walter only finds it possible to acknowledge in his final words as he lies dying; then he can seriously repeat the statement he had made flippantly to Keyes earlier in the film: "I love you, too."[13] Keyes of course makes a similar acknowledgement in his line, "Closer than that, Walter," so the film in a sense is a journey "straight down the line" not merely to the "cemetery" but to self-discovery. And if one takes her final speech seriously, Phyllis achieves a similar epiphany. But the focus of the film is on the two men, and *Double Indemnity* is important not merely as an outstanding example of the *film noir* in which the protagonist succumbs to destructive forces but as a graphic illustration of the latent homosexuality that often underlies the conception of *la belle dame sans merci*.

3

A Dive into the Black Pool:
Edward Dmytryk's *Murder, My Sweet*

JUST as Raymond Chandler modified Dashiell Hammett's conception of the private detective—making his hero Philip Marlowe more conventionally romantic and idealistic (beneath his veneer of toughness) than Sam Spade—so Edward Dmytryk's adaptation of Chandler's *Farewell, My Lovely*, as *Murder, My Sweet* (1944) varies considerably in its conception of its protagonist from the model of ruthless male dominance established by Humphrey Bogart as Sam Spade in John Huston's version of *The Maltese Falcon*. Although many viewers undoubtedly regard Bogart as also the definitive Philip Marlowe on the basis of his portrayal of that role in *The Big Sleep* (1946), I agree with the left-handed compliment Robin Wood pays to Dick Powell's performance in *Murder, My Sweet*:

> The ideal Marlowe—from the point of view of fidelity to the original—is Dick Powell in Edward Dmytryk's [film]. Powell has exactly the slickness and boyishness, the tough superficiality of Chandler's Marlowe. Incarnated by Bogart, the character achieves a sympathy and maturity he never had in the books. . . . [1]

Dmytryk himself described in only slightly different terms the performance he sought and received from Powell: "I wanted Marlowe played as I believed Chandler visualized him—really an Eagle scout, a do-gooder, with a patina of toughness, only skin deep."[2] Marlowe, as conceived by both Chandler and Dmytryk, is a much more vulnerable character than Spade as conceived by Hammett and Huston.

Because he senses his vulnerability (Marlowe at one point in the film characterizes himself as "a toad on a wet rock; a snake was looking at the back of my neck"), the private detective throughout the film strives to overcome his weakness by thrusting himself into dangerous situations in which he risks (and usually receives) physical punishment and at times is threatened with death. Even though he knows he is no match for the enormous thug, Marlowe throws a punch at Moose Malloy (Mike

Mazurki) in Jules Amthor's penthouse—and is strangled to the brink of unconsciousness as a result. Then, after he revives slightly, he takes a more effective punch at Amthor (Otto Krueger) who has been directing Moose's actions. The result—by no means unexpected—is that Amthor in cold fury pistol-whips the detective into full unconsciousness—then ships him off to Dr. Sonderborg to be drugged and questioned. Possibly the latter fate could not have been avoided even if Marlowe had not acted aggressively, but he certainly could have avoided a number of bruises by simply standing still with his hands in his pockets. Avoiding physical aches and pains, however, is not nearly so important to Marlowe as striving to assert his toughness.

His value system is pretty clearly expressed by two speeches in the film—one by Marlowe himself, the other by Ann Grayle (Anne Shirley). As Marlowe is slowly coming out of his drug-induced stupor at Dr. Sonderborg's house, he tells himself,

> Okay, Marlowe, . . . you're a tough guy. You've been sapped twice, choked, beaten silly with a gun, shot in the arm until you're as crazy a couple of waltzing mice. Now let's see you do something really tough—like puttin' your pants on.

The ostensible tone of the speech is self-deprecating irony, but in his heavily sedated condition a simple act like putting his trousers on actually is a test requiring considerable mental and physical "toughness." His desire to prove himself "tough" compelled him to take punches at Malloy and Amthor: surviving the physical punishment that was heaped on him in retaliation is an additional proof. Ann describes the same pattern of behavior in terms of a sports metaphor:

> You go barging around without a very clear idea of what you're doing; everybody bats you down, smacks you over the head, fills you full of stuff, and you keep right on hitting between tackle and end. I don't think you even know which side you're on.

Ann is only partially correct because Marlowe in his own mind undoubtedly sees himself on the side of justice, but he feels he is surrounded by other players whose commitments are uncertain ("I don't know which side anybody's on," he tells Ann). Slamming into others is his method of getting them to reveal which team they are playing for. But it is equally important to him to test his strength, skill, endurance—his toughness—by hitting as hard as he can and not giving way when he is hit himself.

If Marlowe's intention throughout much of the film is to prove his manhood by demonstrating his toughness, one could draw the conclusion that he conspicuously fails at this attempt. Certainly no tribute to his manliness is offered by the policeman who addresses him in the opening line of the film: "I remember you as pretty nosy little fellow, son." He is specifically addressed in terms that suggest the police essentially regard him as a child: "little fellow, son." The impression of Marlowe's childlike vulnerability is increased by the bandage he wears over his eyes, which deprives him of visual awareness of his surroundings and of the policemen who are interrogating him. The private detective seems so uncertain of himself in this sequence that he can only respond feebly to one policeman's implication that he is guilty of murder: "Maybe I didn't do it." The whole introductory sequence creates the mistaken impression that the flashback film we are about to view will not be a detective's story of his successful investigation but rather a criminal's confession of the events that led to his moral downfall. Indeed, when Lieutenant Randall asks if Marlowe wants to make a statement, the blindfolded man's reply seems to border on an admission of guilt: "You've got the rope under my ears, huh?" A viewer unfamiliar with Chandler's novel could easily expect the story that follows to be essentially like Walter Neff's.

Even though there seems to be little possibility that Dmytryk's film was influenced by Wilder's—*Murder, My Sweet* was actually released two months before *Double Indemnity*, 1 July 1944 vs. 1 September 1944[3]—there are many apparent similarities between the two films. Not only do both employ retrospective narration; in both the fatal woman is a beautiful bleached blonde who makes little attempt to conceal her deadly intentions. In each film when the blonde is introduced, the gaze of the male protagonist (and the camera representing his gaze) is fixed on the woman's exposed (and elegantly shaped) leg. In both films the fatal woman has a stepdaughter who holds out the possibility of innocent love to the male protagonist to counter his sexual obsession with the older woman. To be sure, through most of the film Helen Grayle (Claire Trevor) doesn't seem to pose a seriously threatening temptation to Philip Marlowe, simply because he doesn't spend that much time with her. But toward the end of the film Helen does ask the detective to kill Jules Amthor for her. This request is preceded by a scene in which she takes off the trench coat she has been wearing and stands before the detective in her slip. A reaction shot shows Marlowe's gaze as riveted upon her body as it was in his original glimpse of her leg. As she displays her goods, she suggests her availability, explaining that her husband is sixty-five and that although he is "in love" with her, she is merely "fond" of him. When Helen directly tells him, "I want you to help me kill Amthor," Marlowe's response displays no apparent moral outrage and implicitly acknowledges his vulnerability to her sexual appeal: "Why me. Because I'm handy and know how to use a gun? Or just because I wear pants?" Marlowe seems to assume that any man would be vulnerable to her appeal, and certainly he offers no further verbal or physical resistance when she leans up against him to make a final appeal to his sympathy (". . . I need help. I need you.") and to kiss him—as if to seal their deal.

In the end, the viewer of course assumes that Marlowe would not have helped Helen Grayle to kill Amthor; but in truth he gets no opportunity to demonstrate his intentions in regard to Amthor since the man is already dead (killed by Moose Malloy) by the time the detective finds him. Helen Grayle, therefore, does not ultimately have the opportunity to destroy Marlowe's morals, but the detective does—rather carelessly, it would seem—give her the opportunity to kill him. Marlowe has made an arrangement with Moose Malloy to enter the beach house and confront Helen (who is really Velma Valento, Moose's former girl friend) when the detective draws open the curtains over a big picture window facing the ocean. But despite what he has set up and his knowledge of how dangerous Helen is (she not only betrayed Moose and sent him to prison in the past, she has also recently beaten Lin Marriott to death with a sap), Marlowe allows her to draw a gun on him before he can draw his own, does not resist when Mr. Grayle take his pistol from him, and never attempts to pull the curtain strings. He had the opportunity to disarm Helen, when Ann broke a plaster bust and her stepmother briefly glanced in the direction of the sound, but the detective merely looked toward the crash himself. It would seem that Marlowe would have passively allowed Helen Grayle to shoot him dead—if her husband had not shot her first. Later, when Moose and Mr. Grayle confront each other, Marlowe does make an effort to intervene, but is merely knocked out (and temporarily blinded) while the two men kill each other. Philip Marlowe in this film is strikingly ineffectual in comparison to Sam Spade.[4]

Marlowe's temporary blindness is perhaps the key to the underlying meaning of the film. The detective is unable to defend himself from Helen Grayle because he is paralyzed by guilt over his desire for her. Blindness is an appropriate punishment for this desire because it is essentially Oedipal. Although only three characters in the film are literally related (the members of the Grayle family), they combine with several other characters to symbolize the Freudian family. Helen is the all-desired mother. Raymond Chandler gave her the doubly symbolic name of Helen Grayle. Helen was classical literature's prime example of the beautiful woman who causes death and destruction (although Helen in the film only kills one man, Lin Marriott, she is the indirect cause of the deaths of Amthor, Malloy, and Mr. Grayle as well). The association of her with the Holy Grail is obviously ironic, but she is nevertheless the object of Moose Malloy's quest. Although in the course of the film she proves herself to be not only worthless but malignant, both Moose and her husband mistakenly regard her as an object of supreme value. As the symbol of the ultimately desirable mother, she has the same sort of significance to her "son."

Marlowe is established by the opening line of the film as a "son." The role is reinforced by his association with numerous characters who play the role of father to him. Mr. Grayle is not only the husband of the desired woman; he is literally old enough to be Marlowe's father. Other older men in different ways attempt to exert a sort paternal authority over Marlowe: Amthor and Sonderborg subdue him physically and seek to control his mind; Randall and Nulty as policemen are society's spokesmen for the superego. In the detective's relationship with Moose Malloy, the distinction is not in terms of age or authority, but simply in terms of size. When Moose first appears to Marlowe, the ex-con is literally larger than life. By "placing a large . . . pane of glass between [Marlowe's] desk and the camera," the director created a giant size image of Moose Malloy apparently reflected in the upper pane of the detective's office window.[5] Dmytryk also exaggerated the contrast in height between the two actors: ". . . Dick [Powell] walked in the gutter while Mike [Mazurki] walked up on the curb, or Dick stood in stocking feet while Mike stood on a box."[6] The effect is to suggest the contrast in stature not between two men but between a man and a boy—or between father and son.

The other "son" in the film—even more immature than Marlowe—is Lin Marriott. As Marlowe will later be tempted to do, Marriott has aspired to an intimate relationship with Helen Grayle. But he is so completely lacking in the maturity and confidence of manhood that he has to hire Marlowe as protection when he goes to an assignation with jewel robbers. Or so it seems at first; toward the end of the film Marlowe concludes that Marriott was conspiring with Helen Grayle to set the detective up for the kill. In either case, Marriott displays the weakness of a child, acting not on his own initiative but simply following a woman's orders. Marriott's fate—being bludgeoned to death by the woman whose orders he was following—indicates how fatal subservience to a desired female can be for a male. In yielding—or perhaps never even achieving—male authority, Marriott represents the fate that could befall Marlowe if his attraction to Helen led him to become her accomplice.

The final character of significance in the film, Ann Grayle, plays the role of "daughter" just as Marlowe plays the "son." Although she appears to be in her twenties, Marlowe repeatedly refers to her as "the kid," and

Helen Grayle refers to her as a "child." Although Marlowe has only a symbolic Oedipal relationship with Helen Grayle, one of Ann's speeches suggests a rather literal Electra complex on her part in regard to her father: "I'm fond of my father. It's more than being fond. . . ." And certainly she is extremely jealous of her foster mother. In the beach house with Marlowe she delivers a speech denouncing men: "Sometimes I hate men—all men, old men, young men, beautiful young men who use rose water and . . . almost-heels who are private detectives." The primary reason she hates all of these men is that representatives of each class are attracted to her stepmother: her father ("old men"), Lin Marriott ("beautiful young men who use rose water"), and Marlowe ("almost-heels who are private detectives"). She is gratified, therefore, when Helen appears in the room, giving Ann the opportunity to condemn the true object of her animosity: "I hate their women, too—especially the big league blondes, beautiful, expensive babes who know what they've got . . . and inside, blue steel—cold, cold like that, only not that clean." But in response to this speech Helen merely gives a slight, superior smile and remarks, "Your slip shows, dear"—driving Ann from the room in apparent defeat. The fact Helen's brief cliché could triumph over Ann's far more elaborate insult indicates the innate authority that parental figures hold over even a rebellious child. Ann's only chance for an equal relationship is with the other "kid"—Marlowe.

Marlowe and Ann largely stand by (although Marlowe at the end lies unconscious on the floor) as the three "adults"—Helen Grayle, Mr. Grayle, and Moose Malloy—destroy each other in the climax of the film. Both of the "children" seem to realize that they aren't strong enough to stand up to the desired or hated mother and that only the father possesses sufficient authority to do so. Although Marlowe as the Oedipal son may desire the death of the father figure, guilt over both his desire for the mother and his jealous hatred of the father effectively paralyze him and make him incapable of action. As in a dream, the film splits the father into two opposed figures who are powerful enough to destroy each other. The deaths then release the children from their perverse obsessions, freeing them to seek happiness with each other. Ann and Marlowe kiss whole-heartedly for the first time at the end of the film. The happy ending—with the heroine suffering no apparent psychological damage from the demises of both the beloved father and the hated stepmother—is rather reminiscent of a fairy tale. Even Marlowe's blindness is no more than an appropriate temporary punishment for his sin of gazing with lust upon the forbidden woman.

Two of the parental figures in the film are developed more interestingly and complexly—perhaps even tragically—than the childlike hero and heroine. A character that is expanded upon considerably from Chandler's novel is Helen Grayle's husband, whose devotion to her may exceed even Moose Malloy's. In a scene that scriptwriter John Paxton added to the original story, Mr. Grayle explains to Marlowe his feelings toward his wife. He begins, "I have only two interests in life: my jade and my wife." Then he seemingly notices his daughter standing beside him and hastily adds, "Oh, and of course my daughter here." But after making this concession, he sums up, "But my wife's the most important." The linking of Helen with the jade is important because it indicates that he regards the two in similar ways. Both the jade and Helen are possessions, which are valued chiefly for their beauty. His daughter, although important to him, is simply not valued in the same terms.

Grayle's most pathetic speech of the film is uttered in the same sequence: "I've played a little game with myself. I've pretended that she would have become my wife even if I had been unable to give her wealth. I've enjoyed pretending that. It's given me great happiness." Grayle knows that his felicity in his marriage is based on fantasy, but until he senses he is "losing her" he is perfectly content with this illusory relationship. If Helen is primarily a possession to him, why should he care any more about her true attitude toward him than he does about the opinions of his jade. But when he understands he is losing her, he is particularly disturbed that he doesn't "know why. I don't understand what's happened." His lack of comprehension tortures him because it reveals how little he knows about his wife. He is shocked to discover that she has had a life of her own totally separate from him, that she has goals and fears he knows nothing of—in short, that she is an independent human being and not a possession.

Grayle shoots and kills his wife just as she is about to shoot Marlowe, but he does not act for the purpose of saving the detective. As Grayle tells Moose Malloy a couple of minutes later, "It was the only thing I could do. . . . I couldn't let her go. I loved her too much." If he allowed Helen to kill Marlowe, she would have condemned herself to flight or capture by the police leading to imprisonment or execution. Any consequence of her pulling the trigger would lead to her removal from his sphere of life. Shooting her, therefore, is his last attempt to keep her, or at least prevent her from leading an independent existence anywhere else. In behaving thusly, Grayle is much more selfish than Moose, who wanted to *see* Velma, but claims he would have been content to allow her to continue with any autonomous existence she had established for herself ("I wasn't going to bother her none if she done all right. . . .").

When Moose tells Grayle, "You shouldn't of killed her," and moves menacingly toward the older man, it is uncertain whether his anger is on behalf of himself (because he has been deprived of his opportunity of speaking to the woman he loves) or Velma (because she can no longer continue the opulent life she has gained for herself). Grayle's motives for shooting Malloy are similarly ambiguous. At first it would seem that he snatches Marlowe's pistol up from the floor merely in self-defense. But in John Paxton's script, when Marlowe hears that Grayle is dead as well as Malloy, he asks "(thoughtfully, rhetorically), 'Yeh? He did it himself?'"[7] Grayle's apparent suicide would suggest that he didn't pick up the gun in self-defense, but to kill Malloy as well as himself on the assumption that neither of them would want to live without Helen/ Velma. In the film, however, Randall tells Marlowe that despite being fatally shot Moose lived long enough to the turn the gun on the older man and kill him. The film, therefore, is not absolutely clear about the motivations behind the double killing, but it is at least certain that the two men would never have shot each other if they had not both been in love with Velma/Helen.

Mrs. Grayle's own motivations for wreaking havoc receive no more persuasive explanation than Ann's "She was evil! All evil!" Helen herself admits to Marlowe, "I haven't been good . . . not halfway good. . . . I haven't even been very smart. . . ." Her only stated goal behind her destructive actions is "peace." When she first asks Marlowe to help her kill Amthor, she says, "It's the only way I'll ever have peace." In the same sequence she repeats, "I need help . . . and peace. . . ." Finally toward the end of the film she says, ". . . I can't go back now—and I'm so close to peace, so close. . . ." Here she sees "peace" as the consequence of killing Amthor and freeing herself of the burden of further blackmail. A minute or so later, after Marlowe lets slip the information that Moose has already killed Amthor, Helen decides peace is to be achieved by shooting Marlowe, the man who could expose her murder of Marriott. Committing murder, of course, has never traditionally proved to be an effective means of gaining peace of mind, and Helen's pursuit of serenity is as much deceived as the love that Moose and Mr. Grayle bear toward her.

Something she says to Marlowe just before she is shot reveals the inherent insecurity of Velma/Helen's existence. She asks Marlowe what his name is and, after he answers, comments. "Philip . . . Philip Marlowe. Name for a duke, you're just a nice mug. . . . I've got a name like a duchess, Mrs. Lewin Lockridge Grayle. . . . Just a couple of mugs . . ." Even if she could successfully hide her lower-class origins and criminal past from the world at large, Mrs. Grayle can never truly be at peace, for she knows she is basically just a mug leading an unauthentic existence. She kills Marriott and wishes to kill Amthor and Marlowe in order to hide her past, but ultimately it is her own knowledge of that past which cannot be suppressed and is a perpetual source of anxiety for her. For that reason, the only peace she can achieve is the one that her husband gives to her: the peace of death.

Murder, My Sweet represents the positive pole of *film noir* in its happy ending, which allows the hero to reclaim his innocence by uniting himself with the innocent heroine. Other aspects of the film would seem to be in the standard mode: detective hero and *femme fatale*. But if Claire Trevor's Helen Grayle is very much the classic fatal woman—seductive, immoral, and ruthless in the pursuit of her ends—Dick Powell's Marlowe is not at all the self-sufficient hero capable of dominating his circumstances in the manner of Humphrey Bogart's Sam Spade (or later, Bogart's Marlowe). The only time in the film that Powell's Marlowe demonstrates anything resembling heroic competence is in his escape from Dr. Sonderborg's clinic. Nearly all of the rest of his encounters with the forces of evil end in exactly the same manner: Marlowe is hit on the head, the image on the screen grows blurry, and blackness closes in from the sides. The first time Marlowe is knocked out, he describes the experience this way: "A black pool opened at my feet. I dived in. It had no bottom." The last time he says, "That old black pit opened up again. . . . It was blacker than the others . . . and deeper. I didn't expect to hit bottom." But each time there is a bottom, an end to the blackness followed by a return to consciousness. The true bottomless black pool or pit is death, which Marlowe is allowed to evade in the course of the film in spite of several foretastes of it.

What probably remains with most viewers of film, however, is not its happy ending but the dark images of Marlowe's helplessness and ultimate vulnerability. Among the most striking images are those of his dream after he has been knocked out by Amthor and drugged by Dr. Sonderborg. At the beginning of the dream Marlowe is mounting stairs (struggling to ascend to consciousness?), but he is confronted by giant images of Amthor and Malloy (suggesting again a child's view of the dominating adults of his world). Marlowe backs away from Moose to fall backward down the stairs; the fall continues into a black vortex, which dissolves into a series of doors (seemingly hovering in dark space amidst cobwebs) that Marlowe approaches in his shirt sleeves. He struggles with the door, unable to open it, then turns to see, again, a close-up of Moose Malloy (saying, "Shouldn'ta hit me") which dissolves into a similar sized image of the head and shoulders of a man in a white coat. Marlowe succeeds in opening the first door and passing through it. The man in the white coat, now seen to be holding a hypodermic simply passes ghost-like through the door without needing to open it. Marlowe continues to have difficulty opening the doors, and the man in the white coat, unimpeded, comes closer and closer to him. Finally Marlowe opens the last door to find on the other side the doctor he was fleeing from; in a giant close-up the hypodermic comes forward and the doctor's thumb can be seen pressing the plunger. Marlowe staggers backward through the doorway and falls again into the black vortex. The latter part of the dream is explained shortly afterwards as representing the course of drug treatment Marlowe was submitted to by Dr. Sonderborg on Amthor's orders. But the rational explanation for the dream does not altogether dispel its eerie power—especially not the message of the doors sequence: that what you run away from is very often exactly what you reach in the end. Such lessons from the film's imagery are likely to linger longer with sensitive viewers than its tidy plot resolutions.

4

Love in the Dark: Howard Hawks's Film Version of *The Big Sleep*

In 1944 and 1946 probably the two best film adaptations of Raymond Chandler's fiction were released: *Murder, My Sweet*, Edward Dmytryk's treatment of *Farewell, My Lovely*, and Howard Hawks's version of *The Big Sleep*. *Murder, My Sweet*, although it alters the climax somewhat and omits various secondary characters and events, is on the whole quite faithful to the original conception of Chandler's novel. *The Big Sleep* on the other hand changes the author's fundamental theme. In the last analysis Chandler's novel is concerned with the inevitability of death ("the big sleep") and the unavoidability of moral corruption ("the nastiness"). At the end of the novel Marlowe has glimpsed his own mortality and recognized that he himself has not been able to escape complicity with evil: "Me, I was part of the nastiness now."[1] In Hawks's film, Marlowe is not merely an avenger who destroys the forces of evil (those that have not already destroyed each other) but a redemptive force. To be sure the redemption Marlowe offers is not religious in nature but the standard Hollywood version of a morally teetering individual saved through the love of a good person of the opposite sex. *The Big Sleep* only varies from the norm in that the person requiring redemption in this case is female and the redeemer male.

The romantic emphasis of Hawks's film diminishes the role of the fatal woman who was essential to Chandler's conception in the novel. In this sense the film version of *The Big Sleep* is not suitable to my study, but it is of interest because of the way in which it varies from the norm. In general, Hawks subordinates important concerns of Chandler's novel such as mystery, mortality, and morality to a primary focus on the love relationship between Philip Marlowe and Vivian Sternwood, which didn't exist in the book. This change in Chandler's plot was the simple result of the casting decision that was the genesis of the film. According to Gerald Mast, after the box office success of *To Have and to Have Not* (1945), Warners Brothers studio wanted Hawks to supply "another

Bogart-Bacall vehicle."[2] Hawks purchased rights to *The Big Sleep* and instructed his script writers to convert it into such a vehicle.

The intentions of the resulting film are made quite clear by its credit sequence. We first see a man and woman in silhouette (curiously they don't actually seem to be Bogart and Bacall); the man lights the woman's cigarette, then his own. The first credits are the names Humphrey Bogart over the man's silhouette and Lauren Bacall over the woman's—signaling rather clearly that the stars are the most important things about the production (the title appears next). When the names of the supporting cast appear, the woman puts her cigarette down in an ash try in the lower left corner of the screen, and the man then places his cigarette beside hers. The final image of the sequence is simply of the two cigarettes lying side by side, both still burning with smoke rising from them. (The image will be repeated at the end of the movie.) The symbolism of the shot seems fairly blatant: the two cigarettes represent the two people who will also end up lying together (passions smoldering). More specifically the film is about the man and the woman overcoming initial antagonism or conflict of interest to be brought together like the two cigarettes.

In the film as in the book the conflict between Marlowe and Vivian derives from her belief that her younger sister Carmen (Martha Vickers) has killed a man named Regan (first name Rusty in the book, Shawn in the film). In the book Carmen has definitely committed this crime and tries to repeat it with Marlowe; the film leaves the issue of Carmen's guilt rather ambiguous, but least offers the possibility that Eddie Mars or his henchman Canino killed Regan and simply framed Carmen who was too drunk to know what she had done. In any case Vivian believes her sister to be Regan's killer, and her chief intention through most of the film is to prevent Marlowe from discovering what Carmen has done. Her motivation is stated succinctly in an exchange with Marlowe after he has brought Carmen back drunk or drugged from the scene of Geiger's murder. He remarks to Vivian, "You're pretty fond of your sister, aren't you? Would do anything for her." She replies, "Anything." In the same scene Marlowe indicates that he already has suspicion about Carmen's involvement in Regan's disappearance. After Vivian says that following one of her binges Carmen "never remembers" what she has done, Marlowe asks, "Just what did she forget about Shawn Regan?" Vivian's facial expression and her nervous counter question—"What did she [Carmen] tell you?"—indicate to Marlowe that he has been on target (as he indicates in his reply to Vivian's query: "Not half so much as you just did").

Until very near the end of the film Vivian strives to deflect Marlowe from investigating Regan's disappearance. She tries ordering him off the case, charming him, kissing him, pretending that Regan has been found in Mexico where she has gone to join him, and finally claiming she herself killed the man. None of these techniques proves effective in deterring Marlowe. For instance, after they kiss in his car, Marlowe says to Vivian, "All right. Now that's settled—what's Eddie Mars got on you?" This question, which Marlowe repeats several times, replaces the one he asked her toward the end of their first interview: "Just what is it you're afraid of?" Marlowe comes to realize that Eddie Mars has some kind of hold on Vivian, that the focal point of her fears is some piece of knowledge that the gambler possesses.

In both the novel and the film Vivian believes she is concealing her sister's murder of Regan not only for Carmen's sake but for their father's. But in the book the concealment seems much less honorable than in the film because the dead man is Vivian's (third) husband not just her father's employee. Vivian's statement in the book that she cared nothing for Regan ("'I didn't love him'"[3]) is an admission of emotional deficiency (her father was able to love Regan; why couldn't she?). So is the very number of her marriages; as Mast says, ". . . one divorce implies the kind of mistake anybody could make, but three divorces indicates a three-time loser—a sign of moral instability and emotional superficiality."[4] In Hawks's film Vivian has only been married and divorced once and seems leery of making a second mistake. Even when she admits her love for Marlowe, her declaration is half reluctant: "I guess I'm in love with you."

Vivian in the movie is attributed with the same character traits by her father as was Vivian in the book: she "is spoilt, exacting, smart, ruthless" (Sternwood in the book said "quite ruthless"[5]). But it is not a flaw for her to be exacting when she meets a man like Marlowe whom she can truly respect; nor in the film's perspective is her ruthlessness a flaw when it enables her to help Marlowe destroy the personifications of criminal evil, Canino and Mars. Intelligence, of course, is only a flaw in the eyes of unintelligent or insecure males, so from Marlowe's perspective her only true fault is being spoilt—something he will not continue to let her be. At the end of the film Marlowe asks Vivian, "What's wrong with you?" She answers, "Nothing you can't fix"—a reply that Bogart and Bacall with their obvious rapport have managed to make seem quite persuasive.

As a love story The Big Sleep probably "works" for most viewers, but what of the film as a mystery? Donald Willis said, "It's the whodunit carried to its logical extreme. . . . There are always several pieces missing from the puzzle, even after the movie's over."[6] How satisfactory is a mystery film that doesn't adequately solve the problems it presents to its audience? Before trying to answer this question we should consider some of the reasons why the plot of The Big Sleep is so incomprehensible.

First of all, the film retains scenes from Chandler's novel but omits the details that make the scenes understandable. The moral guidelines of the Hays Code lie heavy upon the film. In the front room of Geiger's book store, Marlowe sees an extremely nervous man seek and gain entrance to the back room. Later he sees Joe Brody loading up the books from the back room into a truck and taking them away. But the film never tells us what makes the man nervous or the books valuable: that Geiger has been running a pornographic lending library. In the book Carmen is completely naked when her picture is taken in Geiger's house; that's why Owen Taylor, the Sternwood chauffeur who loves Carmen, shoots Geiger and why the photo has blackmail value for Joe Brody after he takes it from Taylor. But in the film Carmen is fully clothed and neither the murder nor the blackmail makes much sense. (In the book Carmen is also naked when Marlowe finds her in his apartment, but this scene works about as well in the film with her clothed.) The film fails to make explicit the fact that Carol Lundgren, Geiger's chauffeur, was also his employer's homosexual lover—an omission that makes Lundgren's murder of Joe Brody seems rather under motivated. When Harry Jones (Elisha Cook, Jr.) revealed his romantic interest in Agnes to Marlowe, Chandler had the detective say, "She's too big for you. . . . She'll roll on you and smother you"—a remark that truly deserved Harry's rejoinder: "That's kind of a dirty crack, brother."[7] But in the film Marlowe only speaks the first sentence, which hardly merits the same response from Jones—which nevertheless occurs. Many of the unsolved mysteries of Hawks's film find simple explanation in the pages of Chandler's novel.

In an oft-repeated story, Hawks claimed there was one mystery that did not. At least when he called Chandler to find out who killed Owen Taylor, the writer didn't know. The film possibly makes a firmer decision on this than Chandler did. When Joe Brody tells Marlowe how he sapped Taylor and took the picture of Carmen from him but then left the unconscious young man in the Sternwood car at the side of the road, he never once looks the detective in the eye even though Marlowe initially asked him to do so and keeps walking around him to get in visual range. When Marlowe suggests that Brody may have sent Taylor's car off the dock into the sea, Brody merely says, "You can't prove I did it." The movie's strong hints that Brody did kill Owen Taylor make the former's death by the hand of Lundgren seem more just—even if he is being executed for Geiger's murder, which he didn't commit.

For Marlowe, though, the key killing in the film is one that—unlike those of Geiger, Taylor, Brody—appears totally unjust. Canino's only possible practical motive for forcing Harry Jones to drink cyanide is to conceal the hiding place of Eddie Mars's wife—a problem that could have been dealt with simply by moving her to another location. Canino's true motivation, therefore, would seem to be pure sadism or the pleasure he derives from killing. Marlowe is deeply disturbed by Jones's death for a number of reasons. One is his feeling toward Jones. As he tells Vivian, Jones was "a funny little guy. Harmless. I liked him." Another thing that bothers him is that Jones died to protect Agnes, who by no means deserved to be protected. She is unfazed when Marlowe tells her, "Your little man died to keep you out of trouble," and merely complains to him about how *she* "got a raw deal." Finally, and perhaps most importantly, Marlowe is distressed by his own powerlessness to have prevented the killing. Because he was unarmed, he stood by in the next room while Canino made Jones drink the whisky laced with cyanide. The way he tells it to Vivian, "Canino . . . got to him first, while I stood around like a sap." No more than Bogart as Sam Spade does Bogart as Philip Marlowe like to "play the sap"; it is as much necessary for him kill Canino to assuage his sense of powerlessness and gullibility as to avenge Harry Jones.

Marlowe's shooting of Canino is a cold-blooded execution, not an act of self-defense. Canino has apparently fired all of his rounds into the car where Vivian cried that Marlowe was, when the detective steps out from behind the car and says, "Over here, Canino." He does not say, "Drop your gun and put your hands up, Canino," although Marlowe surely had the option at this point to capture the killer and turn him over to the police. Instead he says what he does so that Canino will see him as he pumps three rounds into the hit man's chest. Marlowe's killing of Eddie Mars is equally ruthless even if it is the gambler's own henchmen who (somewhat carelessly) gun down their boss when he emerges from Geiger's front door. Mars certainly wouldn't have so emerged if Marlowe had not fired several rounds at him, at least one of them wounding the gambler in the arm. Marlowe's desires for vengeance and self-assertion seem not to have been satisfied by the execution of Canino; it is further necessary for him to punish Canino's employer, the ultimate source of evil in the film.

After Mars's death, Marlowe announces over the phone to the police that the gambler "killed Regan." But Marlowe's only evidence for this assertion is the fact that Mars didn't seem to recognize Carmen when he encountered her at Geiger's house earlier in the film—something that could easily have been pretense on both their parts. In pinning the murder of Regan on Mars the film fundamentally alters Chandler's plot in which the source of evil was the fatal woman, the psychopathic Carmen, who shot Regan because he was unreceptive to her sexual advances—and later attempted to kill Marlowe for the same reason. Yet even though he has blamed Regan's murder on Mars, Marlowe still tells

Vivian, "You'll have to send Carmen away. . . . They have places for that. Maybe they can cure her; it's been done before." Why would Carmen need to be sent away if she hasn't done anything worse than being sexually irresponsible, getting drunk, and allowing herself to be framed by Eddie Mars? Marlowe's asking Vivian "to send Carmen away" again comes from Chandler's novel, but the reason behind the request has been made obscure in the film. It is almost as if Marlowe has decided to pin Regan's killing on Mars to give him additional reason for engineering the killing of the gambler, but he still knows deep down that it really was Carmen who slew the Irishman.

The killings of Canino and Mars are also significant in that they bring Marlowe and Vivian together. After she has deceived Canino, giving Marlowe the opportunity to shoot the killer, the detective has new respect for Vivian: "You looked good, awful good. I didn't know they made 'em like that any more." Whether admiration for Marlowe's efficiency as a killer has inspired Vivian's declaration, "I guess I'm in love with you," is uncertain; but his gratitude for her assistance in the destruction of Canino certainly influences his own repetition of the line. Doubtlessly her help in setting up Mars for the kill further cements the relationship. At the end of Chandler's novel Marlowe, having killed Canino and been willing to further cover up Carmen's shooting of Regan, feels guilty because he is "part of the nastiness now." In Hawks's film, involvement in two homicides merely seems to be an aphrodisiac. (To be sure, such was also the case with Vivian in the novel: after giving Marlowe "a long slow clinging kiss" she murmured ecstatically, "'Killer.'"[8] In the book, though, such an attitude was presented as a character flaw.)

The flip side of Marlowe's ruthlessness toward Canino and Mars is the disregard for his own safety or welfare that he displays at various points in the film. He wises off to both Eddie Mars and Joe Brody on occasions when the other man happens to be holding a gun on him, inspiring both men to make the same comment: "You take chances. . . ." He takes an even greater chance when he blunders into Art Huck's garage without any apparent plan in mind and allows the garage owner to pin his arms from behind while Canino steps forward and knocks him cold with a fist holding a roll of coins. Being knocked out and trussed up are for Marlowe merely steps towards revenge on Canino and romantic fulfillment with Vivian since she is in Huck's house waiting to release him from his bonds, but it is hard to see how the detective could have known in advance that this would be the case. It is almost as if he initially approached Canino with two opposed goals in mind: to avenge Jones by killing Canino or to pay with the sacrifice of his own life for his failure to intervene and prevent Harry's murder. The decision over which course will be taken he leaves up to fate.

The incoherence of the plot of Hawks's *The Big Sleep* is not in the last analysis a serious flaw of the film. Rather it makes a sort of existential statement. The audience beholds a confused and ultimately inscrutable world (visually represented by the pervasive fog that surrounds the settings of the concluding sequences), in which nothing is finally certain but death. Through this world moves the detective, who not only knows that choices must be made without adequate knowledge upon which to base them but who makes them firmly and unhesitatingly. The film ends with Marlowe and Vivian together in Geiger's darkened living room; they hear sirens and look in their direction, then look toward each other. Even though the sirens are those of the police, coming to rescue Marlowe and Vivian from Eddie Mars's thugs outside, their sound seems more ominous than encouraging[9] and must have at least faintly reminded many members of the audience when the film was released in 1946 of the sound of air-raid sirens. The final message of the film, therefore, would seem to be that in an uncertain and threatening world it is nevertheless possible to find fulfillment in commitment to another person. Two people can turn—at least temporarily—from the chaos of the world outside to gaze upon each other.

Hawks's focus on the romance between Marlowe and Vivian deflects his film from the typical *noir* concentration on *la belle dame sans merci*. As Annette Kuhn points out, "In the first part of *The Big Sleep*, it is Vivian's sister Carmen who functions as repository of the menacing aspects of feminine sexuality, with its threat of castration and disruption of the patriarchal order."[10] In the second half of *The Big Sleep*, though, the film more or less forgets about Carmen until Marlowe's afterthought at the end. Hawks has claimed in an interview that he originally planned to use Chandler's ending but was prevented from doing so "by the censors" who "wrote the scene" that now ends the film.[11] But the altered ending seems in many ways more characteristic of Hawks than the one originally intended: Hawks's filmic world is male dominated, and as David Thomson remarks, "*The Big Sleep* is a seemingly infinite realization of male fantasies."[12] The movie is filled with attractive women, all of them (with the exception of Agnes) apparently willing to offer themselves to Marlowe if he gives them the slightest encouragement (or in the case of Carmen even if he doesn't): the woman in the Acme book store (Dorothy Malone) (who closes up the shop to spend the afternoon with Marlowe behind drawn shades) is the most obvious example, but a female cab driver gives Marlowe her phone number and tells him to call at night because "I work during the day." It is not surprising that in this world composed chiefly of dominant males and cheerfully compliant females the ultimate source of evil has to be a domineering male, Eddie Mars, and not the psychotically subversive Carmen.

5

Out of the Past: The Private Eye as Tragic Hero

For many (among whom the present writer includes himself) Jacques Tourneur's *Out of the Past* is the masterpiece of *film noir*. It includes all the classic elements of the genre: a convoluted but not entirely impenetrable plot, atmospheric night scenes, a wise-cracking private detective as protagonist, an extremely seductive and totally devious *belle dame sans merci,* and various stock supporting characters (thugs, a secondary *femme fatale,* a good girl to contrast the evil ones, and a sidekick for the hero). *Out of the Past* also contributes some interestingly novel elements: the classic nocturnal city and interior scenes are contrasted by brightly lit exteriors in ruggedly beautiful mountainous areas; the hero's chief sidekick is a deaf-mute—who employs a highly unusual method to dispose of a gunman menacing the protagonist (pulling him off a cliff with a cast fishing line). But the chief merits of the film reside in its conceptions of its male protagonist and his female antagonist.

It is perhaps only my personal tastes that lead me to conclude that Jane Greer is the most attractive female lead of all the *noir* films of the forties; but certainly the character she plays in this film, Kathie Moffett, is a more plausible deceiver of men than earlier fatal females such as Phyllis Dietrichson or Helen Grayle. While it is difficult to imagine any man with reasonable intelligence and a survival instinct being taken in by the hard, obviously experienced, dyed blondes, Phyllis and Helen, it is much easier to believe that an otherwise intelligent private detective like Jeff Markham would accept the word of a soft, young, natural brunette like Kathie. Although early in the film she admits to having shot her former lover and only attempts to justify the act by saying, "I hate him," it is relatively easy for both Jeff and the viewer to think that Whit must have done something to deserve both her hatred and his wounding. This conclusion is still possible at the end of the film when Whit lies dead on his living room floor after having been shot by Kathie a second time, but by then it is clear that the woman kills purely out of self-interest and does not require any other emotional incentive.

Tom Flinn has pointed out that the hero of *Out of the Past,* Jeff

Bailey (the surname taken by Markham after the ending of his initial involvement with Kathie) occupies "a niche somewhere between Philip Marlowe and Walter Neff. . . ."[1] The connection with the screen portrayals of Marlowe is more obvious because screenwriter Geoffrey Homes (Daniel Mainwaring) apparently "tailored [the part of Jeff Bailey] to fit the screen personality of Humphrey Bogart"; and when Bogart was unavailable for the film, RKO first assigned the role to Dick Powell before finally giving it to Robert Mitchum.[2] Like Marlowe, Bailey is a private detective who at the beginning of his flashback has the reputation of being "smart" and "honest," but like Walter Neff he succumbs to the temptation to betray the ethics of his profession because of his attraction to a woman. However, Markham/Bailey does not fall morally to nearly the same degree as Neff. Walter commits murder for Phyllis Dietrichson in an attempt to defraud his insurance company: Jeff merely fails to fulfill his contract with Whit Sterling to return Kathie to him. Although he is later hunted by the police as a murderer, he never actually kills anyone in the course of the film. He was a mere bystander when Kathie shot his former partner, Jack Fisher—and even when the deaf and dumb boy pulled the thug Stefanos off the cliff. Jeff therefore seems far less deserving of being shot to death by Kathie (as he is at the end of the film) than Walter Neff did to be fatally wounded by Phyllis. Because Jeff's fate is obviously not poetically just, perhaps we should consider whether it might not in some sense deserve to be regarded as tragic.

Although Jeff Markham/Bailey is not the sort of prosperous and renowned individual Aristotle considered suitable to tragedy, he does quite well fit the Greek philosopher's description of the moral character of the tragic hero: he is neither "a perfectly good man" nor an "utter villain"; instead he is a "character between these two extremes—. . . a man who is not eminently good and just, yet whose misfortune is brought about not by vice or depravity, but by some error or frailty"[3]. In this respect Bailey/Markham probably seems more "tragic" to contemporary viewers of *Out of the Past* than he would have to many members of the original 1947 audience, who were conditioned to judge his out-of-wedlock relationship with Kathie as a manifestation of depravity or vice. But in an era of less stringent sexual ethics Markham's sin seems to reside more in his deceiving of his employer than in the affair with Kathie, which is less a moral error than an error in judgment issuing from his faulty perception of her character. It is of course Jeff's error in becoming involved with Kathie that ultimately dooms him. Like many tragic heroes, though, Jeff Bailey struggles against his fate until the very end; and this struggle, though it does not save him, gives him a dignity almost completely lacking in a defeated *noir* protagonist like Walter Neff.

The opening of the film chiefly does two things: establish a vague sort of threat to Jeff Bailey's current existence and indicate what he values in that life—the things he will later struggle to avoid losing. The credit sequence opens with shots of mountain scenery, then an aerial view of a cultivated valley, a ground level shot of road signs, a dark car passing a sign reading "Bridgeport," and finally—with the camera apparently mounted above the back of the car—a man in dark overcoat and hat driving a convertible with top down into the town. Although we do not immediately learn his name, the dark intruder is Joe Stefanos, seeking out Jeff Bailey (Markham) on behalf of the gambler Whit Sterling (Kirk Douglas). Stefanos learns from the deaf-mute boy at the gas station that Bailey is somewhere outside of town, and we and he learn from gossip at the local restaurant that Jeff has gone fishing with a girl named Ann (Virginia Huston), object also of the romantic interest of the young game warden Jim.

When we first see Jeff Bailey he is walking along the shore of a rippling lake, a fishing rod in his hand, mildly complaining to Ann, "They're just not feeding today." This is just the first of a series of increasingly severe frustrations Jeff will experience in the course of the film as he fails to achieve the exact goals he has set out to accomplish. Ann envies Jeff's experience of the world and says to him, "You've been a lot of places, haven't you?" (She seems to be probing in an attempt to find out something about his background.) His reply—"One too many"—indicates there is one particular thing in his past that he regrets. He offers no further comment on his previous experiences but tells Ann of his desire to build a house on the lake and live there with her. This aspiration, like his decisions to live in this remote part of the country and to have a relationship with an innocent girl like Ann, reveals Bailey's pursuit of sanctuary—his impulse to take refuge from a world, from other people that have proved too difficult for him to deal with. (Ann displays her complete subservience to Jeff in almost everything she says, but perhaps most notably in her action of lighting his cigarette for him as they are leaving the lake. She apparently doesn't smoke herself but carries matches for him.) At this moment the arrival of the deaf-mute with the news of Stefanos's arrival demonstrates just how futile such a desire is for Jeff.

Jeff's interview with Stefanos that follows at the gas station is full of unspoken menace. Stefanos makes clear to the audience that Jeff is living under an assumed name ("Of course, there's a different name up on the [gas station] sign") and says that his employer, Whit, wishes to see him. Stefanos's words depict Whit as a generous, thoughtful, forgiving individual but of course imply the exact opposite: "Whit never steered you to anything bad, did he? Why he never even squawked when you blew the best thing he ever gave you." Seeming to acknowledge that he did blow something and that he owes Whit as a result, Jeff agrees to drive up to Tahoe to talk with the man.

In the next scene Jeff is clad differently: in a hat and trench coat, where in the earlier scenes he was bare headed and wore a short jacket. As Tom Flinn remarks, the change in apparel is "an important iconographic clue that [Jeff] is about to resume his former profession" of private investigator.[4]. He drives up to Ann's house and honks for her. As she runs out to the car, her mother's voice can be heard complaining about "a man who won't even come to the door," and Ann then feels she must reassure Jeff not to "worry about" her parents. But the mere fact that Jeff does not go to the front door and have a friendly conversation with her parents before going off with Ann shows that in some sense *he* believes that he is not respectable enough for them—and perhaps for her. His behavior of driving up and honking for her is that of a teenager from the wrong side of the tracks dating a girl he knows to be out of his class, not that of the mature man Jeff should be at his present age. His immature attitude suggests that his struggle in the latter part of the film is not merely for survival, but for maturity—to prove he is man enough to control his own destiny.

The story from his past that Jeff tells Ann is, as with so many of the stories of *film noir*, "essentially Oedipal."[5] The gambler Whit Sterling hired Markham to find and bring back to him a woman, Kathie Moffett, obviously his mistress, who had shot and wounded him as well as stealing $40,000 of his money. Jeff found Kathie but, instead of returning her to Whit, fell in love with her and accompanied her on her flight—until the relationship abruptly ended with her shooting of his former partner, who had tracked them down. In this story Whit is the powerful father figure—strong enough to have survived Kathie's murderous (castrating) attack. Kathie is the mother in whose arms the son Jeff seeks to usurp the father. He appears successful for a time in this attempt—until Kathie's shooting of Jack Fisher demonstrates to Jeff her willingness to murder (castrate) not merely the father but any male who interferes with her goals or desires. Hence, her destructiveness could potentially be unleashed on Jeff (and is at the end of the film).

Michael Walsh has persuasively argued that the life Jeff Bailey is leading in Bridgeport is his attempt to free himself from his vulnerability within the earlier Oedipal situation:

> Jeff Bailey struggles to overcome his fixation on the traumas of the past, to achieve passage from Kathy [*sic*], the object of threat and dependence, to Anne [*sic*], the object of docility and security, and to translate the sibling

rivalry with Stephanos [sic] which suggests Whit's paternity into the assumption of his own paternity in his relationship with the deaf boy.[6]

But when Jeff first visits Whit at his house in Tahoe and discovers Kathie is once again living with the gambler, he finds he has not succeeded in reversing the original Oedipal situation. He has not managed to become a powerful father figure; he is still the son vulnerable to being killed or castrated by the father Whit, the mother Kathie, or the sibling Stefanos. And he can only overcome the fear attendant on this vulnerablity by killing or castrating (depriving them of their power over him) the threatening members of this "family" or by allowing himself to be killed or castrated by them.

Such, it seems to me, is the psychosexual underpinning of the film, but the literal events and the characters' more apparent motivations also deserve examination. In his own eyes Jeff probably begins compromising his moral values when he first accepts the offer of $10,000 from Whit to undertake the search for Kathie. Markham must realize that he may be taking part in a vendetta. If he finds the girl and brings her back, "What happens to her?" he asks Whit. "I won't touch her," Whit claims, having already told an altogether unconvincing story about how he lost $40,000 on a race horse that finished dead last, then purchased the horse, and put it out to pasture where it lived happily ever after. Can Jeff have any reasonable confidence that a professional gambler, an "operator" (Jeff's word) would treat a woman who shot him and stole from him with similar mercy? Even before he meets and falls in love with Kathie, Markham must have qualms about completing the assignment from Sterling.

But as soon as he does meet her, any impulse to satisfy his professional obligation simply melts away. He first sees Kathie—wearing a broad-brimmed hat and a light dress—as she enters a cafe (La Mar Azul) in Acapulco. She passes from the bright sunlight outside into dark shadow under the arched doorway and back into light as she sits at a table next to Jeff's. His comment in voice-over on her appearance—"And then I saw her . . . coming out of the sun"—invests her with an otherworldly, almost transcendent quality (as does his description of her second entrance: "And then she walked in out of the moonlight—smiling"). He will later say—after their affair has continued for some time—"There was still that something about her that got me—a kind of magic or whatever it was." Only after she shoots Fisher, does Jeff perceive the magic is black rather than white—and her otherworldly quality demonic rather than divine.

To an extent, however, Jeff is not deceived by Kathie even at the outset of their relationship. When she recommends a little bar to him, he knows that she won't show up on the first night he goes there. But he goes anyway and remarks of himself, "I knew where I was and what I was doing—I just thought what a sucker I was." Knowledge of how she has manipulated him doesn't make him any less manipulable. When she admits that she shot Whit but claims she didn't steal the money from him and cries out to Jeff, "Don't you believe me?"—he offers no opinion on her honesty or lack thereof, but merely says, "Baby, I don't care," and embraces her passionately. This is perhaps the definitive moment of his fall: when he decides that such things as truth, justice, innocence or guilt are much less important to him than his passion for Kathie.

The setting in which Jeff decides to embrace Kathie rather than his principles is also highly significant. They are sitting together on a moonlit beach next to a group of hanging fishing nets. Jeff has presumably come to Mexico to capture or net Kathie for Whit, but he has actually become ensnared in her web. In a later scene Kathie and Jeff are driven back to her cottage by a gathering rain storm. Inside, she picks up a towel, tosses it to him, and then goes over to dry his hair (roughly) with it. After she puts on a record, he takes the towel and starts to dry her hair in the same manner, but winds up flinging away the towel and knocking a lamp to the floor as he kisses her. The wind from the storm blows the front door open, and the camera tracks toward the opening. There is a cut to the outside with the camera tracking and panning a bit to watch the rain, then a cut to the inside with Jeff walking over to close the door. Although the viewer is entitled to believe there is no significant time gap between Jeff's flinging of the towel and his rising to close the door (the shots are connected by straight cuts without any fades or other standard indicators of passage of time), it is also easy to imagine an elided scene of violent love making upon the couch or floor in which the participants were so swept away by their emotions that they neglected to observe the open door (and fallen lamp) until their passions were spent. In any case, the storm clearly symbolizes the violence of passion and the blown open door the loss of defenses against it. Jeff's shutting of the door comes too late, for as the scene proceeds he asks Kathie to run off with him, undeterred by her warning that Whit "won't forget."

After a suspenseful interlude in which Whit and Joe Stefanos turn up in Acapulco right as Jeff and Kathie are about to leave together (but just miss seeing her and therefore go off believing she has taken a ship to South America), the couple move up to California, where they hide out successfully until by chance Jeff is seen by his former partner Jack Fisher at a race track. Jeff and Kathie split up, and Jeff endeavors—effectively, he thinks—to shake Fisher from his tail; but Fisher has followed Kathie instead. This is merely one of many instances in the film in which Jeff takes skillful evasive action, which nevertheless does not accomplish the goal he sought.

In a cabin out in the woods Jeff and his former partner slug it out (their stature as combatants heightened by a low camera angle) as Kathie looks on. In her reaction shots, the shadows of the fighting men flit across Kathie's face, and her upper right arm moves slightly as if she were groping for something in her purse down below the bottom edge of the frame. But the camera is on the two men when a shot rings out and Fisher collapses to the floor. On first viewing, the audience is probably as surprised as Jeff (in his slack-jawed close-up) to see Kathie standing calmly, holding a smoking automatic at waist level. When he is able to speak, Jeff expresses dismay: "You didn't have to kill him." But Kathie coolly explains, "Yes, I did. You wouldn't have killed him. You would have beaten him up and thrown him out. . . . You wouldn't have killed him." She has perceived Jeff's flaw as her protector against Whit: the detective is not ruthless enough. It is undoubtedly this realization rather than any revulsion against the murder she has committed that determines Kathie to flee the scene at this moment (carelessly leaving behind her bankbook recording the $40,000 deposit that informs Jeff she indeed did steal Whit's money).

The murder of Fisher and the discovery of the bankbook completely disillusion Jeff about Kathie so that he treats her with ironic contempt when he next meets her at Whit's house at Lake Tahoe. He characterizes her as "a leaf that the wind blows from one gutter to another," and responds to her protestations of helplessness with the comment, "You can't help anything you do—even murder." Frank Krutnik accurately assesses Jeff's primary motivation in this scene: "The debasement of Kathie mirrors her previous over-evaluation in that it represents Jeff's attempt to disavow his earlier romantic idealisation of her."[7]

Although she claims to him that she has told no one about the death of Fisher, he knows he has no reason to believe she is telling the truth about this.

Jeff also knows he has no reason to trust Whit. When they meet at Tahoe, Whit says, "I always remember what any man did for me." Jeff says, "Or didn't." Whit says, "Perhaps." The exchange indicates that both Whit and Jeff know the detective betrayed his employer in the matter of the pursuit of Kathie. Why then does Jeff accept a job from Whit, knowing the gambler has ample reason to desire vengeance on him? Perhaps the primary reason was expressed by Jeff to Ann as they drove up to the gate of Whit's estate: "I've got to. I'm tired of running." Possibly he can square things with the gambler by doing what the man asks him to. Possibly, by vigilance he can foil any scheme to double cross or frame him. Possibly neither will Whit be trustworthy nor will he, Jeff, be wary enough to insulate himself from betrayal; in that case he will probably die—but then, too, he will no longer have to run.

The job Jeff accepts—stealing incriminating tax papers of Whit from his former lawyer, Leonard Eels—is not one that an honest private detective would undertake. But once he is on the job in San Francisco, it becomes apparent that Jeff like Spade and Marlowe before him is merely pretending to cooperate with the criminals in order mislead them. He attempts to warn Eels that his secretary, Meta Carson (Rhonda Fleming), is part of a plot involving both him and Jeff ("It could be that I'm the patsy, and you're on the spot"); but when he returns to the lawyer's apartment to explain the situation more fully, he finds the man dead. He then hides the body next door in an apartment that is being redecorated and sets about trying to scotch what he now perceives as a plot to frame him for murder.

In her willingness to set up for murder a man who loves her and to steal Whit's tax papers from her employer's office, Meta Carson is obviously a sort of double for Kathie. It is not surprising, therefore, that Jeff encounters Kathie in Meta's apartment and overhears her call up Eels's apartment house and identify herself as the lawyer's secretary. Kathie explains to Jeff the foundation for the frame: in a safe in Eels's office is a document, written by her, charging him with the murder of Fisher ("They made me sign it," she asserts). Jeff is not deeply impressed by Kathie's new helpfulness ("You're wonderful. You're magnificent. You can change sides so smoothly"), but he uses the information she has given him to steal the tax papers from the gambling club where Meta has deposited them and informs Whit's underlings that he will trade them for the letter in Eels's office accusing him of murder. Unfortunately, just before Meta and Kathie arrive together to pick up the letter at the office, the police drive up with the superintendent of Eels's apartment house—a consequence of the discovery of the body. On the other hand, given the amply demonstrated unreliability of Kathie and Meta, neither Jeff nor the audience could have complete confidence the result would have been better for him if the women had got to the letter first.

Because of the discovery of the letter by the police, Jeff Bailey is publicly proclaimed the murderer of both Fisher and Eels, and he must devise a new strategy to avoid prison and the gas chamber. The deal he finally strikes with Whit involves the exchange of the gambler's tax papers for his incrimination of the recently deceased Stefanos for the murder of Eels, and Kathie for the killing of Fisher, plus $50,000 getaway money for Jeff. He also succeeds in utterly disillusioning Whit about Kathie—to the point where the gambler tells her if that she doesn't "take the rap and play along," he will personally kill her and make sure her death is extremely slow and exceedingly painful.

But when Jeff returns the following night, he finds Whit lying face up, dead on his living room floor. Kathie then enters from the back to say, "You can't make deals with a dead man, Jeff." For this simple reason, his plan to save himself has failed. He now has no one to back up his contention that Kathie killed Fisher or Stefanos killed Eels. Should he go to the police, it would merely be his word against Kathie's, and he knows she was probably correct in her earlier contention: "They'll believe me." Although they have jockeyed for power all through the second half of the film, Jeff is forced to acknowledge that Kathie is "running the show now."

Kathie's exact attitude toward Jeff in the latter part of the movie is probably difficult for both him and the viewer to gage. She seems quite content to frame Jeff for the murders of Fisher and Eels until he starts mounting an effective resistance to the scheme. Even after she has aided her former lover to the extent of telling him where he could find Whit's papers, she sends Stefanos after the deaf-mute, packing a .45 to shoot Jeff when the boy joins him. This incident later inspires a typical exchange:

> Kathie [half hurt, half indignant]. "You think I sent Joe?"
> Jeff [ironic]. "Oh, you're wonderful, Kathie."

But even though she is willing to have Jeff either sent to prison or murdered, Kathie also seems still to be in love with him. When they meet in Meta's apartment, she tells him, "We can go back to Acapulco and start all over as though nothing had happened." It is easy in the context of the scene to think that she is merely trying to con him, to deflect his anger at her betrayal of him. But even after she has killed Whit, she still expresses the dream of returning to the love she and Jeff once shared: "I want to go back to Mexico. I want to walk out of the sun again and find you waiting." She is willing to acknowledge that their earlier love was flawed, but says that was because Jeff failed to perceive her realistically: "I never told you I was anything but what I am. You just wanted to imagine I was. That's why I left you." Despite her villainy Kathie shares the dream of most normal women (and men): she wants to be loved for what she truly is.

If Jeff finds that hard to do, she'll give him further incentive by threatening that if he doesn't go off with her, she'll pin all of the murders on him (including that of Whit): "Someone has to take the blame," she observes. But her clinching argument, the one he yields to in the end is this: "You're no good for anyone but me. You're no good, and neither am I. . . . We deserve each other." Although he doesn't initially respond to this argument, a minute or two later when she says they "deserve a break," he acknowledges, "We deserve each other."

He is willing to accede to her opinion in this matter because it echoes one he has heard earlier that evening. Jim, Ann's other suitor, has told him, "I don't know whether I'm good enough for her, but I know you aren't." At that time he parried Jim's criticism by saying, "That's one difference. The other is that she loves me." But this rejoinder is not so effective if Jim is actually right, and Jeff *is* unworthy of Ann—something he must have begun to suspect in their final tryst, if not before then. The blond Ann is the diametric opposite of the brunette Kathie in numerous significant ways other than hair color. Where Kathie is sly, manipulative, deceitful, Ann is the epitome of honesty and trust. On the last occasion Jeff meets her, he at one point says to her (with near incredulity), "You believe everything I say, don't you." To which Ann replies with a perfectly straight face and shining eyes, "Everything you say to me I believe." A moment later he mutters, "I don't know why I do this." The reference of the "this" is obscure, but Jeff could very well be wondering why he is striving to maintain a relationship with a woman so totally unlike not merely his previous lover Kathie but himself as well.

For any viewer of the film with some experience and a measure of common sense Ann seems far too good to be true. But if we ignore the possibility—as the film seems to want us to—of her being a hypocrite, pretending to Jeff and perhaps herself as well to be far more innocent than a woman in her early twenties has any right to be, we have to view her as essentially childlike in her naivete. Jeff's relationship with her seems, therefore, more like that of father and daughter than that of man and mate. Certainly his relationship with the deaf-mute boy seems more nearly one between equals than that with Ann. Jeff was probably attracted to Ann by her stark contrast with Kathie; but her stark contrast with him as well probably would eventually have doomed the relationship, even if Kathie had not polished it off more quickly.

Ann's virtue is so extreme she even defends her rival Kathie: "She can't be all bad. No one is." Jeff replies, "Well, she comes the closest." But Kathie's badness is only an extension of Jeff's own badness. He is shocked to discover she has killed Fisher and then Whit, but he certainly didn't like either of these men himself. He clearly derived satisfaction both from beating up Fisher and from blackmailing Whit. In each case his hostility toward the other man was largely based on fear—fear that Fisher would report his and Kathie's whereabouts to Whit, fear that the gambler would exact dreadful revenge. But the physical beating of Fisher and the successful blackmailing of Whit were at best only temporary solutions, offering immediate emotional satisfaction but no long term relief. Beaten up and thrown out, Fisher would merely stagger off to a telephone and call Whit. Once he got hold of his tax papers, Whit would have no reason not to send other agents forth to track down and destroy Jeff. Kathie's solutions to her similar problems—killing both Fisher and Whit—were considerably more effective albeit ruthless. She at least got these enemies off her back once and for all. What she has done in both cases is what Jeff secretly desires but is prevented from doing by his moral censor. His recognition of this fact is likely what makes him admit to Kathie in the end that "We deserve each other."

Jeff's goals in the second half of the film undergo a progressive modification. His original goal when he arrives at Tahoe is to square things with Whit by doing a job for him. He knows there will be risks involved, but is willing to take them because he is "tired of running." After he meets Kathie at Whit's house and knows she has told the gambler about their relationship, he also knows the job he has been given must in some way be a booby trap for him. His goal at that point is the one he expresses to Meta Carson: "Just remember, I'm coming out of this in one piece, Miss Carson." After he find Eels's body, he realizes his chances of coming out of the whole affair intact are not good, so he revises his goal. When Kathie tells him, "I don't want to die," he replies, "Neither do I, Baby; but if I have to, I'm gonna die last." But in the end he is not successful in achieving even this limited goal, for Kathie shoots him at the road block before the state trooper machine-guns her.

We are to assume that Jeff has set up the road block because he is previously seen going over to the downstairs phone and picking it up as Kathie goes upstairs to complete her packing, even if we do not actually hear him making the call. He could obviously have performed other actions that would have proved less immediately fatal to him (e.g., knocking out Kathie, tying her up, and then calling the police to collect them both at Tahoe—she might ultimately have succeeded in framing him for the murders, but he would seem to have a better chance with the legal system than at the road block). One must conclude, therefore, that Jeff quite deliberately chooses the method of stopping Kathie that is most likely to prove fatal to both of them. This seems to him an appropriate fate because not only has Kathie become to him the embodiment of evil, she has also become the embodiment of the evil he now recognizes within himself.

The film ends with a brief coda. Screenwriter Geoffrey Homes (Daniel Mainwaring) has said in a interview that he had intended the movie to end with the deaths of Jeff and Kathie, but the studio protested: "Well, the front office said, 'Jesus you can't end with them dead there. You've got to put something on it.'"[8] This ending—in which the deaf mute boy nods "yes" when Ann asks if Jeff was going away with Kathie, and then salutes Jeff's name over the gas station as Ann drives away with Jim—

is obviously a sentimental touch, but in a way it is perfectly appropriate to the rest of the film. When Jeff betrayed his principles to go off with Kathie that first time down in Acapulco, he in effect condemned himself to go with her all the way. He shows resilience and ingenuity in the second half of the film as he struggles to extract himself from the net Kathie and Whit have cast upon him; but his efforts, although heroic, are futile. The only way he can ultimately be free of Kathie and her influence upon him is by truly going with her all the way—to death. Jeff's ultimate heroism is his willingness to accept this fate.

6

"With You Around, Ma, Nothin' Can Stop Me": The Tangled Emotions of Cody Jarrett

THE writers of the screenplay for *White Heat* have specifically stated that they conceived of the film as a sort of "Greek tragedy" with "Freudian implications."[1] Although "Freudian implications" can be detected in nearly all the films I've discussed thus far, the threatening figure of the "phallic mother" is somewhat concealed in these films in that she is represented by a woman roughly the same age as the protagonist (even though father figures are more consistently older). In *White Heat* the mother figure is quite literally Cody Jarrett's mother, but she demonstrates her usurpation of phallic authority in the standard symbolic manner of taking up a gun to threaten the life of a man. The fact that Cody (James Cagney) in an emotional sense is still not weaned from Ma (Margaret Wycherly) is demonstrated in numerous places in the film, but nowhere more vividly than in the famous scene where Cody sits in her lap as he recovers from a fierce headache. Cody regards his mother as an altogether positive influence on his life: she comforts when he is in pain, assists him in his career of crime (at one point she says to him, "I'll help you, Cody, like always"), and builds up his ego (when he informs her of his plan to serve time for a crime he didn't commit to avoid more severe punishment for a job he did pull, she announces proudly, "You're the smartest there is, Cody"). But despite, or perhaps because of, the warmth of Cody's feelings for his mother, her influence on him in the end is entirely destructive. As Jack Shadoian puts it, "[Cody] acts because of and on behalf of his mother, and the course she sets is ruinous."[2] Purely in numerical terms Ma Jarrett is the most fatal of the fatal women considered in this book, because she has inspired all of Cody's killings and fostered the delusion of smartness that causes Cody to lead his gang to their deaths at the end of the film.

Ma Jarrett, though, is not the only fatal or phallic woman in the film. Although Cody never realizes it, his wife Verna (Virginia Mayo) is the true killer of his mother. Verna shot Ma in the back when the old woman had the drop on Big Ed (Steve Cochran). When Verna tranfers her allegiance back to Cody, she then helps to set up Big Ed for his execution. An additional fatal role is played by a man who has in a sense assumed a female role. The undercover agent, Hank Fallon (Edmond O'Brien), who has assumed the guise of Vic Pardo to gain Cody Jarrett's friendship in prison, realizes that in order to ingratiate himself with the gangster he in some sense has to "take Mama's place." Although he does not encourage Jarrett to kill as Ma might, he makes no move to prevent Jarrett from killing either. And at the end of the film he deliberately takes upon himself the role of the executioner of the man whose friendship he had won under false pretenses. While the relationship between Cody and Ma is destructive (to many other people as well as ultimately to themselves), they are nevertheless unwavering in their loyalty to each other and thus more likely to gain sympathy from the audience than is the duplicitous undercover agent.

I wish to focus in this chapter on the relationships between the murderous Cody Jarrett and the three destructive people who most influence his life in the course of the film; but before I do that, I'd like to consider another aspect of *White Heat*, which I think also tends to sway the audience's sympathies more to the villainous protagonist than to the representatives of law and order. Although the film is typically categorized as a gangster movie, the authors of the screenplay didn't regard it as such:

> "We never thought of it as a gangster film, or of Cody as a gangster. It had, in fact, much more of an *outlaw* feeling for us. Gangsters are mobsters, have mob muscle and back-up and 'connections.' Bandits . . . had to do it on their own, and they had from the Wild West days." At one point in the script draft, the screenwriters actually described Cody Jarrett as "the last outlaw."[3]

Even though Cody Jarrett does have a "connection" in the person of "The Trader" (who buys stolen money from him for forty per cent of its face value and then fences it in Europe), Cody does operate more in the manner of a Western outlaw than an urban gangster. Cody's first robbery in *White Heat* is simply a reenactment of *The Great Train Robbery* (1903), except that Cody and his gang arrive at and depart from the scene of the robbery in cars rather than on horseback.

As the train emerges from a tunnel Cody leaps onto the engine tender from a bridge above the entrance and quickly takes command of the engine cab by leveling his pistol at the engineer and the fireman. With the train stopped other members of the gang approach the mail car from within and outside the train, exchanging shots with guards and finally blowing open the door of the car with dynamite. All aspects of the robbery could have as easily been carried out in the late nineteenth-century. When the gang hides out after the robbery in a mountain cabin, their circumstances are even more primitive because Cody won't let them heat the cabin lest smoke from a fire give away their location. At this point, personality distinctions occur, dividing characters like Cody and Ma who endure the harsh conditions without complaint (until Cody's headache makes Ma worry that the thin mountain air is bad for him) from the spoiled urban types like Verna and Big Ed who bitch and moan about the cold. Even with the momentary lapse from authority caused by his headache, Cody Jarrett is clearly dominant in the nineteenth-century world suggested by these opening sequences of the film. It is when the gang drives off to a distinctly mid-twentieth-century California city that Cody begins to lose his absolute control.

This section of the film introduces Cody's adversary, the Treasury agent Philip Evans (John Archer), who is as distinctly a twentieth-century man as Cody is a nineteenth-century man. The government agents have linked Cody to the train robbery by spectographic analysis of dust on the clothes of a dead (but unidentified) gang member, and the discovery that a fingerprint on the cellophane of a cigarette pack in the dead man's pocket belongs to a "known member" of the Jarrett gang. When the Treasury agents by chance spot Ma Jarrett in a supermarket, they try to follow her car to Cody, utilizing less technologically sophisticated but still essentially scientific means: "the ABC method" (in which three pursuing cars in radio contact are employed to tail the vehicle under surveillance). Ironically, the agents lose Ma's car, and Evans only finds it again when he spots it in a motel parking lot he has ordered his own car into so that it can turn around in order to return to headquarters. Evans at that point has to send his car away because it is in "dead spot" for radio transmission and needs to be sent "up the hill" to call the other cars for back-up. When Cody returns to his car, Evans must confront him alone, and Jarrett's cunning and superior reflexes enable him to seize a hidden gun and wound the Treasury agent. In this part of the film the nineteenth-century criminal proves superior to the twentieth-century resources of the forces of law and order. (Cody also manages to negate the scientific evidence the Treasury agents have against him in connection with the California train robbery by the ploy of confessing to a lesser crime committed in Illinois on the same day.) But with the weight of both the superior numbers of the government agents and their advanced technology against him, Cody Jarrett is obviously in a situation where his triumphs can only be temporary.

In the middle portion of the film, the chief weapon the Treasury agents employ against Jarrett is the undercover agent Fallon, whose pretending to be Jarrett's friend in order to "get [him] and his gang" probably makes a rather bad impression on many members of the audience—even if Shadoian's characterization of Fallon as a "payroll Judas" may be a bit extreme (the similarities between Cody and Jesus are rather slender).[4] More appropriate is Shadoian's contention that "Fallon is an automaton, a machine (Cody's big mistake is thinking he is a person). . . ."[5] Fallon has been given a psychological profile of Jarrett so that he knows what to do to elicit a favorable emotional response from Cody; but in order to manipulate him toward the ends the government seeks, Fallon cannot genuinely share in any of the emotions he evokes. What has always been disturbing to this viewer is how little trouble Fallon seems to have in maintaining this split between outward emotion and inner objectivity (or perhaps frigidity). The chief technological scheme proposed by the federal agents in this part of the film is the oscillator they have installed in the car that Fallon and Jarrett are supposed to use in their escape from prison. The oscillator will transmit a signal that can be picked up by receivers in government cars to locate the position of Jarrett's vehicle. This plan collapses when Jarrett goes berserk after he hears of his mother's death and is hospitalized, preventing his proposed escape with Fallon. But then Jarrett recovers his wits sufficiently to improvise an escape from the prison infirmary in the car of one of the psychiatrists called in to examine him (later in the escape he appropriates the doctor's suit). The careful planning of the government agents has been overturned by both Jarrett's unpredictable emotional volatility and his capacity for decisive (and brutal) spontaneous action.

But in the third and final section of the film the government's technology is finally allowed to function successfully. Fallon in his guise as Vic Pardo has been brought along by Jarrett in his escape (along with two other cellmates). He improvises an oscillator from Verna's malfunctioning radio and attaches it to the underside of the truck in which Jarrett and his gang are being driven to the site of their heist (a petrochemical plant). As soon as Evans gets the word from Fallon (via a soaped-in message on restroom mirror), the government agents deploy their receiving and direction finding equipment to track the Jarrett gang. This part of the film is composed of a montage of alternating shots: long shots of the gang's truck and of the government's cars with rotating ring antennas atop them, interior shots of the gang inside the tank of the gas truck and of the Treasury agents in their cars—two in the front seat with a technician in the back listening through headphones to the oscillator signal and adjusting the direction finder—and long shot of the big wall map at headquarters on which the truck is tracked by the intersection of degree lines drawn from the locations of the tracking cars. When the truck stops at the petrochemical plant, the government agents know exactly where to deploy their forces.

This portion of the film presents an obvious clash between the Old and the New. The government agents employ the latest (ca. 1949) technology to track Cody Jarrett. Even though he and his gang are literally travelling in the tank of a modern gasoline truck, in Jarrett's mind they are being transported in something far more ancient. Cody got his idea for this scheme of getting the gang into the petrochemical plant in the belly of the gas truck from a story Ma told him as a child— the story of the Trojan horse. From the perspective of the Treasury agents, what they are tracking is a group of thugs bent on armed robbery. To Cody Jarrett, he and his gang are in a sense Greek warriors seeking plunder that is somehow rightfully theirs. It might seem that the view of the Treasury agents is ultimately endorsed in that the New seems to triumph decisively over the Old: Jarrett and all the members of his gang are killed (or arrested in the case of Verna and The Trader). Thomas Clark accordingly defines the central theme of the film as "the infringement on and the final destruction of old values and alien ways of life [represented by the bandit Cody Jarrett] by progress in the form a new social-technological order [represented by the Treasury agents]."[6] But in a way Cody Jarrett's defeat is a kind of triumph that makes the apparent victory of the government agents and modern technology seem paltry.

When toward the end of the film Cody snickers and announces, "They think they've got Cody Jarrett. They haven't got Cody Jarrett"—his statements may be taken as sheer bravado if not pure insanity. But in the strictest sense these statements are true: the government agents do not take Cody Jarrett into custody, nor do they succeed in killing him. Cody does not even permit the last surviving member of his gang to be captured. When Riley chooses not to follow Cody up to the top of the Hortonsphere petrol tank and walks with his hands up toward the federal agents, saying, "Don't shoot," it is Cody who shoots him in the back and then laughs in triumph. When Fallon shoots Cody twice with a long-range, high-powered rifle, he brings Cody down to his knees but clearly has not killed him. Dumfounded, Fallon asks, "What's holding him up?" The only apparent answer is Jarrett's determination not to be "gotten" by his foes. Only one man can get Cody Jarrett, and that is Cody himself: that is why he deliberately fires his final shots into the Hortonsphere, igniting it and setting off a series of explosions throughout the petrochemical plant. That this way of dying is not a defeat but a victory to Cody is clear from his final words: "Made it, Ma, top of the world." Fallon is given the final words of the film, and he seeks to undermine Cody's triumph: "He finally got to the top of the world, and it blew up right in his face." Fallon seems to think Cody would have regarded this fate as undesirable—the just punishment of the gods on his hubris. But this is the fate Cody desires, and it is a defeat for the federal agents who have not managed to capture Cody or kill him cleanly. Instead their technological know-how has led to what appears to be the total destruction of the petrochemical plant (another Horton-sphere blows up just before "The End" appears on the screen against a background of flames). Although modern technology was used to entrap Cody Jarrett, he was able to turn the technology upon itself by firing into the Hortonsphere and blowing up the trap. One would hardly expect the owners of the petrochemical plant to congratulate the Treasury agents on their zeal in protecting the plant's payroll at the cost of destroying all its physical assets.

Frank Krutnik describes the conflict of *White Heat* in these terms: "The technological armoury of the postwar police force . . . is pitted against Jarrett's raw, psychotically assertive masculine dynamism, seeking to contain him as a figure of the past (of America, of the movies)."[7] I will add that Jarrett is "a figure of the past" of the human race as well—of the raw primitive instinct of aggression, which—as Freud argues—has not disappeared from the human psyche although civilization seeks to restrain it. Jack Shadoian appropriately describes Cody Jarrett as "a less fantastical King Kong" because both the giant ape and the anachronistic outlaw represent the rampant id.[8] Few members of any audience of *White Heat* (either in 1949 or now) would probably wish to model their lives on Cody Jarrett's, but the coldly rational, "scientific" agents of law and order are not desirable either. Cody at least *feels* and invites emotional identification from the audience no matter how twisted some of his feelings may be.

If from one symbolic perspective Cody Jarrett represents the id, viewed more realistically he is simply a psychological mess. Two dominant and opposed traits of Cody are revealed in the opening sequences at the train robbery and the mountain hideaway. One is his utter ruthlessness, which is demonstated by his cold-blooded shooting of the train engineer and fireman after they have heard his first name spoken by Zuckie, the gang member recruited to drive the engine, and then later by his treatment of Zuckie after the latter is scalded by a steam blast from the engine. As Zuckie writhes in pain on the ground beside the tracks, Cody snaps, "C'mon, let's get out of here," and walks briskly off, although three other members of the gang do, on their own initiative, help Zuckie up from where he lies. When Cody decides it is time for the gang to evacuate the mountain cabin and move on, Zuckie begs to be taken along. Cody says he can't take a chance on being stopped by police with Zuckie in the car (presumably because of his injured appearance) but will send a doctor back to the cabin for him. The only "doctor" that Cody sends, however, is another member of the gang, a "specialist" to whom Cody hands a revolver with instructions to put Zuckie out of his misery.

The scenes in which Cody is utterly, cold-bloodedly in control are sharply contrasted by the scene in which he suddenly closes his eyes, moans, and topples to the floor (inadvertently firing the gun he was holding when the attack came upon him). Verna tells Big Ed it is the second attack Cody has had in a month, and Big Ed offers, "He's nuts. Just like his old man." Cody then stumbles into a bedroom, falls again to the floor, crawls to a bed, lurches up onto it, where he lies on his face pounding on the mattress with his fists. The head-on camera angle foreshortens Cagney making him look rather like a small child having a tantrum. Ma then sits beside him on the bed, kneading the back of his neck until gradually the headache dissipates. Once Cody is back on his feet he tells Ma the effect of the headache is "like havin' a red hot buzzsaw inside my head." His first inclination is to go back into the living room where the gang is, but Ma advises that he doesn't want to be seen in his current vulnerable state: "Might give some of 'em ideas." In the climax of the sequence Cody sits on his mother's lap (a scene spared from ridiculousness by keeping the camera close enough to the actors that we see only their heads and the upper portions of their bodies) and says lovingly to her, "Always thinkin' about your Cody, aren't you, Ma?" The headache demonstrates that there are times when Cody does not have iron control over events around him, but instead is subject to forces which overwhelm him and reduce him to childish vulnerability. To regain the semblance of indomitability he is dependent on his mother as both his physician and a sort of stage manager. His grateful remark to her as he sits on her lap reveals the degree of his dependency on her: he is *her* Cody, her child, not in any sense his own man.

The two contrasting impressions—of the ruthless, domineering Cody and the vulnerable dependent Cody—are perhaps causally related, the first deriving from the second. Cody has to try to *appear* ruthlessly indomitable because he knows that he is essentially a weak child utterly dependent on his mother. But the ruthless role is also the role his mother *wants* him to play—perhaps because it was the role played by his father before his breakdown into madness. Indeed, violence seems to be a tradition of the entire family. Ma felt it was the proper thing for her to do when she went after Big Ed with a gun (and she probably would have killed him if Verna hadn't shot her in the back). Since criminal violence is the norm for the Jarrett family, the way in which Cody demonstrates to his mother that he is a "good boy" is by behaving badly in the eyes of society. As Shadoian said, Ma Jarrett has set the "course" for Cody's life, and this course is "ruinous."

But even though Ma's influence on Cody has appalling consequences not only for him but for the victims of his crimes (not to mention the members of his gang), Ma is actually portrayed in the film largely as a sympathetic character. As a sociopath herself she has no sense that she is leading Cody astray or encouraging him to do anything wrong. Nor despite the obvious Oedipal nature of their relationship is there anything sexually seductive in her behavior toward her son (as, for instance, in the cases of Raymond's mother in *The Manchurian Candidate* or Lilly in *The Grifters*). She simply treats him as if he were still a little child: when he is in physical pain (from the headaches), she comforts him and makes the pain go away; she advises him on how to behave with his peers ("Don't let 'em see you like this. Might give 'em ideas"), and she lavishes praise upon him when he does something clever ("You're the smartest there is, Cody"). When Ma goes after Big Ed, her behavior is much like that of a mother charging next door to retrieve a toy a bigger child has taken away from her little boy. Cody, being in prison, cannot retrieve his own property and indeed seems not even particularly disturbed by the loss of Verna ("Forget it, Ma. It was in the cards for Big Ed to make his try"), but Ma takes his cause as her own and will express what she regards as the proper degree of indignation even if he does not: "No one does what he's done to you, Son, and gets away with it." It would be an understatement to say that Ma has failed to inculcate good values in her son, but her unswerving loyalty and devotion to Cody make her easily the most admirable of the three characters with whom he is intimately involved in the film.

Verna is utterly faithless to Cody, but her infidelity seems to bother him very little, as if he never expected or perhaps even wanted loyalty from her. Cody's only significant emotional tie is with his mother. Verna is important to him merely as a source of sexual gratification and as a display object. The fact that he regards her primarily as a possession is indicated by his response when Ma asks incredulously, "Don't you care?" after he has responded blasely to the news of Big Ed and Verna having run off together: "Sure I care! What's mine's, mine!" Early in the film Cody gets upset when Verna offers to pour Big Ed a cup of coffee, and the viewer might assume he is motivated by jealousy; but the actual words he speaks indicate what is most important to him: "My wife don't wait on nobody." Verna belongs to him and as his possession should serve only his needs. Unlike Jeff in *Out of the Past* Cody seems never to have gone through any stage of idealizing the object of his lust. From the beginning of the film Cody talks to Verna as Jeff did to Kathie after his disillusionment with her. As the gang is about to depart from the mountain hideaway, Verna enters the room where Cody is about to close the suitcase containing the money stolen in the train robbery. She suggests they take all the money and run out on the rest of the gang: "It's your suitcase, Cody. Why don't you keep it all?" Cody's smiling comeback to her—"You're cute"—is both a straightforward tribute to her physical appearance and an ironic jab at her greed and selfishness. Verna's place in Cody's life is symbolically indicated by a later scene in a motel. Verna is standing on a chair to admire a new fur coat in the dresser mirror when she makes a sneering comment about Ma's devotion to Cody ("Ya like strawberries, don't ya? Well, she just had to get some for her boy"). Cody kicks the chair out from under her and dumps her backward onto a conveniently located coach. Verna's physical position at the outset of the scene is that of the woman up on a pedestal. But Cody has not placed her there: only her own self-admiration has. And he makes sure she does not stay there after she offers thinly veiled criticism of the true object of worship in his life.

Cody's willingness to take Verna back after she has been with Big Ed is not so much a sign of generosity or forgiveness on his part as it a sign of his total indifference to her as a person. A clue to the essence of her character is given in a brief scene just before Cody gives himself up for the hotel robbery in Illinois. Verna asks what she will do with herself while Cody is in prison. Ma sardonically suggests, "Same as you did before he married ya." Cody warns, "Better not, Baby, I'll be back." The implication seems to be that Verna was a prostitute before marrying Cody (or at least that she made her living off men), and she clearly seems to disregard Cody's warning in her later involvement with Big Ed. She therefore is terrified after hearing of Cody's escape and has little confidence in Big Ed's ability to protect her. (When he claims to be "ready" for Cody, she attributes supernatural powers to his rival: "Cody ain't human. Fill him full of lead, and he'll still come at ya"—a statement that is prophetic of the ending of the film.) But when she slips out of the house to try to escape in a car, Cody intercepts her in the garage. Cody is obviously totally disbelieving of her protestations that Big Ed forced her into the relationship and that she truly loves Cody and is happy to be "rescued" by him. But she does come up with one lie that deflects his vengeance from her.

When Cody accuses her of having stood by when Big Ed killed Ma—"Didn't even raise a finger to help her"—Verna truthfully responds, ". . . you got it wrong, Cody." Then she comes up with the lie that saves her: she him tells that it was Big Ed who "got her in the back." Why does Cody believe this lie? It may be because Ma was the most powerful person in his life, and he cannot even conceive that someone as insignificant as Verna could have had the power to kill her—even by shooting her in the back. After Cody takes his revenge on Big Ed appropriately (in Cody's misinformed view) by waiting to shoot him in the back as he is trying to flee, he politely offers his left arm (the one not holding the pistol) to Verna to assist her in descending the stairs—then kicks Big Ed's body the remainder of the way down the stairs to clear the obstruction in their way. This gesture seems consciously symbolic on Cody's part—a message both to Verna and the members of his gang (who have entered at the foot of the stairs) about what happens to people to get in his way.

Even though it may at first seem unbelievable to the audience, Cody's relationship with Verna from this point on in the film goes back to being exactly what it was before—as if her interlude with Big Ed had never taken place. Verna herself seems to have trouble believing this is the case. When she comes to Cody whining about her radio not working and pleading to be allowed to go down to "San Berdoo" to get it fixed, he tells her, "Nobody leaves here unless I say so," and raises his hand toward her face. She cringes away, obviously expecting to be slapped; but he smiles and says, "What's a matter baby? I'm not gonna hurt ya." Then he kisses her in a manner that could be taken as tender—if he did not in the next moment advise her to "go and read your comic books." Verna has never been anything more to Cody than a sexual object and a sort of pet he can tease for his amusement. She is no less suitable for fulfilling these roles after her betrayal of him than she was before. On their last night together before the petrochemical plant job, he cheerfully piggybacks her off to bed.[9]

In a scene outside at night with "Vic Pardo" Cody indicates most directly how little Verna means to him emotionally. When he acknowleges that he is "lonesome," Vic looks back toward the house and asks, "What about . . . ?" Cody says, "You mean Verna?" and nods contemptuously: "All I ever had was Ma." And so long as he had Ma, he didn't want anyone in his life who would be emotional competition for her. With Ma gone it is not Verna who fills the vacuum she has left but rather Vic Pardo.

Fallon realizes at the outset of his undercover job that in some sense his role is to "take Mama's place." He finally succeeds in filling this role when Cody collapses with one of his headaches in the prison shop. The primary source of the headache is Cody's anxiety over Ma's determination to go after Big Ed: he rehears her threat against his rival in her voice-over just before he collapses (a montage of shots of shop machinery in operation—drills and grinders—is more an analogy of what Cody feels happening in his head than a noise-related cause of the headache). As Cody's head throbs in his (justifiable) fear of the danger Ma is placing herself in, Vic Pardo slips in to do for him almost exactly what Ma has done for him in similar situations of pain. He massages the back of Cody's neck and also his ego: "Come on, Cody, don't let it beat ya!

You're top man, aren't ya? Why, I been readin' about ya since I was a kid, always hopin' I could join up with ya. Ya don't want those two-bit mugs to see Cody Jarrett down on his knees, do ya?" Pardo not only gives Cody physical relief, he shows the same concern for Cody's image in the eyes of others that Ma did in the first headache scene.

When Cody and Vic plot a prison escape in their cell, most of the continuous shot shows Cody's face on the left side of the screen and Pardo's on the right (Pardo is lying in his upper bunk, and Cody is standing beside it). The chain holding up Pardo's bed passes diagonally in front of his face, and the shadow of the chain runs down Cody's face like a scar or trickle of blood (blood, of course, always looks black in black and white movies). The chain in juxtaposition with Pardo/Fallon suggests the prison bondage from which the two men are plotting their escape but also the undercover detective's plan to incarcerate Cody for the more serious crime for which he has thus far escaped punishment. Tom Conley interprets the shadow down Cody's face as "a patch or scar left by the sadism of confinement,"[10] but the scar or blood image seems more prophetic of the pain and suffering that will come to him as a consequence of his betrayal by Pardo/Fallon.

After Ma's death, Cody's emotional reliance on Vic Pardo is significantly increased. He summons Pardo from his prison cell to come along on the improvised prison escape even though Pardo's participation at this point serves no practical purpose (Riley has already supplied Cody with the gun he needed for the escape). He later tells The Trader that he plans to split "fifty-fifty" with Pardo, even though Pardo seems to be making no greater contribution to the proposed payroll robbery than any other member of the gang. Cody's only justification for being so generous with Pardo is—"I split even with Ma, didn't I?"—a comment that indicates how emotionally dependent on the younger man Cody has become. When he encounters Vic outside the house on the night before the big job, Cody is initially suspicious and questions the younger man about what he is trying to do. Pardo deflects his suspicions by saying he just wanted to see his wife: "I haven't seen her in a long time. I'm human, ya know, like everyone else." In reality Pardo/Fallon is *not* "human, like everyone else" in the way he pretends to be here, but Cody assumes that Pardo's need for his wife parallels his own need for Ma and that they share the same basic feelings: "You're just lonesome, like me."

In the film there is no evidence at all, however, that Fallon is capable of feeling lonesome like other people. He seems to have no wife or girlfriend, and after the completion of his last undercover job he was looking forward not to getting together with friends or family but to engaging in the essentially solitary activity of fishing. While there is no reason to think that Fallon would necessarily respond truthfully to

Cody's question, "Your mother alive?"—the answer of the undercover agent nevertheless has the ring of truth: "She died before I even knew her." Fallon seems like a man who has never known what it feels like to be dependent on another person and to invest that person with overwhelming significance. When Cody tells him about talking to Ma out in the woods and what a "good feelin'" it was, the occasional reaction shots of Pardo/Fallon indicate how little he comprehends Cody's feelings. It is particularly ironic when, after both men go back inside the house and are drinking with Verna, Cody proposes, "We'll pick up your wife after the job tomorrow. And we'll all take a little trip—just the four of us." Cody is unaware not only that Vic has no wife but that both his own wife and his apparent friend will betray him the following day.

In the end no one is truly with Cody on his final day other than Ma. When Bo Creel exposes Fallon, Cody can only laugh at the bitter joke that he trusted a "copper" and "treated him like a kid brother." From this point on Cody Jarrett follows the advice of no other person in the gang and consults solely with Ma. When the authorities order him to "come out with [his] hands up," Cody repeats their words and then looks upward to address his mother: "How do ya' like that, Ma?" He then fires at them with a rifle as if that was what Ma urged him to do. When talking about Ma with Pardo/Fallon the night before, Cody had said of his mother, ". . . times when I was losin' my grip, there she'd be right behind, raising me back up again." The scene at the petrochemical plant is definitely one in which Cody is losing his grip, but his sense of Ma's presence gets him up to the top of the Hortonsphere, then gets him twice again on his feet after Fallon has repeatedly shot him with a long range rifle. His final words are not only are addressed to Ma; they are her words: what she has said to him previously when she raised him back up again (as in the headache scene at the mountain hideway): "Top of the the world!"

Patrick McGilligan correctly characterizes Cody's fate at the end of the film as "not the formulaic cops and robbers death, but a suicide, a blinded Samson tearing down the columns of his enemies. . . ."[11] Cody's triumph is, of course, only a psychopathic triumph; but for him, blowing himself up with the Hortonsphere is enormously satisfying in two ways: it is the ultimate aggressive, destructive act of an aggressive and destructive man—and it is his way of reuniting himself with Ma.[12] It is also a triumph over Fallon whose psychological significance for Jarrett has changed with the discovery of his true identity. Vic Pardo was a surrogate for Ma and also a supportive kid brother. Fallon with his long-range, high-powered rifle is a phallic rival, if not the castrating father. His weapon is far larger than Cody's and should be more lethal, but it is not capable of destroying Cody—while his snub-nosed little pistol is powerful enough to blow up the world.

Humphrey Bogart as Sam Spade and Mary Astor as Brigid O'Shaughnessy in *The Maltese Falcon*

Barbara Stanwyck as Phyllis Dietrichson in *Double Indemnity*

Claire Trevor as Helen Grayle and Dick Powell as Philip Marlowe in *Murder, My Sweet*

Lauren Bacall as Vivian Sternwood and Humphrey Bogart as Philip Marlowe in *The Big Sleep*

Jane Greer as Kathie Moffett in *Out of the Past* (the taller of the shadows behind her belongs to Robert Mitchum as Jeff Markham)

James Cagney as Cody Jarrett and Margaret Wycherly as Ma Jarrett in *White Heat*

James Stewart as Scottie and Kim Novak as Madeleine/Judy in *Vertigo*

Lee Marvin as Walker and Angie Dickinson as Chris in *Point Blank*

7

A Dreamer and His Dream:
Another Way of Looking at Hitchcock's *Vertigo*

T HE critics who voted *Vertigo* one of the best films of all time in the *Sight and Sound* poll of 1982 were plainly undeterred by the fact that its plot is relatively preposterous. Although Robin Wood ranks *Vertigo* as "one of the four or five most profound and beautiful films the cinema has yet given us," he also admits "the whole plot is quite fantastic—no one would ever set about murdering his wife in *that* way."[1] And even if a person would go about murdering his wife in *that* way, the film is riddled with secondary improbabilities.

Faced with the plot of *Vertigo* the reflective viewer is confronted with a number of questions, which if not impossible to answer (critical ingenuity can explain almost anything), resist easy resolution. How did Scottie (James Stewart) get down from the rooftop gutter, suffering no more serious injuries than those requiring (only temporarily) a walking stick and corset? How did Madeleine (Kim Novak) get in and out of the second story room at the McKittrick Hotel without being seen by the manageress, who claims she has "been right [there] all the time . . ."? How did Elster (Tom Helmore) know that Scottie would recognize "Madeleine's" description of the "old whitewashed Spanish church with cloister" in her dream as the Mission San Juan Bautista and would insist on taking her there to prove that her dream visions had a basis in reality? And how could Elster have been certain that no one would climb to the top of the bell tower after "Madeleine's suicide" and find him lurking there with Judy, his wife's double? And finally, to change the interrogative pronoun for once, why on earth would Judy put on Carlotta Valdes's necklace (Elster's gift to her) just when she and Scottie had found happiness together? In truth none of these questions has any very plausible answer, and as a result *Vertigo* does not so much resemble the typical Hitchcock thriller with its surface probability as it does a "long, demanding, surrealist dream."[2]

It is, of course, not a literal dream—any more than a realistic film, even a documentary, is a literal representation of reality. Reality is not a series of images, from appropriate distances and angles, and sounds edited together to provide either narrative or interpretive coherence. So the dream of *Vertigo* for the most part maintains a semblance of the narrative continuity viewers have come to expect from the thriller genre. Nevertheless, from a psychological standpoint, *Vertigo* is best understood as a dreamlike representation of the inner conflicts of its protagonist: more specifically of the conflict within John "Scottie" Ferguson between eros and thanatos—between his longing for love and sexual fulfillment and an equally strong, if not stronger, death wish.

In the opening sequence of *Vertigo* a presumed criminal is pursued across the rooftops of San Francisco by a uniformed police officer and (behind him) Scottie Ferguson. Scottie misjudges a leap onto a peaked slate roof and winds up hanging from a gutter a number of stories above the street. Trying to give Scottie a hand to pull him to safety, the uniformed officer plunges to his death in the street below. In the words of Robin Wood, "We do not see, and are never told how [Scottie] got down from the gutter: there seems no possible way he *could* have got down."[3] But there is of course a way for Scottie to "get down": to let go of or lose his hold on the gutter and plunge to his death as the policeman had. This fate seems far more probable than his surviving such a fall or the fire department getting there in time to save him. I am therefore going to pursue the perhaps radical notion that *Vertigo* may best be regarded as an extended equivalent of Ambrose Bierce's story (and Robert Enrico's film) "An Occurrence at Owl Creek Bridge": that everything after the opening sequence is the dream or fantasy of a dying man (it makes no difference whether the dream occurs while he hangs from the gutter, as he falls to the street, or when he lies dying on the pavement).

Wood reports that "the sensation of vertigo . . . has been explained . . . by psychologists as arising from the tension between the desire to fall and the dread of falling. . . ."[4] If this explanation is correct, it makes *Vertigo* a particularly appropriate title for the film, the majority of which is concerned with Scottie's "desire to fall" and "dread of falling"—or his yearning for death and his fear of death. If the film is regarded as Scottie's dream, it's true subject is the tension between Scottie's desire to live meaningfully—to find something or someone of supreme value to live for—and his urge to die—to cease from all onerous struggle and plunge into oblivion: in other words, to find some reason to hang on to the gutter (his precarious existence) or yield to his impulse simply to let go. Madeleine/Judy is the ambiguous embodiment of this struggle, for she represents both the object of supreme value for which Scottie would wish to live and the appeal of death itself.

Scottie's dream necessarily begins with him safely down from the gutter, having suffered no more serious damage than can be corrected with the temporary aid of a cane and a corset. (I will ignore the phallic implications of the cane but remark that the corset could perhaps suggest the kind of restricted, bound-in emotional life Scottie has apparently lived up to this point.) Scottie is with Midge (Barbara Bel Geddes), a woman he once considered linking his life to in matrimony. Midge is obviously quite a bit younger than Scottie and also than Elster even though she was supposedly in college with both of them—as if she were more the memory of a woman as she used to be, rather than the actual contemporary of Ferguson. Scottie's casual and rather insensitive manner of speaking to her clearly reveals that she is not of overwhelming impor-tance to him—if he needs something to live for, she cannot be it.

Two more things are important in this sequence. Scottie tells Midge of his appointment with Elster, thus setting up the chain of events that will lead him to the woman he will consider worth living for; and he makes an attempt to overcome his vertigo by slowly ascending a steplad-der. Unfortunately on the third step, he glances out Midge's window, sees the avenue below, experiences the view as he had that of the street down below the gutter, and winds up collapsing into Midge's arms. The scene demonstrates that the threat of death by falling is still very much with Scottie despite his apparent rescue from the gutter of the building with the tile roof.

Elster then introduces Scottie to the idea of Madeleine being possessed by "someone dead" from "the past." To save Madeleine from the grip of the dead becomes Scottie's way of saving himself from death. Scottie is initially intrigued by Madeleine's beauty as he sees her glide across the floor of Ernie's restaurant (wearing the same style of black evening dress in her first appearance that Judy will die in at the end of the film). He is then additionally fascinated by her mysteriousness as he follows her about San Francisco and perceives her link with Carlotta Valdes who died approximately a hundred years before.

The style of the film, which is not especially dreamlike in the first two scenes with Midge and Elster, becomes increasingly so after the introduction of Madeleine. Her bodily movements are almost uniformly slow, measured, graceful—as if she were moving through a different atmosphere than that of normal everyday life. The scene in the church-yard, where Scottie first beholds the grave of Carlotta Valdes, Hitchcock says, was shot "through a fog filter" to give it "a dreamlike, mysterious quality."[5] His first day's observation of Madeleine then culminates in her unexplained—and apparently unexplainable—disappearance from the McKittrick hotel: an event which is later recapitulated in her seem-ing disappearance from the redwood forest, although in that case Scottie finally finds her behind a tree.

Through his second meeting with Elster, in which Scottie is told about

Madeleine's blood relationship with the dead Carlotta, the detective has no reciprocal involvement with the object of his surveillance. Elster has asked him to watch her and this, aside from the additional research at Pop Leibel's bookstore, is all that Scottie has done. But his relationship with Madeleine enters an entirely new phase after Scottie fishes her out of San Francisco Bay.

Now Scottie has not merely observed Madeleine; he has saved her life. (He has also observed her much more closely: after the rescue the film resumes with Madeleine found in Scottie's bed, apparently completely undressed—her clothes are seen hanging in his kitchen.) His having saved her in this instance convinces him that he can save her altogether. He has entered the realm of fairy tale or legend and become the knight whose role is to rescue the damsel in distress. In keeping with the atmosphere of fable or myth, Scottie and Madeleine the following day enter the equivalent of an enchanted forest: Redwood State Park. But even though Scottie has psychologically entered the realm of romance in his relationship with Madeleine, part of him remains the "hard-headed Scot" (as Elster had referred to him earlier), so the means by which he seeks to save his damsel in distress are rational ones.

He listens to Madeleine recount her dream, which reveals her identification with Carlotta and her sense of the imminence of her own death, and thinks there must be some explanation for what initially appears uncanny. He says, more to himself than to Madeleine, "If I could just find the key . . . the beginning . . . and put it together." But then he rejects the reasonable explanation Madeleine proposes—"If I'm mad— that would explain it, wouldn't it?"—because it is not consistent with his romantic fantasies about her. Later he thinks he has found a satisfactory explanation in his theory that the Spanish building in Madeleine's dream is actually the Mission San Juan Bautista, which she has visited in the past even though she doesn't remember having done so. He says he will take her to the Mission, she will remember when she had been there before, and then she will "be free." He is trying to impose his practical, commonsensical view of reality on her, thinking that if she can be brought to view things as he does, then *he,* and not Carlotta Valdes, will possess her.

When they get to the Mission, though, Madeleine does not remember any previous visit of her own to the place; she only recalls the experiences of Carlotta more than a hundred years before. She ignores Scottie's attempt to identify "Carlotta's" memories with objects currently found at the Mission and his increasingly desperate pleas for rational interpretation: "You see—there's an answer for everything." Then after their final embrace in the livery stable, she rushes off to ascend the tower (which he cannot climb more than part way because of his vertigo) and plunge (apparently) to her doom. Both the rational and romantic sides of his nature have suffered crushing defeat: the uncanny has triumphed over his endeavors to explain it away; he has failed to rescue the lady in distress.

If Scottie has dreamed his involvement with Madeleine, she possesses more than one kind of symbolic significance within his subconscious. In the Jungian sense, she is his anima—the feminine intuitive side of his nature that he is striving not only to recognize but to achieve union with. It is not surprising, therefore, that his attempts to impose his masculine reason upon her lead only to her destruction. But she is also the possibility of romantic, sexual fulfillment that Scottie has apparently not previously achieved in his life (certainly not with Midge)—a reason for going on with his life. Conversely, she also represents the lure of death itself: she has identified herself with her dead grandmother and ultimately dies by a fall just as Scottie the dreamer may be in the process of doing (the tile roof she lands upon echoes the one he was clinging to at the beginning). Scottie's attempts to save Madeleine represent his struggle to stay alive, which, of course, proves futile.

After hearing the caustic analysis of his behavior by the magistrate at Madeleine's inquest (the judge would seem to embody Scottie's own self-condemning superego), Scottie experiences an obvious nightmare. He sees Elster standing with a woman, but it is Carlotta Valdes (dressed as in her portrait in the museum) instead of Madeleine. Now Madeleine has achieved complete identity with the dead. Scottie moves through the graveyard in which Carlotta is buried and approaches an open grave—which Madeleine had earlier beheld in one of her dreams and identified as *her* grave. Scottie falls into the grave, but then he falls toward the mission roof Madeleine landed upon—and finally into nothingness (represented by a brilliantly white screen devoid of all objects other than Scottie's plummeting black silhouette). This would all seem to be the logical conclusion to the dream of a man who has fallen to his death. Having failed to achieve union with his anima, to gain the romantic fulfillment that would give him a reason for life, to deny the all-powerful hold of death over what is desirable in life—having failed in all these attempts in his dream involvement with Madeleine, what recourse does Scottie have but accept his own death by falling (of which Madeleine's death is merely a displaced representation)? The film would seem to have here reached logical conclusion.

But of course it goes on. Human beings are rarely eager to accept the finality of their own deaths. Scottie constructs a new dream in an attempt to deny the ultimate implications of the first one. He converts his fall to death in the last segment of his dream into a less conclusive mental breakdown: he has not lost his life but merely his consciousness for a time. The new dream begins as the first one did with a scene involving Midge. The purpose of the scene for the dreamer is to restore his self-esteem: even though he is totally unresponsive, Midge remains completely devoted to Scottie. Having brought him this boost to his ego, Midge disappears from the film because she can do no more for Scottie: she cannot provide the romantic fulfillment he has come regard as the only thing truly worth living for.

In the final shots of her in the film, Midge is not actually with Scottie: she discusses his case with the doctor at the hospital and then walks off alone down an empty corridor into a fade out. This is not the first time Midge has appeared in the film in a brief sequence from which Scottie is absent. Earlier, from her car she observed Madeleine leaving Scottie's apartment. Then we saw her chuckling to herself as she put the finishing touches on a painting which we shortly afterwards discover to be her portrait of herself as Carlotta Valdes. This scene is balanced by her defacing of the painting and denouncing herself as "stupid, stupid" after Scottie walks out her following his viewing of it.

While these scenes involving Midge without Scottie present might seem inconsistent with an interpretation of the film as Scottie's dream or fantasy, they are not so if one keeps in mind the purpose they might have for the dreamer. Each of the scenes stresses Midge's devotion to Scottie. The scene outside his apartment establishes her jealousy of Madeleine; the portrait is her way of suggesting that he should abandon his romantic obsessions with an inaccessible woman and focus his attentions on her; her chuckle before he views the painting is a sort of self-congratulation on her method of conveying this advice to him (and, of course, of announcing her availability); and her behavior after he has walked out on her displays her bitterness at his rejection of her as in any way a semblance of his romantic ideal. Finally, the scene with the doctor indicates her continuing devotion to Scottie even after she has acknowledged his love for the dead Madeleine. Even though Scottie does not reciprocate Midge's love, her unswerving commitment to him is of course gratifying to his ego. Her function in his dream is that of a second string object of wish fulfillment—one that can satisfy superficial ego needs but not his deepest desires.

To regain a strong sense of purpose to his existence he has to resurrect Madeleine. Shortly after the recuperated Scottie meets Judy Barton, we have the flashback scene and the letter with voice-over that reveal how Elster had employed Judy as tool in his plot to murder his wife. Again this material might at first seem inconsistent with the interpretation of the bulk of the film as Scottie's dream—since he neither witnesses the flashback nor reads the letter. But we have to distinguish between Scottie the dreamer and Scottie the character in the dream. Scottie the character cannot know that Judy actually *was* Madeleine because that knowledge would make his "resurrection" of his former lover far too easy. But Scottie the dreamer must know that Judy was Madeleine because only then could she truly *become* Madeleine. In his first dream Scottie kept trying to find rational explanations for the uncanny: the possession of Madeleine by Carlotta and the premonitions of death. Now in the second dream he comes up with a rational explanation that works: the whole thing was a plot by Elster.

As he remakes her, Scottie is so obsessed with his dream of Madeleine that he will not permit Judy to be Judy. She must dress exactly like Madeleine, make up her face the same way, color her hair the same color, and finally pin it into the same bun. Judy protests nearly every step of the way because her true hope, expressed in the letter she never sends him is "that I could make you love me again, *as I am, for myself* . . ." (italics added). But Scottie has no interest in Judy's avowed tastes or preferences: he must make her into his ideal of the perfect woman (an ideal that was significantly created by another man). As Robin Wood astutely points out, what Scottie does in an extreme form is merely what many men do when they experience "'romantic love,' with its demand for perfect union and its tendency to construct the loved person as an idealized fantasy figure, the necessary condition for perfect union being the denial of otherness and autonomy."[6] But in real life the woman usually persists in asserting her true identity (or at least her own conception of it), refusing to conform entirely to the man's ideal; the guilt-ridden Judy, on the other hand, feels she can only atone for her sins by sacrificing her true self to satisfy Scottie's desires.

After a heavily filtered shot in which Judy enters from her lavatory perfectly reconstituted as Madeleine, wearing a grey suit identical to the one Madeleine wore the day of her death, Scottie embraces her, and the camera circles the couple as the background changes from Judy's apartment to the livery stable where they kissed shortly before the fall from the tower. This return to the earlier scene has two quite opposed implications. One, Scottie has triumphed, brought back the past, reclaimed the love he lost. Two, just as he lost Madeleine the first time right after their passionate embrace in the stable so he may be about to lose her again. Mixed implications of triumph and defeat are apparent throughout the whole final third of the film.

On the one hand Scottie has demonstrated great power in molding Judy into the perfect semblance of Madeleine. In so far as he has in effect brought her back from the dead, his power could be said to be godlike. There are obvious sexual connotations here as well. Scottie's vertigo, like L. B. Jefferies's broken leg in *Rear Window*, can easily be seen as a symbol of sexual impotence.[7] After Scottie kisses Madeleine

in the barn, he is unable to consummate their sexual relationship because his vertigo prevents him from following her to the top of the tower
to stop her from throwing herself off. Freud's theory of dream symbolism
helps to interpret this sequence: "Symbols such as a staircase or going
upstairs . . . represent sexual intercourse."[8] (In this respect, it is significant that Scottie can only ascend three steps in Midge's apartment and
then topples into her arms in the manner of a weak and terrified child—
rather than a man.) After kissing Judy/Madeleine in her apartment/
the livery stable, Scottie rather obviously is able to consummate their
relationship. (Following the fade after the embrace, Judy is wearing a
different dress, and both characters are smiling contentedly.) It is not
surprising, therefore, that in the final sequence of the film Scottie *can*
ascend to the top of the tower with Judy.

Yet in this same sequence Scottie is made aware of his true powerlessness. He has not truly resurrected Madeleine because the Madeleine
he knew never really existed. The woman he loved was merely a fiction
composed by Elster. There is small triumph for him in persuading Judy
to play a part she had already played once before. Scottie's return to
the Mission with Judy is his attempt to relive the earlier scene with
Madeleine and bring it to a different conclusion. When he persuaded
Madeleine to go to the Mission with him, he promised her what the
result would be: "You'll be free." Now he tells Judy that if she will enact
the role of Madeleine and ascend the tower with him, "when it's done,
we'll both be free." But of course when it's done, only Judy is free, just
as Madeleine was at the end of the first visit to the mission—freed by
death from the demands of life. Even though Scottie manages to climb
to the top of the tower with Judy/Madeleine this time, the end result is
the same: the woman plunges to her death. In the last analysis, Scottie
has no more control over the circumstances governing life and death in
the second visit to the Mission than he had in the first.

Scottie discovers that Judy actually *is* Madeleine when she (quite
improbably) asks him to fasten Carlotta's necklace about her throat.
The necklace reveals not only that Judy is the dead Madeleine but that
she is also the dead Carlotta. She is death itself which he has mistaken
for life. She has to fall from the tower a second time because it is
his destiny to join her through his own fatal fall. In the somewhat
overdetermined final sequence, death also appears as the black shape
that rises up from the stairwell. In this respect the fact that the shape
resolves itself into the figure of a nun when she steps into the light is
less significant than the first black anonymous image—the idea that
death can unexpectedly intrude into life at any moment.[9]

The final shot of the film shows Scottie standing at the very edge of
the tower top, his arms slightly spread as they were earlier when he

stood before Carlotta/Madeleine's grave inhis dream (within a dream). That shot preceded his plunge into the grave, then down upon the lower Mission roof, then into oblivion. This shot also seems, therefore, to precede a dive into nothingness. If we interpret the preponderance of the film as a dying man's dream, then although the dream in both its major parts has initially raised the possibilities of new life—of emotional fulfillment and mastery of fate—the final message it enforces with iron rigor is the necessity of yielding to the inevitability of death. As Lesley Brill has put it, "*Vertigo* is a film of trying not to plunge into the abyss, and failing."[10]

Taken literally, *Vertigo* is the story of a man incidentally destroyed by a beautiful young woman and an older man in their plot to commit the perfect murder of another woman. Although she herself is a victim of Elster, Judy/Madeleine nevertheless causes devastating harm to Scottie, driving him to mental breakdown, then leaving him at the end of the film perched on the brink of the void. But if both Judy/Madeleine and her mentor Elster are seen as products of Scottie's imagination, as characters in *his* dream, then they become not objective forces conspiring to undo him, but rather projections of destructive elements within his own nature. They are in effect embodiments of his death wish, and they teach him not to resist but to accept his fall into the abyss.

But from another point of view, Elster and Judy/Madeleine represent Scottie's mother and father or rather his childhood psychosexual conceptions of them that linger in his unconscious. Teresa de Lauretis is surely correct when she argues that Scottie is not in love with Madeleine "but her narrative image, . . . the desire for the dead Mother which Madeleine represents and mediates for him."[11] Madeleine represents herself to Scottie as a woman who is psychically merging with or being taken over by her own grandmother. In the symbolism of Scottie's dream she represents his own dead mother—the infinitely desirable mother of the oedipal stage of his early childhood. (Whether Scottie's real mother, who is never mentioned in the film, is in fact alive or dead is irrelevant; the desirable young woman of his early childhood no longer exists and is dead that sense.) In trying to save Madeleine's life, Scottie is really trying to bring the mother of his early childhood back to life so that he can possess her sexually. In this respect his inability to ascend the stairs, in order to save her and to possess her, merely recapitulates his childhood sexual inadequacy and the loss of the beautiful young mother that he could do nothing to prevent.

A double meaning, therefore, can be found in the sentences de Lauretis quotes from Hitchcock's interview in Truffaut's book:

> I was intrigued by the hero's attempts to re-create the image of a dead woman through another one who's alive. . . . To put it plainly, the man wants to go to bed with a woman who's dead; he is indulging in a form of necrophilia.[12]

Hitchcock seems merely to be speaking of the second part of the film when Scottie remakes Judy as Madeleine and apparently goes to bed with her once the illusion is complete. But this section of the movie simply reveals the creative process that underlay the presentation of Madeleine in the first part: she is the disguised image of supreme object of his desires—the mother of early childhood. When Scottie drags Judy up to the top of the tower with him, he twice uses the same phrase: "You're my second chance." "This is my second chance." He is probably speaking of his second chance to prove his manhood by ascending the tower, but Scottie's whole pursuit of Madeleine was for him another chance to achieve the object of his desire that he had failed to gain as a child. Shortly before the end of the film Scottie announces despairingly to Judy, "It's too late; there's no bringing her back"—acknowledging the futility of his whole attempt. Then he kisses Judy passionately— apparently deciding that if he cannot have the true object of his desires, a reasonable facsimile is certainly better than nothing. But then the unexpected intrusion of the nun into the love scene on the tower sweeps Judy to her death and leaves Scottie with exactly nothing, other than an overwhelming sense of irreparable loss.

An additional symbolic significance of the nun needs to be considered here. Psychoanalysts have commented on the ways in which American detective novels and films "[split] the maternal image" into two opposed types of female characters: the *femme fatale* representing "the sexual night-time mother" and the faithful secretary or sidekick, "the . . . de-sexualized daytime mother."[13] In *Vertigo* Midge is clearly the daytime mother, and both she ("Mother is here," she tells Scottie in the hospital scene) and Scottie ("Oh, Midge, don't be so motherly," he protests in the opening apartment scene) consciously see her in that role. For this reason, Scottie is unable to develop a strong erotic interest in her. It is not the known, daytime mother who excites his interest but the unknown, nocturnal mother. The nun whose appearance sends Judy/Madeleine to her doom is another version of the daytime mother. She is the mother as moral authority, upholder of religious values. In real life it is perhaps this aspect of the mother that most effectively squelches the child's erotic desire for her and drives it deep into his unconscious. Thus, it is quite appropriate that in Scottie's dream the nun should deprive him of the final semblance of the prime object of his desires.

If the film is an oedipal dream, the role of the father might seem rather underdeveloped. As the husband of Madeleine and the lover of Judy, Elster of course plays the paternal role—an idea underlined by his appearance in Scottie's transitional dream standing beside an animate Carlotta from the painting. The shot clearly suggests that Elster's true mate is the dead (grand)mother. But Scottie manifests little open aggression towards this father figure beyond ignoring Elster's proffered hand-shake after the inquest. Nevertheless, the film makes Elster the ultimate source of evil in the story, the direct cause of Madeleine's death, the indirect cause of Judy's. He *deserves* killing for his crimes even though the ending of *Vertigo* leaves him unpunished. By making Elster the arch villain, the dreamer justifies his feelings of hostility and aggression to-ward the father; by leaving him unpunished, he acknowledges his inabil-ity to defeat or overcome his great rival.

Freud argues that civilization inevitably frustrates the instinctive de-sires and drives of humankind. One of the basic taboos in all societies is against incest, and Freud comments that "this is perhaps the most drastic mutilation which man's erotic life has in all times experienced."[14] The male remains frustrated throughout his life following his early recog-nition that he cannot erotically possess his mother. If Freud's theory has a measure of validity, one can see Scottie's dream as a disguised quest for the erotic fulfillment he missed out on as a child, leading to his final anguished recognition that true satisfaction of his desires is unattainable. (Even if we assume that Scottie had sexual intercourse with Judy/Madeleine, this scene is not presented—as if the dreamer were unable to imagine it—and in any case it was merely sex with a substitute.) Having achieved such recognition, the dreamer is perhaps ready for the death his dream (as wish fulfillment) had sought to forestall. Scottie has finally realized that the only way to achieve union with the dead mother is through his own death.

8

A Revenger's Tragedy:
John Boorman's *Point Blank*

MORE than a quarter of a century after its initial release John Boorman's first American film, *Point Blank*, remains, if not his best, his most innovative and thought-teasing production. Classified as a "gangster thriller" in *Halliwell's Film Guide*, *Point Blank* is actually more of an updated version of the sort of Jacobean revenge tragedy written by Tourneur and Webster, in which vengeance is achieved only at serious cost to, if not total destruction of the avenger's humanity. The film also continually forces us as viewers to question the reality of what we are seeing. *Point Blank*'s plot is extremely simple: a betrayed man called Walker seeks revenge upon his betrayers, his wife and best friend, and also seeks money from the criminal organization that provided the motivation for the betrayal. One significant problem with this simple story, however, is that there is no believable way in which Walker could have survived to carry out his vengeance.

Far more obviously than Hitchcock's *Vertigo*, Boorman's film lends itself to the interpretation that virtually the entire film is the dream of a dying man. In the pre-credit sequence Lee Marvin's Walker is shot twice at close range (point blank) and collapses into the corner of a cell in the abandoned Alcatraz Prison. Even if Walker is not dead but has only been seriously wounded, it seems not merely improbable but virtually impossible that he could make it alive from the island to the mainland. As the post-credits portion of the film begins, we see Walker on an excursion boat approaching Alcatraz and hear the voice-over of a female tour guide explaining how "treacherous currents" in the ocean about the island "render[ed] it virtually escape proof." A new character, Yost (Keenan Wynn), approaches Walker and asks, "How did you make it . . . ?" How indeed? If the currents could keep perfectly healthy prisoners from swimming to the mainland, how could a badly wounded man succeed where they had failed?

Of course the heroes of action adventure films commonly survive tribulations that would prove fatal to the ordinary person. And the viewer may simply choose to attribute Walker's survival to the superior physical strength and extraordinary good fortune with which action heroes are not infrequently blessed. But such is not the impression given by the shots that conclude the opening credit sequence: we see Walker stagger into the waters off Alcatraz Island and flounder in them, clearly lacking the strength to swim a few yards let alone the miles to the mainland. Nor do we then get an insert shot of Walker being fished out of the ocean by deck hands on a fortuitously placed fishing vessel. No plausible explanation whatsoever is provided for his survival: with no transition the film cuts from Walker apparently helpless in the ocean to him standing in perfectly good health on the deck of the tour boat. It seems logical, therefore, to conclude that what we see must in some sense be deceptive: Walker couldn't have and *didn't* get back to the shore alive. If we take that view, it still leaves us with more than one way of understanding the bulk of the film. One possibility is suggested by James Michael Martin: ". . . Walker is . . . a revived restless spirit, an exterminating angel brought back by the gods, returned to the living to stalk his betrayers and avenge his own death. . . ."[1] In other words, the film is not a standard action-adventure but a ghost story. If one grants this ghost enough corporeality to go to bed with a woman (his former sister-in-law Chris, played by Angie Dickinson) and to manhandle any number of thugs, this interpretation of *Point Blank* works well enough—except for the very ending of the movie. Does it really make sense for an avenging spirit to discover he has merely been used by a living gangster to cement the latter's worldly position? (In the end Walker discovers that the helpful Yost is really Fairfax, the boss of the Organization.)

The interpretation that I personally prefer is that the invulnerable Walker who stalks through the film is not a Superman or a ghost but merely the wish-fulfillment projection of a man who has lapsed into dream as he dies back on Alcatraz Island. In an interview with Michel Ciment, Boorman himself says, "Seeing the film, one should be able to imagine that this whole story of vengeance is taking place inside [Walker's] head at the moment of his death"—although he then adds, "In any case, that's a possible interpretation."[2] Despite Boorman's less than total commitment to this interpretation, it is the one I have chosen to explore for the bulk of this chapter because for me it is the one that gives strongest meaning to the film. I would be less than honest, however, if I didn't admit that some parts of *Point Blank* (particularly those which seem intended as satiric of American capitalist society) are rather inconsistent with such a view. At some of these I will glance briefly toward the end of the essay.

One thing that reinforces the impression that *Point Blank* is a dream is Boorman's use of a full range of non-realistic techniques employed by French New Wave directors, particularly Alain Resnais. Fragmented flashbacks, slow motion, freeze frames, disorienting editing (as Stephen Farber points out, sequences seldom begin with conventional establishing shots: ". . . we're constantly being thrust into a scene before we have our bearings, forced to catch up with what's going on"[3]) are some of the devices that make the film resemble a dream with its irrational dislocations and obsessive repetitions. These techniques are all established within the long credit sequence that opens the movie.

An opening credit announces the name of the production company (Metro-Goldwyn-Mayer) against a red background. The red screen dissolves into a tight close-up of Lee Marvin's (Walker's) face. As the camera pulls back, a shadow falls across Walker; a shot rings out, then another as he lurches backward to collapse in the corner of a dimly lit room with the shadows of bars visible on the walls above him. As we look down at the body, Walker's voice-over helps us to identify the setting and start to move toward an understanding of what we have just seen happen: "Cell . . . prison cell—how did I get here?" Flashbacks immediately begin to offer partial answers to the question. Extremely drunk at what appears to be a stag party, Walker is accosted by his friend Mal Reese (John Vernon), who pleads that he needs Walker's "help." To gain Walker's full attention, Mal knocks him to the floor and lies on top of him as he begs for his friend's assistance. We then cut to a daylight scene at the prison as Mal explains how they will intercept a "drop" at Alcatraz and hijack the money. A woman, who will later be identified as Walker's wife, is seen in the courtyard down below the two men up on a catwalk. Mal assures Walker there will be minimal violence when they take the money from the two men who have received it from the helicopter delivery: "We just hit 'em on the head, and that's it."

But when the heist actually occurs, Mal shoots and kills the men. Perhaps it is this deviation from the original scenario that makes Walker say to Mal, "We blew it," as his friend is gloating over the success of the operation. Shortly afterwards Mal realizes that things have not gone as well as he had believed: after he finishes counting the money, he says in disappointment, "It's not as much as I thought." To get the money he needs to pay off his debt to the "Organization" he will have to appropriate Walker's share. To this end he sends Walker's wife Lynne (Sharon Acker) to distract him, then shoots his friend after calling Lynne away. At this point both Walker and the viewer have a fairly good idea of how he came to be lying wounded in the corner of a prison cell.

These highly condensed opening scenes not only explain how Walker came to be shot, they also suggest how he must feel about it. The man lying in the corner of the prison cell has been doubly betrayed: his wife has connived with his best friend to bring him to the brink of death. The flashbacks, however, focus more on the friend's betrayal than the wife's. The scene where Mal lies on top of Walker on the floor is more erotically charged than the one between Walker and Lynne on the cell bed. Boorman has said in an interview that he wanted to suggest "homosexual overtones" in the friendship of Walker and Mal and that in the scene on the floor, "Lee's whole playing of that was kind of like a girl who's getting raped and is not sure whether she's enjoying it or not."[4]

Mal is in effect seducing Walker into participating in the robbery with him—partly by appealing to his sympathy ("I owe a bundle to some guys, Walker; I tell you, they're going to kill me if I don't get it"), partly by stressing his need ("I can't make it on my own"), but mostly by pushing the claim of friendship ("You're my friend, Walker"). It is the final appeal to which Walker is most vulnerable, as evidenced by his off-screen voice repeating "my friend" and then summarizing his response to Mal's petition to him in the three words, "Help my friend." The scene on the floor between the two men is staged like a sex scene largely because Walker—like the victim of a seduction—is swept away by his emotions to do something contrary to his own best interests. "Trust me," Mal says four times in succession as they are lying together on the floor. This is exactly the fatal or nearly fatal (depending one's interpretation of the film) error that Walker makes. The bitterness that fuels Walker's drive for vengeance in the first half of the film is fueled by his sense of betrayal by *two* lovers. And his ruthlessness is an overcompensation for his sense of weakness in having succumbed to Mal's emotional (erotic) appeal to him.

After Walker has reviewed the key events that led up to his shooting, he says to himself in voice-over, as his head falls to one side (as in death or unconsciousness) on the cell floor, "Did it happen? A dream. A dream." But it is far more likely that the film that follows is the dream—the wish-fulfillment fantasy of a nearly powerless man seeking to experience in his imagination the irresistible strength and dominance he could not achieve in reality. Walker trusted his wife and friend to his own harm. Walker in the remainder of the film will trust no one. Walker's emotional commitments to Mal and Lynne made him vulnerable. In the rest of the movie he will commit himself to no one, not even apparently to Chris, who is deserving of commitment. Walker was obviously disturbed when he saw Mal shoot down the two men who had picked up the drop from the helicopter. From this point on, he will witness a number of deaths without apparently blinking an eye. (Only Lynne's death is an exception.) The man who lay wounded in the cell in Alcatraz was a victim—a man whose fate was controlled by others. After meeting

Yost on the boat, until almost the very end of the film, Walker will apparently be in control; it will be Lynne, Mal Reese, the members of the "Organization"—his former victimizers—who will be the victims.

Walker's escape from Alcatraz is largely presented in a series of freeze frames: Walker standing in the hall of the cell block, Walker eerily lit from below as he crawls along a catwalk, Walker climbing a barbed wire fence. Jack Shadoian describes the sequence this way: "[Walker] is caught in stark and mythic poses, at peculiar angles and focus, distorted by queer lighting and special lenses. . . . We are given an abstract of the escape, out of time."[5] These images create for me the impression of a man not deeply enough into his dream to create narrative continuity, merely able to call up fragments of the story he wishes to compose. Only on the boat with Yost does the dream begin to unfold smoothly. Yost's function at the end of the film will be quite different, but at this point he appears as a sort of guardian angel willing to aid and abet Walker's quest for righteous vengeance. Most first-time viewers of the film probably interpret Yost as John Michael Martin originally did: ". . . a police detective—willfully allowing (or even ordering) the deaths of . . . Syndicate figures—perhaps because his department has been unable to gather sufficient evidence for conviction."[6] This of course is the realistic way of seeing the guardian angel. In any case Yost's aid is essential to Walker in locating the people he wishes to find—the first of whom is his faithless wife Lynne.

Walker's approach to Lynne is accompanied by a significant sound effect. We first see him striding toward the backtracking camera down corridors of the Los Angeles airport. The corridors are mostly empty except for Walker; his footsteps are loud, echoing, inexorable. They are also heard over the intercut scenes of Lynne waking up in the morning, getting clothes from her closet, making up her face, and then getting a facial and having her hair done at a beauty parlor. The echoing footsteps continue even when we see Walker driving a rental car; they do not stop until he smashes open Lynne's front door, flings her to the floor, and bursts into her bedroom to fire all the rounds from his pistol into her bed. The footsteps remind us of the character's name: Walker. As Shadoian says, "He is The Walker. He pursues with old-fashioned tenacity, on foot. . . ."[7] He moves directly forward, with scarcely any deviation toward his goals: first, vengeance on those who betrayed him; second, attainment of the $93,000—his share from the hijack, which Mal took after shooting him—that he believes the Organization owes him. Of course, the true goal he strides after in both cases is simply justice. Walker believes has been wronged, and his entire being is bent upon only one thing: redress.

Why did Walker fire the six shots into Lynne's empty bed? Did he expect Mal to be lying in it? Is the bed a convenient symbol of Lynne's sexual betrayal of him with Mal, upon which Walker vents his jealous rage instead of directly upon Lynne? (Later, after Fairfax over the telephone turns down his request for the $93,000, Walker expresses his fury by shooting the phone.) Or has the tension built up so strongly within Walker that merely manhandling Lynne is not sufficient outlet for it? He must release it in the almost orgasmic pumping of shots into the bed. Even then the tension is not entirely released: he still has to sweep nearly three full shelves of bottles of colored oils and lotions into a wash basin in Lynne's bathroom before he can go into the living room and collapse—spent—upon her couch.

Lynne's confession to him that follows, unlike most of the film, is rather directly adapted from the novel upon which *Point Blank* is based—*The Hunter* by Richard Stark (Donald Westlake). But although Lynne in the film says many of the same things as Lynne in the book, there is a fundamental difference in the ways in which the speeches are presented. The novelist has Lynne express herself through dialogue with Parker (the novel's equivalent of Walker), who keeps her revelations flowing with probing questions and his own interpretations. In the film Lynne delivers a long monologue—without any prompting from Walker by either word or gesture. Although she addresses Walker from time to time ("Walker, I'm glad you're not dead."), she seldom looks at him and delivers the entire speech in a flat, inexpressive voice—rather giving the impression that we and Walker are eavesdropping directly upon her thoughts. Her monologue drifts, stream-of-consciousness style, from one subject to another:

> You ought to kill me. I can't sleep. Haven't slept. Keep taking pills. Dream about you. How good it must be . . . being dead. Is it? No, no, I can't. Never had the courage. This? [*She glances at the living room.*] Payoff, I guess. I don't know where he is. I really don't. Money? Guy brings it the first of every month. Thousand. Thousand. . . . Just couldn't make it with you, Walker.

But it is appropriate that her monologue should drift, for that is what she has done in her life as well: "Suddenly I began to drift toward Mal. And I, . . . I just went with it." If her speech is in reality Walker's dream, it offers him at least an ego-saving interpretation of her betrayal of him: it was not a considered act, but one of inadvertence. She "drifted" into it, but she now tells him, "That night on Alcatraz . . . I knew it was really you I wanted. I found out too late."

After Walker awakens on Lynne's couch the following morning, he finds her lying dead on her bed, having succumbed to an overdose of her sleeping pills. Again, if we interpret this event as part of Walker's dream, an element of wish-fulfillment is obviously present: in the end Lynne could not live with her betrayal of Walker. He slips his wedding ring on her finger to claim her conclusively as his in her death.

At this point the film or the dream seems to slip slightly out of control. Scriptwriter Alexander Jacobs had written a perfectly coherent sequence in which Walker drank steadily and gradually stripped the apartment as a sort of "wake" for Lynne.[8] What Boorman supplies is a far less coherent sequence, as if the death of Lynne has proved more of a shock to Walker than his psyche was prepared for, and it takes him a while to resume a lucid fantasy. After finding Lynne's body, Walker looks out one of the front windows of the apartment; we see his face from outside the window screen in a telephoto lens shot that is at first slightly blurry but then comes more sharply into focus as Walker recognizes the man lounging on the sidewalk below him—Yost. The "guardian angel" acknowledges Walker with a one-finger wave and a slight smile, as if to ask, "Well, did you get what you wanted?" Walker then returns to Lynne's bedroom where he finds the bed stripped, the bullet holes gone, and his wife's dead body replaced by a live white cat. Walker enters Lynne's bathroom, inadvertently drops another glass bottle of green bath oil into the sink and then looks down where the new oil flows together with those from the broken bottles of the day before. The camera moves closer and closer to the shattered glass and flowing oils to focus on red oils that inevitably suggest blood. Walker then returns to the living room to find it stripped and the front door nailed shut. The significance of this sequence is quite obscure. Stephen Farber speculates, "Perhaps the stripping of the apartment is to be taken as only a fantasy, a visualization of Walker's forlorn state of mind." Then he adds, "But there is no way of knowing."[9] To be sure, there isn't; but my own guess is that the stripped apartment represents Walker's sense of the emptiness of his vengeance on Lynne (and the absence of the bullet holes, the futility of his acts of aggression). The red oil in the sink (which would have long before drained away in real time) represents his guilt for her death (like the blood that Lady Macbeth could not wash off her hands). After beholding the blood and the emptiness Walker goes to sit in a corner of the living room as if he is returning to the corner of the cell in Alcatraz to accept his death there.

But then he suddenly re-hears Mal's voice calling, "Lynne, com'ere," followed by a shot. The sounds symbolize Walker's realization that he has something to live for—vengeance on Mal. The sound of the shot is echoed by hard raps on the front door of the apartment. Walker (now clad in coat and tie) strides purposefully to door to assault and question the deliverer of Lynne's monthly payoff. The fantasy of revenge has restarted and will flow smoothly with only occasional eddies of incoherency to the end of the film. The episode that follows, in which Walker destroys one of Big John Stegman's cars by repeatedly smashing it into the pilings under the Los Angeles freeway in an attempt to force information about Mal out of the car dealer, is one of the best in the film—but also one of the least dreamlike. I will discuss another of its other implications later, but for now I merely want to stress that Stegman introduces an important new character into the film: Lynne's sister Chris: ". . . how's your wife?" Stegman asks Walker. "And her sister?" Lynne hadn't mentioned she had a sister—nor that Mal was trying to put the make on that sister (as Stegman reveals). One suspects the reason Chris hadn't formerly been mentioned is that Walker's imagination had not yet brought her into existence. Chris is, quite simply, a reincarnation of Lynne—but a new, improved Lynne, whose loyalty will unambiguously be to Walker and not to Mal.

Before setting out to find Chris, Walker visits Lynne's grave. Then he passes through the night club Chris operates, as if confronting a set of demonic spirits guarding the entrance to the realm of the dead. Rock music thumps and wails like a heavy electrical storm, a black singer screams like one of the damned in his torment and invites the audience to scream with him, two thugs beset Walker in the darkened backstage area and only allow him to continue on his way after he dispatches them with maximum brutality (he smashes a beer bottle into the face of one and whacks the other in the testicles). After demonstrating his manhood in this manner, he approaches Chris's home, which is a suitable house of the dead because it had belonged to her former lover, a musician who was killed by the Organization. He then finds Chris lying on her bed in much the same position as the dead Lynne. There is even a small plastic container of pills, like Lynne's, on the night table next to her; but Walker sweeps it to the floor with one swipe of the barrel of his pistol— and shakes Chris's shoulder to wake her up. The resurrection has occurred.

Like Lynne, Chris goes to bed with Mal, but unlike Lynne, only to give Walker the opportunity to sneak into his former friend's penthouse apartment. She quickly dresses and departs after Walker has entered and dragged Mal, wrapped only in a sheet, from his bed. In most of the scene that follows Walker, although not lying on Mal as his so-called friend had lain on him in the scene at the stag party, is in the superior position looking down at his betrayer. When Mal repeats his classic line—"Trust me"—it is clear that Walker is now thoroughly in control of the situation and impervious to his former friend's deceptive appeals. In a brief flashback to the scene on the floor, Mal makes a statement, the irony of which was then most immediately applicable to Walker but is now to himself: "We'll live forever." Mal's death a moment later is somewhat ambiguous in visual terms. It *is* possible to interpret what we see on the screen as T. J. Ross does:

> Yanking at the folds of the sheet [Mal] Rees [*sic*] had wrapped round himself, Walker steers the villain to the penthouse balcony over which, with a flick of the wrist, he empties Rees out of his sheet like so much rotten meat being thrown down a garbage disposal chute.[10]

But since Walker does not directly cause the death of anyone else in the film, it seems far more likely that Boorman wanted the audience to think that Mal caused his own demise, that he was tripped over the roof edge by the sheet as he tried to bolt away from his captor. Certainly just before Mal fell to his doom, Walker had said to him, "I'm taking you to Carter; we're gonna do this one together"—indicating that his more pressing concern at the time was collecting his $93,000 rather than gaining the utmost measure of revenge on his betrayer. Later when Chris asks what happened to Mal, Walker says (admittedly without the slightest measure of regret), "he fell"—not "I threw him off the roof." It is part of Walker's power fantasy that he doesn't actually have to *kill* the people he seeks vengeance upon: Lynne (intentionally) and Mal (unintentionally) destroy themselves; members of the "Organization" are shot down by other employees of the same company.

Walker's relentless pursuit in the remainder of the film of the $93,000 he says the Organization "owes" him would on the surface seem to be poorly motivated. How could he really think the Organization owed him money that Mal stole from it? The real reason for Walker's vendetta against the Organization is probably just that the deaths of Lynne and Mal have not satisfied his lust for vengeance. John Michael Martin is surely correct in saying, "Walker is not really interested in collecting his $93,000; only in having justice. He uses the money, as do so many of us in everyday circumstances, as a justification for his ruthlessness."[11] I would add that the $93,000 becomes to him the symbol of *everything* he feels he has been cheated out of in his life—all the things he feels he deserved but did not have, including the love of a faithful wife and the loyalty of a true friend. The money is so important to him only because he becomes fixated on it as something that ought to be attainable.

After the death of Mal, Chris increasingly takes on the role of Walker's anima—offering fundamental criticisms of his rigid, male value system that honors only strength, dominance, and the ruthless pursuit of justice. When he gives her the envelope containing a thousand dollars (Mal's monthly "payoff" to Lynne) as his payment to her for her aid in helping him get to Mal, she says to him, "You died at Alcatraz, all

right." This statement has a double meaning if the film is regarded as
the dream of a dying man; but in its immediate context it implies that
if Walker could consider money a suitable payment for what she did for
him, both his feelings and his awareness of the feelings of others must
be totally atrophied. Over the intercom at Brewster's house she offers a
more thorough-going criticism:

> You're a pathetic sight, Walker, from where I'm standing—chasing shadows.
> You're played out. It's over—finished. What would you do with the money
> if you got it? It wasn't yours in the first place. Why don't you just lie down
> and die?

A part of Walker's psyche is telling him that the continued existence
he has fantasized for himself is hollow. He has made the $93,000 a
symbol of all that he feels he has been unjustly deprived of, but he has
no real right to the money: as Chris says, "It wasn't yours in the first
place." The money is also a dead-end goal: Walker merely wants to
attain it; he has nothing he wishes to attain *with* it. The absence of any
goals for his life beyond the vengeance that has already been achieved
and the money he has no plans for spending indicates that Walker in
truth has virtually nothing to live for. As Chris says, he might just as
well accept his death.

Chris offers him another lesson in this same section of the film. At
one point Chris becomes infuriated with Walker's emotional unrespon-
siveness; she slaps him, then hits him with her purse, and finally pounds
on his chest with her fists until she drops to her knees at his feet in
exhaustion. Throughout her attack Walker is totally unmoved; she might
as well have been beating on a block of granite. In his dream Walker
has recreated himself as a superman—lacking the vulnerability he had
in real life to people like Lynne and Mal. But Chris gradually breaks
through the apparently impenetrable shell he has placed about himself.
First, she causes him irritation by turning on all the electrical appliances
in the house, then she denounces him over the intercom, finally she
decks him with a billiard cue. Only after she has knocked him down
and perhaps out, does Walker embrace Chris—first on the floor of the
billiard room (with Walker lying on top of her as Mal had lain on him
at the stag party), then naked together in bed. The message seems clear:
Walker can only love a woman again after he is forced to acknowledge
his vulnerability. He can experience no pleasure with a woman if he
cannot also experience pain with her.

During the lovemaking another curious sequence of shots occurs. We
cut from Walker and Chris on the floor to them naked in bed. In a cut
that is barely noticeable the two characters roll over and Chris becomes

Lynne. Then in the same manner Walker becomes Mal, and in the final transformation Lynne becomes Chris. Then we are back on the floor of the billiard room with Chris and Walker embracing fully clothed. Finally there is a reprise of them naked in bed. Are the first four bedroom shots merely Walker's fantasy as he lies with Chris on the floor? If so, the first transformation from Chris to Lynne would seem to indicate that the sister for Walker is ultimately a substitute for the wife he lost. Walker's transformation into Mal with both of the women might indicate his sense of being superseded by Mal with Lynne and his retrospective jealousy that Mal had Chris first. But it might also betoken his sense of identification with Mal and the latent homosexual attraction that underlay their relationship. If these scenes are Walker's fantasies, it is significant that in the final shot, following the return to the floor of the billiard room, he is in bed with Chris and no further transformations occur. Even if this scene along with the rest of the film is also his fantasy, he has at least settled for the time being on who he is and whom he wishes to be with.

In the morning, though, Walker seems not to have made any significant progress as a result of his experiences of the night before. He is clearly unwilling to give up his pursuit of the $93,000 in order to remain with Chris. When he accosts Brewster (Carroll O'Connor) after knocking out his bodyguard, the Organization executive accuses him of being "a very bad man, . . . a very destructive man" and asks, "Why do you run around doing things like this? What do you want?" Walker can only reply, "I want my money." Even when Brewster presses his questioning—"What do you *really* want?"—Walker can only look faintly puzzled and dully repeat,"I, I really want my money." Interspersed in the scene are flashbacks to Walker making the same demand of Mal and of Carter (the executive just below Brewster). Walker will not be ready to acknowledge that he doesn't really want the money until the final sequence—the return to Alcatraz Island.

In the prison courtyard Walker sees a helicopter make another money drop and watches Brewster collapse as a shot rings out (he has been hit by the same marksman who earlier killed Carter and Stegman). Then Yost steps out of the darkness to reveal that he is really Fairfax, Brewster's superior in the Organization. He has been using Walker to eliminate his rivals for power in the criminal empire. When he told Walker at the beginning, "I want the Organization," he didn't mean he wanted to bring its members to justice—he meant he wanted to cement his control over it. Fairfax first offers Walker a position in the Organization ("Hey, Walker, come on in with me"); receiving no response, he shouts, "Well, come and get your money then." But instead we see Walker draw back into the shadows of the darkened prison—he is finally seen taking a sideways step into total blackness, which can easily be interpreted as his ultimate acceptance of his death.

The original scriptwriter for *Point Blank*, Alexander Jacobs has criticized Boorman's ending for the film as "evasive." Jacobs had written a fairly conventional happy ending in which Fairfax "falls off [a] parapet and dies" and Walker "is led away by the girl [Chris] out into the world again."[12] But Boorman's ending is perfect if one considers the film to be Walker's dream. In the end the dream coils back on itself. Walker realizes that his two-fold pursuit of vengeance and money has not truly served justice but only the unjust forces of exploitation and destruction. This recognition makes him withdraw, as John Lindsay Brown says, "in a kind of impotence into the shadows, realising at last his own complicity and refusing to act any longer in this world of treachery and deception."[13] It would be better to "lie down and die" rather than to cooperate further. He may even perceive that he originally accepted such complicity when he agreed to assist Mal in the hijack and that for this reason his death in the cell in Alcatraz is no injustice.

The final shot of the film is something of a mind twister. We look down from a bird's-eye perspective on Brewster's body and the package of money lying in the courtyard at Alcatraz. Then the camera zooms back and tilts up to show the San Francisco night skyline and slowly pans the building tops until we see the Bay and an island in the distance. As the camera zooms in on the island and the final credits begin, we perhaps realize with a start that the island we see is Alcatraz! Boorman's final clue that the film operates according to laws quite removed from those of verisimilitude.

But Alexander Jacobs complains that *Point Blank* doesn't consistently operate even according to the laws of surrealism (or dream or myth):

> . . . while it would have been marvelous to have continued our myth that he literally comes from the underground, roams over the surface of the earth for a brief while, then goes back into the shadows—well, by introducing the girl and all sorts of other things, we obviously go away from the essential myth.[14]

While I think "the girl" fits quite well into the dream-like atmosphere of the film (men frequently dream about "girls"), I would agree that certain sequences have the quality less of dream or myth than of social satire.

Most of the scenes involving members of the Organization other than Mal have this quality because Boorman was trying to convey an idea he expresses directly in his interview with Farber: "It seems to me the business world *is* the Organization in America." For this reason the director expected the audience to identify with his protagonist in his campaign against the Organization:

> . . . one of the levels I was working on was to say that Walker was like an ordinary individual with no backing trying to deal with a business corporation or trying to claim from the insurance company and just being rejected and pushed away.[15]

It is exactly such identification that makes several of the scenes in the film so exhilarating. Many a viewer of commercials by auto dealers on late night TV would love to give one or more of them the kind of ride Walker gives Big John Stegman among the pilings under the L.A. Freeway. When we have been thwarted in what we regard as a just claim by some big corporation, we would love to be able to drag one of its chief executives down out of his office the way Walker does with Carter. When we are given the run around on the telephone or have a pressing demand dismissed by some impersonal voice, it would at least be a release to blast the offending message bearer out of existence with a .357 magnum.

But if we identify too closely with Walker in such scenes, we run the risk of missing the central point of the film: Walker is not a real hero, only a dream hero. And the dreamer's values are misplaced. The quest for vengeance and for material reward does not bring self-satisfaction— only the tragic realization of how inextricably one is mired in a fundamentally evil system of greed and exploitation. As Walker disappears into the darkness at the end of the film, he must realize again what he did after Mal's successful completion of the murderous heist: he blew it.

9

"The Worst Part":
Martin Scorsese's *Mean Streets*

MARTIN Scorsese's grittily realistic portrayal of the marginal lives of young men in an Italian neighborhood of New York City focuses primarily on the conflicts of its protagonist Charlie (Harvey Keitel). On a first viewing of the film one might conclude that Charlie's most significant conflict is between ambition and friendship—between his desire to rise within the local Mafia hierarchy and his commitment to his irresponsible friend, Johnny Boy (Robert De Niro). The film would then seem to end tragically, for Charlie's actions ultimately lead to the destruction not only of his ambitions but apparently of his friend as well. But to understand the real tragedy of *Mean Streets* one must understand that the most important thing Charlie has lost at the end the film is not his ambition or his friend but his sense of spiritual purpose.

The friend, Johnny Boy, has played a crucial role in Charlie's undoing, in that his reckless behavior has contributed greatly to the catastophe in the movie's culminating sequence. Because Johnny Boy owes $3,000 to a loan shark and has not only refused to pay the money back but verbally humiliated the man, he has become the victim of a shooting attack while riding in a car with his friend Charlie and cousin Teresa (Amy Robinson). Johnny Boy, Teresa, and Charlie have all been shot and additionally injured (or at least shaken up) by the car wreck that occurred as a consequence of the shooting, but for Charlie the physical wound is the least of the damage he has suffered.

Charlie had hoped to open a restaurant under the patronage of his Mafioso Uncle Giovanni, but his uncle had warned him against associating with the "half-crazy" Johnny Boy ("honorable men go with honorable men") and his epileptic cousin Teresa ("don't get involved"). The fact that he has been shot and wounded on the streets with two people he was admonished to avoid almost certainly spells the end to Charlie's hopes of having his path to prosperity paved by his uncle. (In the original script Giovanni exiles his nephew, giving him a $350 airline ticket with Charlie to fill in his own destination.[1]) But losing his chance for upward mobility through mob-related business ventures probably strikes most viewers of the film as less of a tragedy than it does Charlie. In truth, throughout the course of the film he has never revealed much aptitude for success in either business or organized crime. If he has lost an opportunity through his involvement with Johnny Boy and Teresa, it doesn't seem likely it was one he could have made much of in any case.

The real harm Charlie has sustained is not to his worldly career but to his spiritual self-image. From the very beginning of the film Charlie has entirely contradictory goals and desires. He is quite willing to suck around his uncle in hopes of being set up in business, but he also talks frequently to God about his desire to do penance for his sins. At one point he tells Teresa about his admiration for Francis of Assisi, and she quickly points out the contradiction between his beliefs and his style of life: "St. Francis didn't run numbers." (Charlie denies that he does either, but shortly before in a café he seemed to be accepting a bet from a man on the "4–6–3 combination.") But Charlie still tries to emulate Francis: the saint helped people, and Charlie has made it one of his prime aims in life to give aid to Johnny Boy, whom he describes to Teresa as "just a kid who needs to be helped." On another occasion when Teresa is denouncing her cousin as "crazy"—"he's like an insane person"—Charlie asks rhetorically, "Who's gonna help him if I don't?"

But at the end of the film, Charlie sees that he has not helped Johnny Boy; indeed he has simply brought him in range of the hit man's gun. Scorsese has said in an interview that "Johnny isn't dead. A lot of people think he is, but he isn't";[2] but Charlie certainly has ample reason to think that when Johnny Boy stumbles away from him down the alley, blood gushing from his neck, he is literally on his last legs. Charlie has not only failed to help his friend, he has miscarried in the performance of what he had specifically identified, to both himself and the "Lord," as an act of penance. Indeed he seems to feel less guilt for the pain he has caused both Johnny and Teresa by driving them into the path of the gunman's bullets than for having failed to carry out his commitment to God: in the final shots of the film Charlie is not looking at either his friend or his lover; he is kneeling in the street in an attitude of prayer.

That a religious theme is central to *Mean Streets* is apparent from the very outset of the film. It begins with a completely black screen and Charlie's voice uttering the words, "You don't make up for your sins in Church; you do it in the streets. You do it at home. The rest is bullshit, and you know it." Then in the first real shot of the film we see Charlie waking up in bed. He gets up, walks by a crucifix on the wall, and then looks at himself in his dresser mirror. (This sort of self-examination will occur several times in the film.) It is impossible to know if the opening words came to Charlie in a dream or were simply familiar thoughts he reiterated to himself before opening his eyes. At any rate the crucifix ought to remind both the viewer and Charlie that true penance requires sacrifice; and when he looks at himself in the mirror, he may be wondering if he is capable of it.

Charlie pursues his thoughts about penance in his second appearance in the film in church. Speaking to a statue representing Christ in Mary's arms after His having been taken down from the cross, Charlie seems to be trying to strike a deal with the Lord: "If I do something wrong, I just want to pay for it my way, so I do my own penance for my own sins. What do you say, huh?" In the next sequence in Tony's bar, Charlie looks up from where he is sitting to see Johnny Boy enter, smiling broadly, a girl on either arm. Charlie addresses the deity in voice-over: "All right, okay, thanks a lot, Lord, thanks a lot for opening my eyes. We talk about penance, and you send this through the door." The word "penance" has two meanings which are relevant here: "1. a punishment undergone in token of penitence for sin. 2. a penitential discipline imposed by church authority."[3] Charlie sees Johnny Boy both as a punishment the Lord has imposed on him and as a source of discipline—by taking care of Johnny, helping him through his difficulties, Charlie hopes to work off his own sins. As Michael Bliss puts it, "Charlie apparently sees Johnny as the cross he must bear as a necessary prelude to his redemption."[4]

The meeting of Johnny and Charlie is filmed in an interesting manner. Johnny and the two girls come down beside the bar toward the camera in slow motion. Intercut are reaction shots of Charlie seated at the bar. After he ironically thanks the Lord for his "penance," he studies the approaching Johnny Boy for a long time, then gets down off his stool, turns, and moves off toward the rear—obviously indicating he does not feel ready to accept his penance. But after we see Johnny Boy arrive at the empty stool, the film immediately cuts to him arriving at the same stool with Charlie on it, and the two of them embrace. The escape to the rear of the bar was apparently just a fantasy on Charlie's part—an impulse he chose not really to act upon.

Before Johnny Boy's entrance Charlie has talked to Michael (Richard Romanus) about the loan debt Johnny owes and Charlie has "vouched for." Michael's view of his defaulting debtor is harshly judgmental: Johnny is "a punk kid . . . the biggest jerk-off around." Charlie defends his friend to Michael—"he's really a good kid"—but evinces little faith in him when he talks with Johnny Boy in the back room of Tony's bar. In this and in successive scenes Charlie is repeatedly astonished and dismayed at how minimal an attempt Johnny is making to pay back even a small portion of the money he owes Michael. In the first scene in the back of the bar Charlie wrests money away from Johnny Boy and indicates that he (Charlie) will give the money to Michael if Johnny won't (although we never actually see Charlie do this). Toward the end of the film he gives $22 of his own money to Johnny Boy so that at least *some* payment can be made to Michael. But these interventions on Charlie's part not only prove futile they also seem to be counter-productive.

Charlie does not realize how strong a role pride plays in the financial relationship between Michael and Johnny Boy. Michael's pride makes it absolutely necessary for him to collect at least a significant portion of the money Johnny owes him—or to inflict appropriate punishment on the defaulter. Johnny Boy's pride prohibits him from making any payment that his creditor will regard as more than humiliatingly insignificant. The chief difference in the way the pride of the two characters operates in their conflict is that Michael's pride is offended by Johnny Boy, while the latter's pride is chiefly affronted by Charlie.

Michael is introduced into the film as would-be smart operator. In the first scene in which he appears he is supervising the unloading of a truck. He enters the car of a potential customer and offers to sell him part or all of two shipments of (presumably stolen) German lenses he has bought. The customer examines the "lens" and says, "You bought two shipments of Jap adapters, not lenses." Michael can only repeat, "Jap adapters," and stare forward in dismay. In trying to demonstrate his cleverness and make a big profit, he has only displayed his gullibility and taken a big loss. His one success in the film is when he and Tony (David Proval) cheat two teenaged boys from the suburbs who want to buy fireworks, and even then the boys only give him half of the $40 they said they had to spend. "We got stiffed by them kids," Michael complains as he and Tony drive off. It becomes increasingly important to Michael, therefore, that he make money from his loan to Johnny Boy so that he can restore in his own eyes his self-image as a sharp operator.

When Michael first talks to Charlie about Johnny, he expresses his contempt for his debtor by calling him a "jerk-off"; but as the film goes on and Johnny continues to avoid making any payment, Michael begins to fear the epithet may come to be applied to him: "If that kid thinks he's making a jerk-off out of me, I'm gonna break his legs." Employing violence is thus seen as a last resort for restoring self-respect. Charlie conveys Michael's sentiments when he urges Johnny Boy to show up at Tony's bar on his payday with some money in hand: "This way he doesn't think you're tryin' to make a jerk-off out of him." But that is exactly what Johnny Boy does want to do. When he is forced by Charlie to turn up (late) at the bar, he only gives Michael $10 (even though Charlie had made it possible for him to pay $30). He also tells Michael he had only borrowed money from him because he had already borrowed from everybody else in the neighborhood. Only Michael was a big enough "jerk-off" to lend him money by then. He goes on to rub in the insult: "That's what you are, that's what I think of you—a jerk-off." He then pulls a gun on Michael and drives him from the bar, simultaneously heaping upon him further epithets (of which "asshole" is the most reiter-ated). It is not surprising, therefore, that Michael feels the only possible way of restoring his pride is to get his own (hired) gun and use it upon Johnny Boy.

While Johnny clearly enjoys humiliating Michael, the latter is merely a surrogate for the person he is truly taking his revenge upon: Charlie. Johnny Boy's pride has been hurt repeatedly by Charlie throughout the film. In their first scene together when Johnny comes up to his friend at the bar, Charlie grabs him by the ear to pull him into the back room to discuss the debt to Michael. Johnny Boy protests, "You're making me look bad, Charlie, in front of the girls over here." Later Charlie makes him look bad in front of a different kind of audience. When the group of friends from the neighborhood go together to collect a gambling dept for Jimmy from Joey the pool hall operator, Johnny provokes hostility by muttering insults about the denizens of the hall. Afraid Joey will refuse to pay, Charlie tells Johnny Boy, "Keep your mouth shut." Johnny is highly indignant: "You told me that in front of this asshole!" Charlie not only makes him look bad in front of other people, he makes Johnny Boy look bad to himself by constantly advising him on how to behave. At one point Johnny says to Charlie in exasperation, "I'm so stupid, you gotta look out for me, right?"

But Johnny Boy is also bothered by the fact that Charlie has not *always* looked out for him; on crucial occasions Charlie has chosen to look out for Number One instead of his best friend. On the night streets after a shooting in Tony's bar, Charlie refers to the time Johnny Boy got hit on the head by a cop and says—perhaps only half humorously—"You never recovered from that one, did you?" Johnny points out that one of the reasons he got hurt as badly as he did was that Charlie ran out on him, leaving him as "a punching bag" for the cops. Charlie doesn't deny the charge, merely says that if Johnny Boy had any sense he would have done the same thing. The brief exchange may be a key to the present relationship between the two characters. Charlie feels guilty about running out on his friend; he may even feel that Johnny Boy's irrational and irresponsible behavior may literally be the result of this head injury. If so, taking care of Johnny is not a form of penance he has chosen randomly (because his friend happened to walk in the bar when he was talking to God about the subject); he is basically doing penance for a specific sin (or sins) against Johnny Boy. And because Charlie ran out on him back then, Johnny Boy expects him to do so again—whenever the going gets really tough. Perhaps one reason Johnny gets deeper and deeper into trouble with Michael is because he is always testing the limits of Charlie's commitment to him.

For Johnny Boy, his friend's expected betrayal of him occurs when Charlie refuses to go to his uncle Giovanni as a way of resolving the debt to Michael. In the graveyard scene Johnny says there is only one "way out" of his money problems: "Talk to your uncle." Johnny Boy doesn't know that Charlie has been specifically warned by his uncle not to associate with Johnny or Teresa, and Charlie never explains his fears to him as clearly as he does to Teresa: "Between you and Johnny, you're gonna ruin everything for me." But the motivation of self-interest on Charlie's part is perfectly clear when he responds to Johnny Boy's appeal that he go to his uncle with the comment, "Oh, that it'd be just, just, just really great for you—but not for me." Johnny Boy's cry in a later sequence—"You didn't do nothin' for me, you fuck . . ."—is technically unjust, but Charlie has certainly tried to do nothing that would injure his own future. As Pauline Kael says, Charlie is "Judas the betrayer because of his careful angling to move up the next rung of the ladder."[5] In the end, therefore, Johnny plunges himself into deep trouble as a form of indirect revenge on Charlie.

After the confrontation with Michael in the bar, Johnny Boy smiles and says to Charlie, "You got what you wanted." This statement has a number of possible meanings, but certainly one of them is that by refusing to go to his uncle, Charlie showed that he wanted Johnny to get into trouble with Michael. Since Johnny had no real way of paying the debt, the crisis would have come sooner or later; he merely chose to force it now through his obnoxious behavior to demonstrate to Charlie where his refusal to seek help from Giovanni would ultimately lead. He may also mean that because Charlie has always regarded him as "stupid," he should be happy to have witnessed this classic instance of stupid—i.e., self-destructive—behavior. An underlying meaning of which Johnny Boy is doubtlessly unaware, however, is that he has just acted out aggressive instincts that Charlie possesses and would like to express himself but is ordinarily too cautious, too repressed to do so. Although outwardly disapproving in keeping with his civilized persona, Charlie is really gratified to behold Johnny Boy acting as his own surrogate id.

Earlier in the film, Tony surprises his old friends by revealing that in one of the back rooms of his bar he keeps a pet lion cub. As Johnny Boy and Jimmy cower up on a table and Charlie watches with wary interest, Tony enters the animal's cage to play and cuddle with it, murmuring endearments of a quasi-sexual nature. Tony confides to Charlie that he originally wanted to get a tiger: "William Blake and all that." Just as Blake's "tyger" symbolizes (among other possibilities) an inherent fierceness in animal and human nature that contrasts the gentle innocence represented by the lamb, so Tony's lion would seem to represent a wildness he wishes to embrace. He seems to think he can tame the fierceness of the beast by treating it with affection, but there is always the possibility that it will some day turn upon him and maul him. (The beast may already have done so on a small scale; through much of the film Tony wears a bandage on one hand, but it is uncertain whether the injury was caused by the lion cub or the pool hall fight.) At any rate, Tony, generally the most level-headed of the group of young men in the film, finds an almost erotic satisfaction in consorting with an incarnation of wild instinct. For Charlie, Johnny Boy plays the same role the cub does for Tony: he is Charlie's "tyger."

Another motive for the anger toward Charlie that partially activates Johnny Boy's blow-up against Michael is jealousy. When they were leaving the hotel room where they had made love, Charlie told Teresa he didn't want Johnny Boy to know anything about their relationship. He is then quite upset when Johnny Boy finds Teresa with him in his room. Johnny Boy in turn makes deliberately obnoxious comments like "When is yah gettin' married?" But his jealousy emerges most clearly when Teresa falls to the floor in an epileptic seizure, and Charlie asks for his help in treating her: "She's your fuckin' girl," Johnny snarls and stomps off. Both Charlie's desire to conceal the affair from his friend and Johnny Boy's evident jealousy when he finds out about it point to an element of latent homosexuality in their relationship.

The same idea is raised symbolically in another scene. After a shooting in Tony's bar, Charlie and Johnny Boy escape from the crime scene in Michael's car with a pair of flagrant homosexuals named Benton and Sammy. The balding Benton is restrained and polite, but the younger Sammy is totally out of control. He shouts propositions out the car windows to attractive men on the street: "Hey, Beautiful!" Benton tries to calm him down: "Sammy, behave yourself." But Sammy replies defiantly, "I won't—I won't! Why should I?" Clearly the relationship between Benton and Sammy is parallel to that of Charlie and Johnny Boy. A reasonable man tries to restrain his irrational and unruly partner but with only minimal success at best. After Benton and Sammy are forced out of the car, and Charlie and Johnny take advantage of the stop to get out themselves, Sammy shouts to the friends as they move away from him down the street, "Hey fellows, yuh goin' my way?" Whether Charlie and Johnny Boy realize it or not, the answer may be "yes—but certainly not all the way."

It is dawn of the following morning when the friends get back to Charlie's apartment, Johnny lies down with Charlie on his bed (both are in their underwear), and the latter then gets up to wander about his rooms. He winds up looking out his window at Teresa's window and sees her get up, pull off her nightgown, and briefly stand nude in full view. A voice-over begins with Charlie telling about a dream of his as the film cuts from him peeping through his window to him naked in bed with Teresa. The viewer might easily take the second scene to be a fantasy inspired by Charlie's view from the window. But as the sequence between the young man and woman continues with perfectly realistic dialogue and behavior on the part of both characters, it becomes apparent that what we see and hear is actually supposed to be happening. The audience has, of course, no idea when the affair between Charlie and Teresa began—whether after the morning at window or before; but because this relationship is introduced after the midpoint of the film, well after the closeness of Charlie and Johnny Boy has been established, it is difficult not to conclude that the woman functions (initially at least) as a mere proxy. Because Charlie's religious and cultural upbringing prohibits him from consciously considering a sexual relationship with Johnny Boy, he has turned to his friend's cousin as acceptable substitute.

In the dream that he tells Teresa about, Charlie has a premature ejaculation, but he comes in blood rather than semen. One obvious implication of the dream is that his sexual affair with Teresa is as likely to be productive of pain and suffering as of pleasure. At first, most of the pain seems to be on her side. When she tells Charlie she loves him, he admits that he "likes" her but says, "I don't love you." When pressed to give a reason for not wanting to "get involved" with her (to the point of sharing an apartment with her), he gives his reason succinctly: "Because you're a cunt." Ostensibly the epithet implies that because she is a sexually available woman, he can't consider her worthy of serious commitment (the classic double standard); but the latent meaning of the phrase is that he can't commit himself whole-heartedly to her because his deepest allegiance is to another man. The same implication comes through when he urges her not to let Johnny Boy know about them— almost as though Johnny were the wife from whom he is hiding his infidelity.

Charlie comes to care more deeply for Teresa, however, than he wants to admit either to her or to himself. After Giovanni warns him about associating with either Johnny Boy or Teresa, he tries to break off with *her.* But she won't accept his perfunctory "I can't see you for a while." She forces him to consider the question he had evaded before when they were walking on the beach: "What are you afraid of?" One thing he is afraid of is what she finally forces him to admit—even though he protests, "I don't want to say that"—that he loves her. Because he loves her and can't bring himself to abandon her—any more than he can abandon Johnny Boy—he has little chance of ever satisfying his uncle enough to be set up in a restaurant by him.

Teresa's role in *Mean Streets* is ambiguous. Her presence in the culminating shooting and car wreck sequence is largely irrelevant. Her being at the scene of the shooting might make Giovanni a touch more irritated with his nephew, but surely he would have been upset enough just that Charlie was with Johnny Boy. (In the original script, Teresa was not in the car—and Johnny Boy was killed, removing him as an influence on Charlie's life—but Giovanni still exiled his nephew.[6]) From Charlie's perspective, though, Teresa is a destructive influence because she would deflect him from the pursuit of his penance. Just as much as Giovannni, she would advise him not to associate with Johnny Boy. When he carries on one of his periodic conversations with God in the car with Teresa and Johnny—and makes the mistake of speaking aloud: "I'm tryin', Lord, I'm tryin'"—Teresa laughs at him. The concept that Charlie's spiritual welfare is bound up with his commitment to Johnny Boy is incomprehensible to her.

It is by no means certain, though, that the filmmaker also regards Teresa as a negative spiritual influence. She is named after Theresa of Avila, the sixteenth-century visionary nun—who was also undoubtedly an epileptic. But according to contemporary lay Catholic standards in this particular section of New York City, the modern Teresa is not a visionary but "the one who's sick in the head" (Giovanni's phrase). Although at times surprisingly foul-mouthed (Teresa to Michael after he has spilled her groceries in attempting to intimidate her into giving a message to Johnny Boy: "Will you just give me my fucking eggplant, please"), Teresa on the whole is a strong, level-headed, caring person whose influence on Charlie would appear to be almost entirely positive according to worldly morality. Surely he would be better off marrying her and getting a legitimate nine-to-five job than trying to rise in the Mafia or continuing to fritter away his time with the heavy-drinking petty criminals who are his "buddies." Charlie has defined his penance as caring for his irresponsible, self-destructive friend Johnny Boy, but what if he is mistaken in that definition? What if the commitment to Johnny Boy, which is doomed never to lead to any positive result, is just Charlie's way of avoiding genuine commitment—linking himself to a person who will help guide his life in an affirmative direction? What if Teresa offers a better way of penance for Charlie than he has conceived for himself? The film may raise such questions in the viewer's mind, but Scorsese doesn't seem to have provided definitive answers.

Although Charlie regards caring for Johnny Boy his penance, one could argue that in committing himself to his friend, Charlie is in reality allying himself with a demonic force. Interspersed with the scenes involving the main characters, Scorsese gives brief shots of activities of the Feast of San Gennaro celebration and of various locations in the neighborhood. One of the latter shows a white statue of Christ on a rooftop. The character in the film who is associated with rooftops is Johnny Boy, who is twice shown up on the roof of his tenement. When I first noted this association of both Christ and Johnny with rooftops, I thought (if it wasn't a coincidental similarity) it meant that, for Charlie, Johnny Boy and Christ were in some sense identified—that is, Charlie defined himself as a Christian through his behavior toward Johnny. But another possibility is that by placing both Christ and Johnny Boy on the rooftops Scorsese is setting Charlie's friend up as the Antichrist. Certainly Johnny Boy's behavior up on his roof is totally hostile and aggressive, lacking the slightest smidgen of mercy and mildness. In the first scene he is shooting a pistol, frightening people in the neighborhood. When Charlie climbs up to ask him what he is doing, Johnny Boy replies, "I'm gonna shoot the light out of the Empire State Building." His behavior is a classic example of purposeless violence, not only because he can't hit the Empire State Building with his shots but because he doesn't care at all where the rounds he has fired into the night may happen to fall. In the second rooftop scene Johnny looks out from his building and makes an obscene gesture—directed not apparently toward any individual but toward the whole world.

Johnny Boy displays his aggression and destructiveness in a number of other scenes. In his first appearance in the film he blows up a mailbox. He provokes the fight in the pool hall and for a brief time stands atop a pool table flailing at his adversaries with a broken cue. As he is returning home earlier on the night of the showdown with Michael, the camera tracks behind him as he strides rapidly along the sidewalk, repeatedly glancing over his shoulder as if trying to elude a pursuer. Not watching where he is going, he bumps into a teenaged boy, then pummels him until the kid slumps to the sidewalk—where Johnny Boy stomps him several times before continuing on his way. If there is anything in the film to indicate that the victimized boy was anything other than innocent bystander, I certainly missed it. All of these instances of Johnny's violent conduct indicate not that he is a bomb waiting to go off but that he is one that has already gone off repeatedly and will some day do serious if not fatal harm to another person (and we have no way of knowing that this has not already happened). He clearly needs to be stopped, and at the end of the film he is—although the method employed scarcely leaves the viewer feeling that moral order has been restored to the cosmos (or the mean streets of New York).

The part that Charlie plays in the final chastisement of Johnny Boy is highly ambiguous. Scorsese has said in an interview:

Some people think . . . that Charlie drives Johnny Boy at the end to meet his fate. They think Charlie sells him out. . . . But that's not the case at

all. The idea is pure random violence, and the idea is that they were followed. Charlie would never sell Johnny out that way.[7]

That one of the major ideas of the film is indeed "pure random violence"
goes nearly without saying. A long-haired boy shoots a man at the urinal
in the bathroom of Tony's bar in a misguided attempt to earn points
with the neighborhood Mafia hierarchy. About a dozen men start bash-
ing each other in the pool hall because someone has called someone
else a "mook." A returned Vietnam veteran suddenly goes berserk at his
welcome-home party. (Somewhat ironically, Tony tries to calm the veteran by saying, "Take it easy. You're in America, Jerry"—as if New York
in this film weren't almost as violent as Saigon.) The viewer of this
movie is definitely conditioned to expect the eruptions of sudden violence. But does that mean Charlie bears no responsibility for the violence directed toward Johnny Boy at the end?

I must agree with Scorsese that Charlie would never *consciously* sell
out Johnny Boy, but there is some indication that his unconscious is
placing not only Johnny Boy but himself and Teresa in jeopardy. Scorsese
says, "the idea is that they were followed"; but in point of fact we don't
see the car with Michael and the gunman (played by Scorsese himself)
until after Charlie has been driving around the city, apparently lost, for
quite some time. In doing this, Charlie is behaving exactly contrary to
Tony's sensible advice: "Don't go drivin' around." It would seem that at
some level of his personality he is deliberately providing an opportunity
for Michael to catch up to them and attempt his revenge on Johnny.

If this is what Charlie is doing, what is he attempting to achieve for
himself? One possibility is that he wants Johnny killed so that he (Charlie) will be relieved of the further burden of taking care of someone who
in the final analysis is unwilling to be helped. It is also possible that he
would like to be freed from his relationship to Teresa, who is placing
demands upon him that he finds increasingly burdensome. Finally he
may want to put himself in the path of a bullet to punish himself for
his desire to be rid of the two people he loves best. If these are Charlie's
goals on some unconscious level, Scorsese (moralist that he is) doesn't
let him achieve them.

As he says in the same interview I quoted from above," . . . people
say they're both dead at the end. They're not. . . . The fact is they
have to go on. That's the worst part."[8] It is interesting that Scorsese
omits any mention of Teresa when he speaks of people incorrectly speculating that "they're both dead"; but I will paraphrase him and say that
none of the three characters is deceased at the end of the film. Johnny
is seriously injured, Teresa probably less so, and Charlie has a bullet
wound in his hand, which Scorsese in another interview refers to as a

"stigmata."[9] This would seem to me to be an ironic stigmata since Charlie has made no deliberate sacrifice of himself or of his welfare for the sake of anyone else. But perhaps Scorsese intends the stigmata to signify the inevitable suffering which Charlie's life must include (whatever his fate in an afterlife).

Throughout the film Charlie tests his ability to bear the fires of hell by holding his hand over various flames (from the candles in the Church, a match, and the grill in a restaurant kitchen). That Charlie is not very successful in withstanding the heat is not the greatest of his problems because he knows there is another kind of pain in hell: "The kind you can feel in your heart—your soul—the spiritual side." And he also knows, ". . . the worst of the two is the spiritual." As Charlie kneels on the pavement after the shooting and the car crash, perhaps for the first time he understands the true pain of hell. Although shortly before the shooting he told the Lord he was "tryin'," he now perceives it wasn't hard enough. Scorsese says, "I think Charlie at the end of Mean Streets learns."[10] What he has chiefly learned is the absolute insufficiency of his penance.

10

"The Injustice of It All": Polanski's Revision of the Private Eye Genre in *Chinatown*

Roman Polanski's *Chinatown* might be described as a serious parody of such 1940s detective films as *The Maltese Falcon* and *The Big Sleep.* Although it doesn't spoof the genre, it employs many of its characteristic features for the ultimate purpose of critiquing its assumptions. As Virginia Wright Wexman has pointed out, specific scenes in *Chinatown* echo those of the earlier films by Huston and Hawks.[1] Like "Miss Wonderly" in *Falcon* the female client at the beginning of Polanski's film pretends to be someone she is not and is employing the detective agency for reasons other than the one she gives. Jack Nicholson as detective Jake Gittes and Faye Dunaway as client Evelyn Mulwray fence verbally in a restaurant scene similar to one between Bogart and Bacall in *Sleep,* and Gittes's repeated remark to Evelyn—"I think you're hiding something"—shows the same wariness as Marlowe's reiterated question to Vivian: "What's Eddie Mars got on you?" And as in numerous detective films there is a confrontation scene in *Chinatown* in which the detective confronts the murderer, Noah Cross (John Huston), one-on-one with evidence of his guilt. The culmination of that scene, however, indicates the difference between Polanski's detective movie and the ones of the '40s: instead of killing the villain or insuring his arrest, Gittes allows Cross's henchman to take away from him the broken glasses that are the evidence of the murderer's presence at the scene of the crime. The film then ends with the villain triumphant, the hero defeated, and the heroine dead—the expected ending of a detective film seems to have been turned completely upside down.

Screenwriter Robert Towne had apparently written a more traditional ending, which director Polanski refused to accept. Polanski writes in his autobiography,

> Towne wanted the evil tycoon to die and his daughter, Evelyn, to live. . . .
> I knew that if *Chinatown* was to be special, not just another thriller where
> the good guys triumph in the final reel, Evelyn had to die. Its dramatic

impact would be lost unless audiences left their seats with a sense of outrage at the injustice of it all.[2]

As I will discuss later, the pessimism of the film's ending actually derives from more than Evelyn's death; but because her demise is at the center of all that goes wrong in the final moments, it is difficult to avoid speculating that the outrage Polanski was trying to create in audiences was the aesthetic equivalent of what he had felt at the senseless slaughter of his wife Sharon Tate at the hands of the Manson gang. If that event did not create, it certainly must have reinforced the bleak philosophical perspective that underlies *Chinatown:* the notions that evil is ineradicable, events are uncontrollable and cannot be foreseen, and life can be snuffed out in an instant.

The film in an almost didactic manner teaches these "truths" to its protagonist Jake Gittes—and through him to the audience. It is significant, though, that Gittes has been taught this lesson before; the film for him constitutes not so much a learning as a relearning experience. As a policeman in Chinatown, Gittes was taught that he couldn't "always tell what's going on" and that his attempts to produce one kind of result could very well create the opposite. When Gittes begins his investigation for "Mrs. Mulwray," he attends a city council meeting at which a proposed dam is being discussed. As Hollis Mulwray testifies for the Water and Power Commission, he says that the new dam would be built on shale similar to that under the Van der Lip Dam, which "gave way" causing "over five hundred lives [to be] lost." He had approved that dam, but says, "I'm not going to make the same mistake twice." After the statement the film cuts to a close-up of Gittes in the audience. Later when he tells Evelyn Mulwray about his experiences in Chinatown, Gittes has the opportunity to make the same kind of statement that Hollis had at the hearing—but he does not. In truth he fully deserves the comment the police Lieutenant Escobar (his former partner in Chinatown) makes to him shortly before the end of the film: "You never learn, do you, Jake?" But such is the cynicism of the film that the only reward Hollis Mulwray receives for having learned his lesson is an early death at the hands of Noah Cross.

The focus of the film, however, is on the slow learner Jake Gittes. After extensive opening credits in the style of 1940s' films, *Chinatown* opens with a scene only peripherally related to its central plot: Gittes's informing a lower class client, Curly, of his wife's infidelity. We initially see black and white stills of a man and woman having sexual intercourse. On the sound track we hear moans, which we initially associate with the love-making couple but which turn out to be the anguished response of the cuckolded husband, who then flings the photos in the air, lurches (sobbing) about the office, and finally winds up with his face pressed against the window blinds. Jake then coolly tells him not to "eat" the Venetian blinds because he "just had 'em installed on Wednesday." When Curly then bitterly announces that his wife is "no good," Jake placidly agrees: "What can I tell you, Kid? You're right. When you're right, you're right, you're right." He then eases Curly out of the office without pressuring him to make immediate payment for the investigative services the agency has performed for him. This scene immediately establishes that Jake Gittes is no idealistic private eye like Philip Marlowe who refuses to do divorce work. The repetition of "you're right" seems to suggest both a boundless cynicism about the morality of women (are any of them any good?) and an extremely limited empathy for Curly's feelings. That Gittes ushers Curly out of the office without pressing any demand for payment seems less like an act of kindness than the manifestation of a desire to be quickly rid of an annoyingly distraught client. When we later learn of Jake's experiences in Chinatown, we can retrospectively interpret his behavior in this opening scene and in much of the rest of the film as a defensive strategy: by regarding other people cynically or not caring too much about their feelings, he protects himself from disillusionment or from painful involvement with others.

In the following scene with "Mrs. Mulwray" there is a possible suggestion that Jake in reality wasn't as indifferent to Curly's suffering as he had appeared. When "Mrs. Mulwray" asks him to find out if her husband is being unfaithful to her, he asks her, ". . . do you love your husband?" When she replies that she does, he advises her to "go home, forget everything"—that way she will spare herself the kind of suffering Curly has experienced through the certain knowledge of a mate's infidelity. But we can't be certain that this advice is not simply Jake's standard ploy with women wanting to have their husbands investigated—a way of warding off customer dissatisfaction when an inquiry produces dismaying results. In any case he is willing enough to take the case when she insists, "I have to know!" Jake treats the actual investigation more or less as a game—a game he is confident he has won when he manages to take photos of Mulwray with the girl in the boat on the lake at Echo Park and on a veranda at the El Macondo Apartments. The name of the park has symbolic resonance because the film is full of echoes—the most obvious one being the echo of Gittes's earlier experience in Chinatown in the final sequence of the film. When Gittes is photographing Mulwray and the girl from a vantage point on the roof of the El Macondo, we see a reflection of the subjects in his camera's lens. This shot might remind the viewer of an earlier one in which Gittes observed Mulwray through the reflection in the circular, rear-view mirror on the driver's side of his car. Again, the film's visual emphasis on reflected images may simply be another way of stressing the echo effect: just as people and events are duplicated in their mirror reflections, so Evelyn Mulwray, for instance, duplicates the woman in Chinatown Jake tried "to keep . . . from being hurt" but only "ended up making sure that she was hurt." But one may also remember these earlier mirror-image shots when Jake—after making love to Evelyn and then following her to the house where her "sister" is being kept—studies his own refec-tion in the mirror of his bathroom. The change clearly marks his passage (which unfortunately for him only seems to be temporary) from the scrutiny of others to self-scrutiny. But Jake is clearly happiest in the early parts of the movie when he is merely observing others in a detached and almost godlike manner (e.g., his view from on high atop the El Macondo roof). His first fall of the film occurs in the sequence immedi-ately thereafter.

Although he didn't expect it, Gittes seems perfectly content to see the results of his investigation spread across the front page of an L.A. newspaper—that is, until another man in the barbershop makes a slight-ing comment. Gittes erupts in response to what he regards as an imputa-tion to his professional honor, leaps out of his barber chair with his face lathered to confront his censurer. His defense partly takes the form of a counterattack: after he finds out that his critic works in the mortgage department of a bank, he snarls, "I don't kick families out of their houses like you bums down at the bank do!" He also asserts, "I make an honest living"—a statement he then repeats in an increasingly fragmentary manner: "make an honest living, . . . an honest living." The repeti-tion, of course, only creates the impression of a man who "doth pro-test too much."

His second fall occurs in the next sequence when the real Evelyn Mulwray walks into his office behind him as he is telling his associates the dirty joke about the man who screwed "like a Chinaman." (The juxtaposition of Evelyn with "Chinaman" is also a slight foreshadowing of the end of the film.) His embarrassment in telling such a story in the presence of a lady is nothing in comparison to that of discovering that he was deceived by a phony client. From this point on he seeks to find out who had used him to discredit Mulwray—not merely for the purpose of defending himself from Mrs. Mulwray's lawsuit (which she tells him she will "drop" even before her husband's body is found), but more importantly, I think, to prove to himself that he is indeed "an honest man."

In the self-motivated investigation that follows, which he is deeply involved in even before Evelyn Mulwray hires him to "find out what happened to [her husband] and who is involved," Gittes finds that the seemingly irrelevant parts of his previous observation of Hollis Mulwray's daily activities are now the relevant parts. After Mulwray's body is found in the Oak Pass Reservoir, his activities at various water sites about the city become clues to someone's motives for murdering him. Gittes slowly comes to the conclusion that Mulwray was murdered for two main reasons: because he was opposed to the new Alto Vallejo Dam and because he had discovered that water was being diverted to the northwest valley, thereby increasing the severity of the water shortage in Los Angeles.

Water is not only the motive for Mulwray's murder and the means of it as well (he is first thought to have drowned in the reservoir, but Gittes later discovers he met his death in the tidal pool in his own yard), it also poses a threat to Jake Gittes as well. When Hollis Mulwray is still alive, Gittes watches him down on the shore from a vantage point just in front of the opening of a big drainage pipe. Suddenly Gittes hears a sound of running water and just barely manages to jump aside as a run-off hurtles by him, splashing him but just missing knocking him off the cliff onto the rocky beach below. He is less lucky when he visits the Oak Pass Reservoir at night after Mulwray's death. He hears shots, jumps down into a flood control channel to get out of the way, and is crouching there when surge of water pours into him, sweeping him down channel until he is slammed up against a chain-link fence, which he manages to climb up and over to avoid drowning. Dismayed by the loss of a new "Florsheim shoe," he is limping along muttering to himself when he encounters Mulvihill, the corrupt former sheriff, and the small thug (played by director Polanski) who slits the detective's nose with a switchblade knife to warn him not to be "nosy."

The loss of the shoe, even though it may seem minor in comparison to the slashed nose, is a significant event in this sequence. When the body of Hollis Mulwray was dragged up from the reservoir, one of his shoes was missing also. The fact that Gittes has almost drowned as Mulwray did and lost a shoe as he had indicates the detective is following in Mulwray's footsteps—which could very well lead him to the grave as they did the older man. Certainly the violence done to his nose makes Gittes want to take up Mulwray's causes—to block the new dam and expose the diversion of water. But his identification with Mulwray goes beyond espousal of the man's causes; he also winds up in bed with Mrs. Mulwray.

The slashed nose may also be a motivating factor in this respect. The cutting of the nose clearly seems to be a symbolic castration. Gittes's sense of his manhood must have suffered a severe blow as he knelt holding his bloody nose while Mulvihill and the diminutive knife-wielder stood over him. Certainly it is noticeable at this point in the film that Gittes does not put up the kind of fight against his adversaries that we would have expected from Sam Spade or Philip Marlowe; he just stands there and lets Mulvihill hold him while a man much smaller than he is carves him like an unresisting hunk of meat. Even the vengeance he fantasizes against the superiors of Mulvihill and the thug ("the big boys") is not the sort of manly action one expects from a tough private eye: he wants to "sue" them. In allowing his nose to be cut and in bearing the marks of this humiliation throughout the rest of the film, J. J. Gittes has suffered a loss that he can only make up for through manly action in his subsequent endeavors. The problem is that if he continues to try to assert himself, continues to be "nosy" as the thug put it, he runs the risk of not just partial but total loss: as the thug warned, "Next time you lose the whole thing."

Jake manages to restore his sense of manhood for a time through two forms of action: violent risk-taking and sexual involvement. When he sees a "KEEP OUT NO TREPASSING [sic]" sign at the entrance to an orchard, he drives right in. Nor does he "Hold it right there" when this command follows a warning shot at his car; instead he guns it and goes roaring off down a lane between trees. When his path is blocked, he backs up and turns down another lane, finally coming to a stop only when holes have been shot in his radiator and tires—and he runs his car into a tree. Confronted by a group of enraged farmers, he makes little attempt to calm them down; he denounces one as a "dumb Okie" and winds up being knocked out by the crutch a crippled farmer has been using as a weapon. (The screen fades to red before black as he passes out.) He has put up a more vigorous resistance here than he did against Mulvihill and the thug, but the results have scarcely been better. Only the inherent decency of the farmers, who have no wish to inflict further harm on a man who has been lying unconscious for several hours, and the arrival of Evelyn Mulwray, who has been summoned as his employer of record, get Jake out of the orchard without further violence occurring that he would doubtless get the worst of.

But the next sequence at the Mar Vista Rest Home allows Gittes to restore his view of himself as a man who is on top of events and can dominate his adversaries when necessary. He makes a significant step in his investigation by discovering that land in the valley has been bought up in huge quantities in the names of unknowing residents of the home; and when he is confronted by Mulvihill in the lobby of the home, Gittes is able to pull the larger man's coat over his head and pound him into submission. He then avoids a further confrontation with the small thug and another henchman when Evelyn drives up just in time to whip him away from their menace. But he has still handled Mulvihill with enough dispatch to restore his self-confidence and make him ready to demonstrate his manhood in another way: with Evelyn in bed.

Just as J. J. Gittes is not quite the classic hard-boiled private eye of earlier films, so Evelyn Mulwray is not quite the *femme fatale* of those films (nor the "good woman" who sometimes appears to balance her). When she first appears in Gittes's office—cool, poised, beautiful—she seems to be the cliché (or more positively, archetype) we have come to expect in private eye films: "In almost every case, the hardboiled hero encounters a beautiful and dangerous woman in the course of his investigations and finds himself very much drawn to her, even to the point of falling in love."[3] In *Chinatown* Gittes *is* drawn to Evelyn—and toward the end may come to love her; but although she does prove to be extremely dangerous to him, it is not at all in the same way that Brigid O'Shaughnessy, Helen Grayle, and Kathie Moffett were.

Evelyn Mulwray is dangerous not because she is cool, hard, and ruthless but because she is neurotic, insecure, and vulnerable. Her behavior in her first appearance in Gittes's office is misleading. Each successive time that Gittes talks to her the self-control she displayed in their first meeting breaks down a little more. Initially she spoke like a well-rehearsed actress delivering her lines in a drawing room comedy. But when Gittes confronts her in later scenes, she becomes increasingly less fluent, groping for replies to his probing questions. (According to Polanski, this manifestation of the inner uncertainty of the character was aided by Faye Dunaway's inability to remember her lines.[4]) Then her poise seems almost totally broken down when with shaking hands she lights a second cigarette—unaware she already has one going—after Gittes asks her a question about her father. But of course the ultimate breakdown comes when she admits in broken phrases (simultaneously weeping) that her sister is also her daughter. This revelation—probably equally shocking to Gittes and the first-time viewer—rather obscures the fact that much remains unknown about Evelyn even by the end of the film.

First of all, did she know that her father had killed her husband? If not, why did she tell Gittes she was dropping her lawsuit against him and later, after the discovery of Mulwray's body, claim to the police that she *had* hired the detective to investigate her husband—if she did not wish to conceal the water plot that lay behind both the discrediting and the murder of her spouse? After she and Jake have made love, she warns him that her "father is a very dangerous man. You don't know how dangerous; you don't know how crazy." When Jake asks if Noah Cross could have killed her husband, she replies, "It's possible." If she knows or at least strongly suspects her father killed Hollis Mulwray, did she initially try to deflect Gittes from finding that out in order to protect her father or merely because she assumed it would do neither Jake nor the public any good to discover this fact since, as she says toward the end of the film, her father "owns the police" and therefore could never be brought to justice?

If Evelyn's knowledge of and motives in regard to the central crime of the film remain obscure, her sexual morality is also highly ambiguous. In the restaurant she tells Gittes that she was glad her husband had a mistress because (she implies without actually stating) it made her feel less guilty about her own affairs. Her comments—like "I don't see any-one for very long, Mr. Gittes"—insinuate that she is a compulsive nym-phomaniac. But of course it is probable Hollis was not really having an affair with Katherine, merely spending time with her as an affectionate stepfather. If Hollis's affair is fictional, are Evelyn's as well? She does prove willing to go to bed with Gittes, but she demonstrates an interest in prolonging the relationship when she wants him to go back home with her after he discovers her with Katherine. Or did she do that only in an attempt to prevent him from revealing the girl's whereabouts to the police or her father (the two possibilities amounting to the same thing if Cross "owns the police")?

If one considers the film carefully, very little can actually be known about Evelyn Mulwray, her life or her motives. The one indisputable fact, aside from her marriage to Hollis Mulwray, seems to be that she committed incest with her father, and a child, Katherine resulted. But even this event is presented ambiguously. When Gittes finally realizes that the incest has occurred, he places his own interpretation upon it. He asks, "He raped you?" Evelyn offers no verbal reply to the question, but she finally shakes her head briefly from side to side. Gittes wants to believe that Evelyn would not have committed incest unless brutally forced to by her father, but her response offers no confirmation of this view, may even reject it. In Robert Towne's screenplay for *Chinatown*, Evelyn explains to Gittes that her father

> had a breakdown . . . the dam broke . . . my mother died . . . he became a little boy . . . I was fifteen . . . he'd ask me what to eat for breakfast, what clothes to wear! . . . it happened . . . then I ran away. . . .[5]

She also says she hates her father not for the incest itself but "for turning his back on [her] after it happened!"[6] None of these lines appear in the finished film, possibly because the director deemed they went too far in mitigating Noah Cross's guilt; but neither does the movie offer any firm evidence that the incest occurred as the result of a rape rather than a seduction to which Evelyn at least half-willingly succumbed.

At any rate, Evelyn plainly feels that she was corrupted by Noah, and she is willing to go to nearly any lengths—even shooting her father, although not fatally—to prevent him from having the same effect on his and her daughter Katherine. John Huston as Noah Cross has been criticized for giving "an essentially, lazy unresonant performance opting for easy charm."[7] But the fact that he doesn't give off an impression of obvious malignancy is one of the most chilling things about the character Noah Cross. He is not so much *immoral* as utterly *amoral*. In regard to the incest he tells Gittes, "I don't blame myself. You see, Mr. Gits [sic], most people never have to face the fact that at the right time and right place, they're capable of anything." For him the act was simply normal human behavior produced by a particular confluence of circumstances. That Evelyn does blame him is merely a sign that she is, as he told Gittes earlier, "a disturbed woman." In Chinatown toward the end of the film Cross can't understand why Evelyn won't "be reasonable" and turn Katherine over to him. After all he is an old man and Katherine is his child as well as Evelyn's: "How many years have I got? She's mine, too." He advises her, "Evelyn, you're a disturbed woman; you cannot hope to provide. . . ." Although it is uncertain what he thought Evelyn couldn't "provide" for Katherine that he could, in the context of the introductory clause it seems most likely he meant that he, a sane man with clear perspective on life, could give the girl the kind of stable existence she could never have with his neurotic elder daughter. Evelyn's objections to him strike Noah as purely irrational.

Noah is as free of remorse for his killing of Hollis Mulwray as he is for the act of incest. Noah speaks fondly of Hollis as he stands beside the pool in which he drowned the man. He admits that Hollis's theories of water management "made this city." But unfortunately Hollis with his opposition to the new dam stood in the way of making the new city: the expanded Los Angeles which will incorporate the irrigated north-west valley. Hollis was fascinated with tidepools: ". . . he used to say . . . that's where life begins. . . ." Hollis looked backwards—to the origins of life and to the Van Der Lip Dam disaster, which he sought to avoid a recurrence of in the future. Noah Cross looks to the future, willing to risk another disaster and willing to sacrifice his best friend to bring to fulfillment his vision of the new Los Angeles. As for the present, he feels as little guilt about diverting water from farmers who currently need it as he did about diverting his seed to his own daughter.

The film ends with the triumph of Noah Cross. He seems as little bothered by the bullet wound he has received as he would be by a mosquito bite as he leads his granddaughter/daughter away from the car in which her mother lies dead. The bleakness of the ending of the film is best understood by comparing it with an ending screenwriter Robert Towne wrote but the director chose not to use. In his autobiography Polanski writes only of the "happy ending" Towne originally wanted,[8] but the "Third Draft" of the screenplay published by Script City contains a tragic ending that nevertheless offers possibilities of hope. Katherine is driven away by Curly (whom Gittes had earlier hired to take both women to Ensenada in his boat) as Gittes and Evelyn prevent Cross from following her. As Evelyn drives off to follow her daughter, she is shot and killed much as in the film. At the end Gittes is led away by his fellow operatives, Walsh and Duffy, while Noah Cross kneels "on the ground, holding Evelyn's body, crying."[9] This ending, while not cheerful, does at least indicate the efforts of Gittes and Evelyn were not in vain because the innocent Katherine does escape for the time being from the evil influence of her conscienceless father/grandfather, who is also shown expressing grief (and possibly even remorse) over his daughter's body. At least some human values are affirmed in this ending.

But in Polanski's ending Katherine is left firmly within the grasp of Noah, who may look upon his dead daughter with a measure of shock as he backs away from the car but is certainly not casting any tears for her. As she is pulled away, Katherine is screaming, "No, no!"—which I take to be her protest against her mother's death but would also be an appropriate response to the sort of future one might envisage her having with Noah. The prime source of evil in the film has gotten his way here just as he has with the water policy of Los Angeles. This scene also includes a final line from Jake Gittes that wasn't present in Towne's third draft. There Gittes's concluding words were his last vigorous denunciation of Noah Cross: "Get him away from [Evelyn's body]. He's responsible for everything! Get him away from her!"[10] In the film itself Jake only mutters the phrase, "as little as possible." The implications of this utterance deserve to be examined at some length.

When he was a police officer in Chinatown he was advised by the District Attorney to do "as little as possible," but he apparently tried to do more than that in an effort to "keep someone from being hurt"—with the result that he made "sure she was hurt." Now his efforts to save Evelyn and Katherine have led only to Evelyn's death and Katherine's possession by Noah Cross. Seeing once again a negative outcome to his striving to do good, Gittes repeats the phrase "as little as possible" as if acknowledging the wisdom of the DA's advice and proclaiming the futility of all struggle against the forces of destruction. On the other hand, if one examines Gittes's behavior in the final sequences of the film, one might reach the conclusion he has done *almost* "as little as possible" to aid Evelyn and Katherine. Whereas in Towne's third draft, Gittes fought vigorously with Cross and Mulvihill to make time for Katherine to escape with Curly,[11] in the film for the most part the detective does little more than stand by handcuffed to a policeman while the burden of defending herself and her sister/daughter is borne almost entirely by

Evelyn. *She* is the one who might have been better off doing as little as possible.

Although most viewers of the film probably find him attractive, J. J. Gittes in the last analysis is a hollow man—the mere semblance of the hardboiled private eye, not the real thing. This detective is a specialist in appearances. Through the first half of the film Gittes wears a different, immaculately pressed suit in almost every sequence—even when the new sequence would seem most likely to be taking place the same day as the preceding one. Production designer Anthea Sylbert apparently conceived of Gittes as man who modeled his wardrobe on the apparel of the popular Hollywood leading men of the time: "His clothing, she thought, would reflect 'an outsider's idea of how a star would dress.'"[12] When Evelyn Mulwray is leaving the morgue after identifying her husband's body, Gittes hustles her past a waiting group of reporters and cameramen, then turns in the door and poses himself—giving them all a big star-smile. The slashed nose and the unsightly bandage Gittes is forced to wear much of the remainder of the film is not only a reminder of his impotence but a sign of how vulnerable his self-created star image is.

Yet I doubt that either Polanski or the audience blame Gittes much for his failure to protect Evelyn and Katherine at the end of the film. The death of Evelyn is technically an accident: a warning shot by the policeman Loach happened to hit her in the back of the head with the exit wound through her eye. But because of heavy symbolic foreshadowing of this event, it doesn't seem at all like an accident. R. Barton Palmer mentions some of the images that prepare us for the final catastrophe: "Cross's glasses . . . found with one lens shattered, the one taillight on Mrs. Mulwray's car which Gittes breaks . . . , and, most importantly, the imperfection in Mrs. Mulwray's eye. . . ."[13] To these may be added the black eye of Curly's wife, a consequence of Gittes's previous investigation, and a foreshadowing of a slightly different nature: Evelyn's involuntary sounding of her car's horn when she puts her head down on the steering wheel the night Gittes finds her with her "sister" presages the prolonged wail of the horn when her dead body slumps against the wheel. With all of these portents, Evelyn Mulwray seems less the victim of chance than of an inexorable fate.

For the director Polanski, Evelyn's death is indeed unavoidable, for it seems likely that to him she represents women who were already dead at the time the film was made. I earlier suggested that the "sense of outrage" Polanski was trying to create in the audience was the equivalent of the outrage he felt at the murder of his pregnant wife, but the character of Evelyn more directly represents a woman other than Sharon Tate. Polanski has said he selected Faye Dunaway for the part "on the ground that her special brand of 'retro' beauty—the same sort of look I remembered in my mother—was essential to the film."[14] Earlier in his autobiography he describes his mother's appearance: "I recall . . . her elegance, the precise way she drew the lines over her plucked eyebrows. . . ."[15] Those same precise lines appear over Evelyn's plucked brows in *Chinatown*. Polanski's mother was picked up by the Nazis during their occupation of Poland; years later he learned "that she had died in a gas chamber only days after being taken away."[16] It is not surprising that J. J. Gittes appears powerless to prevent the death of Evelyn Mulwray when the director of the film could do nothing to save either mother or wife.

Noah Cross does not specifically represent either the Nazis or Charles Manson (or even the all-powerful, all-destructive oedipal father), but he does seem to stand for all the forces of exploitation that dominate our times. Deborah Linderman cites the link between Cross's sexual exploitation of his daughter and his economic exploitation of the water politics of Los Angeles: "[Cross] demonstrates that excesses in capitalist profiteering are inextricable from excesses of the body: one transgression leads to another."[17] Ms. Linderman perhaps ignores that abuses of power and manipulation of people without regard for their feelings and desires probably occur as frequently under socialism as capitalism, but is doubtlessly correct that one form of transgression can give rise to another. When Gittes can't understand why Cross would commit murder to make possible economic development of the valley, he asks, "What can you buy that you can't already afford?" Cross replies, "The future, Mr. Gits, the future." Cross's future is our present; Polanski's film expresses the fear that the Noah Crosses have already bought it and that a fundamental corruption underlies the world in which we live.

11

Eating Their Children: The Honor of the Prizzis

In his fortieth film, shot forty-four years after *The Maltese Falcon*, John Huston returned in *Prizzi's Honor* to the theme of the fatal woman. As in the *Falcon*, in the later film a professional man overcomes his intense sexual attraction to a beautiful woman and arranges—partly to preserve the safety of other members of the profession—to turn her over to the police for a murder she has committed. These are the fundamental similarities between the two movies; some of the differences are as follows. The "professional man" in *Prizzi's Honor* is not a private detective but an "enforcer" for the Mafia family whose name appears in the title, and he must "turn over" the woman not for the sake of those on the side of law enforcement but to spare organized crime from police crackdowns and gang war. Unlike Spade, who professes to have known from early in the film that Brigid O'Shaughnessy killed his partner, Charley Partanna (Jack Nicholson) continually receives unpleasantly surprising revelations from other people about the woman he loves, Irene Walker (Kathleen Turner). Moreover, his decision to turn her over to the police is not freely chosen, as is Spade's, but is forced upon him by the Don of his Mafia family. And, oh yes, the woman Charley turns over to the authorities (or rather leaves to be collected by them) is dead—having been killed by Charley, her husband.

Prizzi's Honor uncovers the cynical core of *The Maltese Falcon*. It is easy for conventional-minded viewers of the earlier film to believe that at the end justice has been done: all the criminals involved in the story are dead or apprehended, and the detective, a designated upholder of society's laws, has triumphed over the evil forces that would intimidate, deceive, bribe, or seduce him. But as Spade admits to Brigid, his primary motive for turning her in to the police is egoistic. He is less concerned with justice than with protecting himself—not merely from any physical threat the deadly Brigid poses to him, but from emotional vulnerability. He has to give her to the police because "all of [him]" wants to let her go free so that he can be with her, and his very desire for her—and to do the things she wishes to be done—threatens his independence. If he allows her continued liberty, she not he will have gained control of his destiny. *Prizzi's Honor* removes the possibility of any illusion that justice is done at the end of the film. True, Irene Walker is a contract killer who deserves the punishment of death for the premeditated murders she has committed, but her executioner is as deeply involved in a bloody life of crime as she. In killing Irene, Charley is only incidentally acting in behalf of forces of law and order; his principal motivation is the preservation of his personal existence. But he is not, like Spade, trying to uphold his autonomy. He is not allowed the illusion of being an independent agent; he is casting off his dependency on Irene, his wife, to acknowledge his greater dependency on his Mafia family. In this film, the hero figure of the 1940s detective films completes his disappearance; unlike Charlie in *Mean Streets* and Jake in *Chinatown*, Charley Partanna doesn't even *intend* to do good in any traditional sense.

In three brief opening scenes before the bulk of the credits, we are given a thumbnail sketch of the formation of Charley's warped value system. In the first shot of the film Charley's father Angelo Partanna and Don Corrado Prizzi look through the window of a hospital nursery at the newly born child, and the Don promises he will be "as one with [his friend] in protecting [the boy's] future." Angelo says he is "honored"—in the film's initial use of one of its key terms. In the second scene we see Charley as a boy in a Cub Scout uniform receiving one of his Christmas presents—a set of brass knuckles. The top of the frame cuts off his head and hence his facial expression, but the boy slips the knucks on his right hand and enthusiastically pounds them against his left palm. The title of the background music for the scene—Tchaikovsky's *Nutcracker*—takes on an additional meaning from the context. The third scene is Charley's initiation as a young man into Don Corrado's Mafia family. The Don reiterates his personal pledge of the opening scene on behalf of the "family": "We protect you." But Charley now is given a reciprocal responsibility: "You protect Prizzi honor." This mutual obligation, sealed by Charley with a drop of blood from his finger, is not to be regarded as a short term thing; as Don Corrado says, "We are one—until death."

In simple terms, therefore, the central conflict in the film is between love and honor, although the latter term is defined in a specialized manner as "*Prizzi's* honor." Before we consider more closely the meaning of this term, though, we should examine "love"—about which the two central characters offer several interesting (albeit mostly second-hand) thoughts.

For Charley Partanna, love occurs in the classic manner of older Hollywood films—at first sight. At the wedding of one of Don Corrado's granddaughters, Charley in speaking to a man behind him happens to glance up and see Irene seated in the balcony. Something about the way she looks in her lavender dress immediately catches his eye, and he keeps turning back to gaze upon her as she fidgets with her pearls, nervously aware of his scrutiny. When the ceremony ends, Charley enlists a photographer to take pictures of the woman who has attracted him. Then at the reception he goes up to her and asks her to dance— apparently not noticing the apprehensive look on her face when he first approaches her nor finding it strange that she takes her purse with her out onto the dance floor, smoothly shifting it from under one arm to the other as they go round. He is extremely upset, however, when she disappears after she has been called away by a boy to answer the telephone. Later that night in desperation he calls his former fiancée, Maerose Prizzi (Anjelica Huston), to find out if she knows anything about the woman in the lavender dress, whose name he unfortunately didn't think to ask for when they were dancing. Awakened early in the morning, Maerose advises him to "go soak [his] head," leaving Charley in despair until he receives a call from a woman who identifies herself as Irene Walker—and he realizes she was the woman in the lavender dress. Undeterred by her announcement that she is now at home in California, Charley makes a date with her for the following day.

Even upon repeated viewings, Irene's motivations in this part of the film may be obscure to many viewers. The reason why she clutched her purse so close to her is probably apparent to most of us when Angelo Partanna later informs his son Charley that Irene was "the outside talent, . . . the specialty hitter" who shot and killed Sal Netturbino for the Prizzi family: the bag undoubtedly held the weapon she was going to use. And the "telephone call" summoned her to the performance of her task. Some viewers may also make the connection between the scam in Las Vegas—carried out by Irene, her husband Marxie Heller, and Luis Palo—and her looks of nervousness and apprehension when Charley first stares at her and then approaches her. She knows he is the Prizzi family's "enforcer" and may fear that her cover has already been blown and that Charley is looking upon her with interest because he knows who she is and plans to "ice" her at the earliest opportunity. When she realizes he is looking upon her not with blood lust but with sexual lust, it undoubtedly comes as a great relief. Her phone call to him from California the following day may be interpreted as an attempt to seize a possible advantage. If she can make Charley fall in love with her, then she can probably escape the vengeance of the Prizzis when they send him as their chief enforcer after the perpetrators of the Vegas scam. Later in the film we learn that Irene seduced Luis Palo to get him to participate in the theft of $722,000 from the casino, then killed him in order to hijack his share. Is there any reason to think that her professions of love for Charley are any more sincere than those she undoubtedly made to Luis?

The film offers no definitive answer to such a question. The novel by Richard Condon upon which the film is based, by directly presenting Irene's inner thoughts, makes clear that she really does love Charley Partanna,[1] although she comes to regret that fact when she realizes the Prizzis have appointed him to "zotz" her.[2] The viewer is allowed to make the same sentimental assumption about Irene's inner feelings in the film but, in the absence of any unambiguous confirmation of such feelings, might also come to the opposite conclusion—that she is a cold, manipulative bitch who merely feigns emotions of which in reality she incapable.

The film's primary focus, as is typical of nearly all movies in the *noir* vein, is upon the male protagonist's emotions, not the female's. Almost from the first moment Charley sees Irene he is firmly convinced that he loves her. Under the influence of a pop psychology article he read in a magazine, he even distinguishes between the emotion he feels and that of being "in love": "*In* love is temporary, then you move on to the next in love." His emotion, he claims, is far deeper and more permanent. Later after he and Irene have been married for a while, he tells her his love "may not be scientific, but it's real." When she is puzzled by his use of the word "scientific," he explains, "I read in a magazine, according to a doctor, everyone's always trying to get what they thought they needed from their mothers, but they didn't get it." In view of the fact that the film establishes in its opening scene that Charley's mother died at his birth, it is clear that for him Irene fills an extremely large gap in his life. What Charley didn't get from his mother was just about everything. Although he doesn't realize it, what Charley is admitting to Irene is that his great need for a nurturing female led him to cast her in the role of the all-providing mother and that this image was what he truly loved and not the real person, Irene Walker (née Maida Walcewicz).

Irene responds to Charley's initial declaration of love by more cautiously saying, "I love you—I think." Although she admits, "It sounds like I hedged it," she goes on to say she has never said anything like that before: "All my life I had to protect myself, and you can't protect yourself from anything when you love somebody." Then, almost with a visible effort, she declares, "I love you, Charley." Although these statements seem to have a ring of truth to them (a professional assassin surely would need to protect herself from emotions of many kinds), if one examines the whole sequence dispassionately, there is little reason to believe that an attractive young woman would be so quickly swept off her feet by a middle-aged man with receding hair, clad in an absurd canary-yellow sports coat, who quoted declarations about love out of mass-circulation magazines. With her dashing red Excalibur sports car Irene would seem to have pretensions to class that a plainspun Mafioso from Brooklyn could hardly measure up to. Again it seems more likely that Irene in the film professes love for Charley and gives herself to him out of a desire to bind him to her and prevent him from killing her on behalf of the Prizzis rather than from any deep and sincere (even if temporary) love for him.

Charley's love for Irene *is* deep and sincere, but it is also temporary or at least less strong in the end than his professional or family commitments. Initially, though, his feeling for Irene is stronger than his sense of obligation to the Prizzis. When he discovers that she is Marxie Heller's wife (actually widow at the exact moment he discovers the relationship), he knows that she must have been involved in the theft from the casino and that she is holding out on him when she gives him only half the money that was stolen; but he has to "believe" her claim of total ignorance regarding the Vegas job because, as he tells her, "I can't change the way I feel about you." He suffers further disillusionment when he learns from his father that she was "the piece man for the Netturbino contract"—and therefore quite likely also to have been the killer of Luis Palo. Yet he says to Maerose Prizzi when he goes to her for advice, "But just the same I love her, Mae; I love her." So on Maerose's advice (which we will consider later in another context) Charley Partanna marries Irene Walker and is only moderately dismayed later on to hear from her that she did kill Luis Palo and hold out $360,000 from the Vegas scam. When she admits having lied to him, she explains, "I only told you what you wanted to be true"—and he cannot dispute her interpretation.

Although their marriage is of brief duration and reaches a stunningly violent conclusion, one of the amusing aspects of *Prizzi's Honor* is the way in which Charley and Irene behave much as any ordinary married couple would. In her review of the film, Pauline Kael characterizes it as "a baroque comedy about people who behave in ordinary ways in grotesque circumstances."[3] This description is most true of the marital behavior of Charley and Irene. Kael mentions Irene's conduct after she has aided Charley in the kidnapping of the banker Filargi by shooting the man's bodyguard and also a woman who had accidentally witnessed the snatch: ". . . she chirps 'See you at dinner' to Charley and pecks him like a suburban housewife as he drives off with the kidnap victim."[4] But Charley's behavior when she offers her services as the "second man" in the abduction is equally conventional: "I didn't get married so my wife could go on working."

Charley does, however, like most modern husbands, come around to supporting his wife's right to work after marriage—and also her right to be paid according to the value of her efforts. Ironically his willingness to present her petition for just payment to his superior, Don Corrado, supplies an additional rationale for her murder. The reasons why Charley is ultimately willing to be persuaded to act as the executioner of the woman he loves need to be considered at some length.

It is important for the viewer of the film to realize that although he is a gangster and an assassin, Charley Partanna adheres to well-defined ethical standards. He has a quite highly developed superego, ingrained in him primarily by his biological father Angelo and Mafia father Don Corrado. Marxie Heller, shortly before Charley "ices" him, refers his assailant as "Straight-Arrow Charley, the All-American hood"—acknowledging the man's reputation for probity within Mafia circles. Charley in his own eyes is an honorable man, but "honor" for him is defined narrowly: it is "Prizzi's honor." The honor of a leading Mafia family is determined by such things as the ability to accumulate vast amounts of illicit wealth and to take ruthless vengeance on those who would betray the family or defeat its ends. Charley Partanna upholds both of these "values" without reservation—that is, until he becomes involved with Irene Walker.

Charley lies to the Prizzis when he tells Dominic Prizzi that he could only recover half of $720,000 from the Vegas theft and that he had believed "Heller's wife" when she told him she knew nothing about the whereabouts of the rest of the money. Later, after he finds out that Dominic—not knowing of their relationship—has hired Irene to "clip" him, Charley decides the Prizzis are setting him up and determines, upon the advice of his father, to kidnap Filargi from the other kidnappers and demand $3,000,000 from the family. Charley makes a significant statement when he agrees upon the plan with his father: "These people can't win all the time." He is not only distancing himself from the Prizzis by referring to them impersonally as "these people," he is also, perhaps for the first time, perceiving their vulnerability ("can't win all the time"). But Charley's rebellion ends the moment his father tells him that Don Corrado is not only willing to meet his demands but genuinely does want him to succeed Dominic as "boss" of the family. (Dominic has been killed by a rival family while Charley was hiding out with Filargi.) It is evident that Charley only turned against the Prizzis when he thought they had abandoned him; once they show him that he remains a highly valued—even indispensable—family member, he is ready to reaffirm the total commitment to the family that had eroded during his involvement with Irene.

The Prizzis have practical reasons for designating Charley as Irene's assassin. The police are putting pressure on the illegal activities of all of the Mafia families in the attempt to force them to turn over "the second man"—the person who shot the police captain's wife who blundered into the kidnapping scene. The other families, knowing that Filargi was connected with the Prizzis, are ready to go to "war" with them, and have already set a fire at Dominic's farewell dinner and later hit Dominic on the street. There can only be peace and the resumption of normal "business" if Irene is given to the police; but she cannot be given over alive because she knows too much about the activities of the Prizzis. As Pop told her when they were planning the second kidnapping of Filargi, "You're very dangerous to the Prizzis, Irene." The appointing of Charley as Irene's killer is also presented by Don Corrado as a practical matter: "You're the only one who can get close enough to do it."

But the real reason the Don selects Charley to make the hit on his own wife is to test where his ultimate loyalty lies. When Charley protests, "She is my *wife*, padrino. I can't kill her!"—the Don reminds him of the oath he swore when he was a young man:

> Charley, you swore an oath of blood—my blood and yours—that you would always put the family before anything else in your life. We are calling on you now to keep that sacred oath. . . . You failed in your oath when you covered up for her part in the Vegas scam. Great sin against your honor. For this you must atone.

Note the religious overtones of the language Don Corrado uses: "*sacred* oath," "great *sin*," "you must *atone*." After the opening credits the first scene in the film takes place in a church, and the opening shot of the sequence is of a stained glass window representing the exalted Christ. As the scene progresses, however, Charley does not look up toward Christ, but rather off to the side toward Irene in the balcony. *She* becomes the object of his worship. Charley never shows any of the concern for his relationship with the deity and his eventual fate in the hereafter that his near namesake repeatedly displayed in Scorsese's *Mean Streets*, but the language and attitudes of Catholicism inform his relationship to the Prizzis. They are his true object of veneration; thus his worship of Irene has been mere idolatry. This false worship which led him to betray his faith in regard to the Las Vegas affair was his great sin and can only be atoned for through his voluntary sacrifice of the idol. (That his quasi-religious commitment to the Prizzis is also idolatry, of course, is something that never occurs to Charley.)

While Charley is trying to decide whether to carry out the hit, his father tells him his dilemma is a natural consequence of his choice to marry a woman from outside of "the environment." He adds, "It mighta been all right if she was straight. But she wasn't." According to Mafia mores, women are allowed to stand separate from the criminal activities of their fathers or mates and deserve respect and consideration for their innocence. But as Don Corrado puts it, rather more bluntly than Angelo, Irene "is a hitter and a thief"; hence, she deserves no more mercy than any man who betrayed the family. But even more telling is another argument Angelo gives his son: "Charley, she is a woman you have known for only a few weeks. She is your wife. We are your life." The Don then reinforces the final idea by changing only a single word: "We are your blood."

Don Corrado's phrasing is, of course, intended once again to remind Charley of the blood oath he swore in becoming a member of the family; but both he and Angelo succeed in bringing Charley to his key realization of the film: "The family is the only place I can be. I know that." While the first sentence could be interpreted as meaning that Charley only feels comfortable or at home when he is with the Prizzis, it seems more likely that in his view he only *exists* within the boundaries of the family. His very sense of who he is incorporates the mutual dependency that abides between him and the Prizzis: he is a man who is protected by the Prizzis and protects Prizzi honor. If he were to break with the Prizzis and go off with Irene, he would lose his fundamental sense of who he is. He must destroy the woman he loves in order to preserve his identity, and the fact that this identity has been imposed upon him by "the environment" is basically irrelevant: it is nevertheless the only identity he has or can conceive of having.

Charley's behavior in this latter part of the film is in most respects more understandable than Irene's. Don Corrado would have wanted to turn her over—dead—to the police in any case; but when he hears Charley convey her request for $900,000, he says, "I'm glad that she's so foolish and grasping; makes it a little easier what we gotta do." When Charlie calls her on the phone from Don Corrado's and tells her the Don has agreed to give her everything she asked for, she knows immediately that he is setting her up for the kill, and after hanging up the phone she mutters, "Oh, Marxie, I should have listened." This remark refers us back to something her first husband had once said about "Sicilians" and which she had repeated to Charley on their wedding day: "They'd rather eat their children than part with money. And they are very fond of children." Having been told this, Irene should have realized that pressing a demand for $900,000 on the Prizzis was decidedly ill-advised. Why would she urge her husband to make a request of Don Corrado that would almost surely provoke a negative (and undoubtedly murderous) reaction?

Many answers are possible to this question, none altogether satisfactory to the exclusion of others. One is that Irene suffers from a classic case of hubris that temporarily clouds her judgment (which clears only with the call from Charley). In the motor home where they are keeping Filargi prisoner, she hears from Charley that the Prizzis are meeting their demands and offering something more: "It's all settled. My end is the two and a half million—plus I am Boss of the Prizzis. . . ." But what she hears is that all of the rewards are going to be Charley's. There is apparently no payment for, no recognition of the essential part she played in the kidnapping. *Amour propre* makes her seek recognition in the form of $900,000. Another possibility is that she is testing not the Prizzis but Charley with her demand. She wants to see if he values her enough to make a request of the Don that the old man will undoubtedly find offensive. Perhaps what she is really hoping for is that Charley will call and say, "The Don is really mad; maybe we'd better clear out our bank accounts and head for South America." The call that does come merely shows her that when the crunch came, Charley chose the Prizzis over her. Another possibility is that unconsciously Irene is seeking ex-actly what comes to her: death. She has been carrying out, according to her own testimony, "three or four hits a year"—"not many if you consider the size of the population," she tells Charley, but still a consid-erable amount of blood to have on one's hands. Although she displays no apparent remorse for any of her hits, it is at least possible that unconsciously she bears deep guilt for her crimes and desires the only punishment that would be just. On the other hand the filmmakers and the author of the original novel may have given no consideration to Irene's underlying psychological motivations; they may merely have wanted to set up a sort of duel scene between husband and wife that through Charley's victory would once more have lent support to one of our culture's prevailing myths—male supremacy.

The actual scene in which Irene shoots at Charley and misses while he pins her neck to the door with a hurled knife (apparently the one he took from Marxie Heller) is ambiguous, despite being presented in slow motion to give the viewer a better opportunity to see exactly what happens. Does Irene miss Charley with her shot because he is in motion to bring the knife up from the floor and hurl it at her? Or does she miss because she finds it difficult to kill the man whose bed she has shared the past few weeks (she had no trouble killing the bodyguard who was also in motion). To my eyes her shot misses to screen right of Charley before he lunges into motion—even though she has taken a highly professional stance, feet firmly planted, gun hand supported (police style) with her other. Kathleen Turner, who played the character, takes the view that Irene "was such an excellent marksmen, it was impossible that she could miss. . . . she was *choosing* to be killed rather than to kill him."[5] But the visual evidence certainly isn't conclusive, and one may just as well take the view that Charley is able to make the kill merely because he is the more highly skilled (and experienced) assassin.

Charley takes his leave of Irene after he parks her car at the airport— with her body in the trunk. Huston gives a close-up of Charley looking downwards sadly, then a close-up of the trunk lid of the red Excalibur. It seems a little odd to have this scene played without Charley actually looking at Irene's body but with him staring instead at the inanimate trunk lid. The director seems to be suggesting, however, that it makes little difference: Irene is now as inanimate as the lid and will have little more significance to Charley in his future life than any other object he once possessed.

When Charley gets back home, he takes a long shower as if trying to wash away the whole experience with Irene. Then he goes out onto his balcony and calls Maerose Prizzi on the phone to invite her out to dinner with him, explaining that Irene "hadda go away; she won't be back." The film ends with Maerose's enthusiastic acceptance of Charley's invitation. The slot that Maerose fills in the plot of *Prizzi's Honor* is that of the "good woman" to whom the *noir* hero sometimes turns (or returns) after his infatuation with the fatal woman is over. It is in its depiction of this "good woman" that the film most obviously displays its cynicism: Maerose is almost as much of a fatal woman as Irene.

Like Charley, Maerose is a product of her background within the "environment" of the Prizzi family. For Charley, the great formative experience was his initiation into the Mafia family and into the system of privileges and obligations his membership entailed. For Maerose, the formative experience was her exile from the family after she got angry at her fiance Charley and went off to Mexico with another man. This offense to Charley's honor was totally unforgivable to her father Dominic, who refused to let her live again in his house so long as Charley remained unmarried. Four years after the incident, Dominic still scorns his daughter: and even though he has allowed her to be invited to his other daughter's wedding, he informs her when she is brought up to him at the reception that she dressed like a "whore" (apparently because her gown leaves her shoulders bare and she has added a salmon-colored sash to the Sicilian women's basic black garb). Her experience of exile has left Maerose with two major goals in life: to regain her place in the family and attain vengeance on those who have scorned her—especially her father.

Her attitude toward Charley is more ambivalent. Unlike her father, he treats her at the wedding reception like an old friend. But she clearly resents his avuncular advice to her to get married to someone outside the family, have a couple of kids, "practice [her] meat balls." She snarls back sarcastically, "Sure, Charley, thanks a hell of a lot. You're a big help." Although Charley later tells Irene about Maerose's disgrace and says that despite the incident they are "still friends," it is evident that Mae rather resents being treated merely as a "friend." That she wants more from Charley is clearly indicated when he comes to her for advice following his unpleasant discoveries about Irene: in additional to their verbal conversation, Maerose suggests they "do it . . . right here on the oriental [carpet] with all the lights on." Despite wanting and receiving sex from Charley, Maerose advises him to marry Irene (". . . just because she's a thief and hitter doesn't mean she isn't a good woman in all the other departments"). Advising him in this manner is not a disinterested act of generosity; she tells him that if he marries Irene (or anyone) she'll "be able to go back in the family." What she doesn't tell him is that she has a scheme for eliminating his new wife shortly after the wedding.

Maerose keeps the pictures of Irene that Charley had brought to show her and uses them to gain identification of Irene as the woman in hot pants who entered Luis Palo's car the night he was killed. She takes this information to Don Corrado and suggests the necessity of punishing Irene with death. Don Corrado responds admiringly: "You're a true Prizzi. . . . You're like me; we forgive nothing." But he also is concerned that killing Irene "would cause Charley great pain." Maerose's straight-faced reply is highly ironic: "What is that, compared to the honor of the Prizzis?" The honor of the Prizzis has caused her four bitter years of exile; now she wants to use that same honor to achieve an end she desires.

Shortly after she returns to her father's house—having made "herself up to look like a ruined spinster"[6]—she tells him that Charley raped her ("Three times. Maybe four"). What she hopes to accomplish with this lie, other than making her father miserable, is uncertain. Dominic almost immediately hires a "hitter" (Irene) to kill Charley and thus gain vengeance for the violation of his daughter. Did Maerose expect this to happen? Does she want revenge on Charley for his part in her dishonor? Or did she think Dominic would go after Charley himself, and the younger man would inevitably prevail, eliminating the tyrannical father she despises. Chances are Maerose had no very clear plan in this in-stance; she merely wanted to stir up trouble, spread a little misery about to gain slight recompense for her own years of suffering.

By the end of the film Maerose has gotten nearly everything she wants. Dominic and Irene are dead. Charley has called up to ask for a date. In the last shot of the film, as Maerose realizes the implications of what Charley has told her, the light upon her grows brighter and brighter, irradiating her like the madonna in a stained glass window on a sunny day. The impression of transcendence created by this shot, however, is by no means altogether appropriate to the resumption of a love affair between two damaged people, who in their union may wreak more havoc upon others than they have in their isolation from one another. The killing in the world of the Prizzis has not stopped with the death of one fatal woman.

Despite all the deaths it contains, Pauline Kael has written of the "daring comic tone" of Prizzi's Honor,[7] and Terence Raftery described it as "a quirky, deadpan Mafia comedy."[8] The filmmaker John Huston was in agreement with the critics:" . . . the picture is a comedy."[9] That the film does not intend for us to take its violence entirely seriously is indicated by the musical score, which accompanies the deaths of Marxie Heller, the bodyguard and the police captain's wife, and Dominic Prizzi with excerpts from light-hearted Rossini overtures. The killing of Irene is backed by a recording of the tune Charley had earlier designated as "our song"—an effect not comic but bitterly ironic. Little in the film invites us to regard Irene's death as tragic (she is basically an "utter villain" who gets exactly what she deserves) or to feel that Charley will suffer long or deeply as a result of killing her. Despite what he had said, it has become clear by the end of the film that he didn't really "love" her—he was merely "in love" with her. Otherwise he would have at least waited a little longer to call Maerose. Ultimately this is a film about people whose social environment has permanently eroded or eaten away their ability to experience significant love in either a religious or secular sense. If we cannot weep for such incomplete human beings, laughter may be the only feasible alternative.

12

"Now It's Dark": The Child's Dream in David Lynch's *Blue Velvet*

N<small>OT</small> only have several critics have noted *Blue Velvet*'s resemblance to a dream and identified the male protagonist Jeffrey Beaumont (Kyle MacLachlan) as the dreamer,[1] but one of them, Tracy Biga, has suggested both a starting and ending point for the dream. Just before Jeffrey goes for the first time to the house of Detective Williams and then meets his daughter Sandy (Laura Dern) after the visit, we have an extreme close-up of the severed ear the young man earlier found in the vacant lot, and the camera appears to descend into the middle ear (which of course it could not literally do with the cut-off external ear). At this point, Biga submits, "We go inside the ear, inside Jeff's mind, and it is not until the final sequence, when the camera zooms out of an extreme close-up of Jeff's ear, that we will return to relative normality."[2] Biga implies that the main part of the film is basically Jeffrey's dream or fantasy, inspired perhaps by his disordered emotions arising as a consequence of his father's stroke, which left the older man lying helpless and apparently near death in the local hospital.

Certainly the possible death of a father could call up from a son's unconscious the long suppressed oedipal desires and fears of early childhood. And such desires and fears are readily apparent in Jeffrey's relationships with Dorothy Vallens (Isabella Rossellini) and Frank Booth (Dennis Hopper) who appear respectively as the seductive mother and the castrating father in the main part of the film. Yet to say that the dream begins with the entry through the ear and ends with the exit from it ignores the fact that the opening and concluding sections of the film are no less dreamlike than the central portion. I would submit that the entire film is Jeffrey's dream and that even though he appears in *Blue Velvet* as a young man of college age, the dream is basically that of a child.

The film opens with the camera fixed on a lightly swaying curtain of blue velvet, in front of which the opening credits run. (The velvet curtain will also return for the closing credits.) The movement is echoed by the brown drapes swaying in the wind in Dorothy Vallens's apartment, but the central fact about the piece of velvet behind the credits is that we cannot know what is causing it to move because *we do not know what lies behind it*. The drapery, therefore, could be regarded as a metaphor both for any first-time viewer's ignorance of the film that follows and for the characters' ignorance of the fates that lie before them. But it is a particularly apt symbol for a child's sense of so many things in the adult world being hidden from him. After his first two meetings with Dorothy Vallens and his surveillance of Frank and the man then only known as "Yellow Coat," Jeffrey tells Sandy, "I've seen something that was always hidden." His excitement as he goes on to say, "I'm in the middle of a mystery, and it's all secret," is distinctly childlike.

The film proper opens with a dissolve from the blue velvet to a shot of a bright blue sky; then the camera tilts down to show intense red roses against the backdrop of an immaculate white picket fence. Successive shots present a red fire engine going down a quiet residential street—with a friendly middle-aged fireman and a docile dog on the running board—yellow flowers in front of a white picket fence, a maternal lady assisting school children across the street. Lynch himself has said he chose to have the camera angle "looking up" in the first shot "because it's a childhood sort of image,"[3] but the entire sequence of images is like the vision of a childhood paradise: bright, highly saturated primary colors; friendly, protective adult guardian figures.

Then the serpent appears in this paradise in the form of the hissing hose that becomes blocked when it is bent over the branch of a bush. In his struggle to disengage the hose from the bush, a hitherto placid middle-aged man grows agitated—until he suddenly grabs his neck, lurches violently, causing his hat to fly off, and collapses to the ground, making inarticulate grunting noises. Water from the now-freed hose sprays straight up into the air, and a neighborhood dog (apparently seeking a drink) snaps at the stream in a manner that seems increasingly vicious as we are brought progressively closer to the scene (by means of an optical printer that makes the image grainier as it gets bigger). A toddler in the yard next door observes the spectacle with emotions that are unreadable: dismay? horror? simple lack of comprehension? But the sequence demonstrates to the audience that the protective adult figures of the preceding sequence are highly vulnerable—and that the well-trained dog on the fire engine is no more the model of animal behavior than the uncontrollable mutt dancing on the chest of the fallen man.

The sequence then ends with perhaps the most famous image of the film. The camera descends toward the well-kept green lawn, penetrates into the grass, and reveals in near darkness a world of insect activity—finally showing two beetle-like creatures engaged in what appears to be mortal combat. Accompanying the images as the camera descends, rustling noises grow louder and louder, at last transmuting to a roar. The symbolism is fairly obvious: when one looks beneath the peaceful surface of *anything*—a lawn, a small town, a clean-cut boy like Jeffrey Beaumont—one discovers violence and destruction. Something in his own physical nature has just attacked Mr. Beaumont as fiercely as the two insects are assaulting each other in the grass beneath him.

Knowledge of such violence in the realm of nature and in human nature is apparently one of those things that have remained hidden from Jeffrey up to this point in his life. Even as he goes to visit his father in the hospital, Jeffrey displays signs of wanting to remain in the realm of childhood innocence and to avoid facing his father's mortality (which of course by extension suggests his own). Walking through a vacant lot, he picks up a stone and flings it as a child would. After beholding his father in the hospital bed—immobilized, unable to speak—Jeffrey on the way back through the same lot again tries to return to a childish frame of mind and throws a couple more stones, this time at a green bottle. Missing the bottle, he looks around for another stone—and finds the severed ear, which will be his entree to knowledge of that which is dark and violent in the world around him and, more importantly, within himself.

The discovery of the ear marks a transition in the form of Jeffrey's dream. Up to this point his parents have appeared only as themselves (the mother is briefly seen drinking coffee, smoking a cigarette, and watching what appears to be a *film noir* on television). Now disguised versions of the parents begin to appear. The first is Detective Williams (to whom Jeffrey brings the ear), who represents the positive aspects of the father: the moral guardian, law upholder. When Jeffrey visits him at his house, Detective Williams says he understands that the young man is "curious to know more" about the investigation involving the ear, but he requests that Jeffrey not only refrain from telling anyone about his discovery but also from even "ask[ing] more about the case." Williams promises, "one day when it's all sewed up, I'll let you know in detail. Right now, though, I can't." To Jeffrey's admission that he is indeed "real curious" Williams offers in a kindly fashion, "I was the same way myself when I was your age." Detective Williams's manner is very much that of a father putting off a son's questions about such subjects as sexuality and the evil in the world that the parent doesn't deem the child ready to know about yet. His willingness to admit that he too was curious about such matters at the child's age merely reinforces the impression that he is denying the young person such knowledge only for the latter's own good. But when we later learn that Frank's associate "Yellow Coat" is really Detective Gordon, Williams's partner, certainly the audience and probably Jeffrey as well must suspect that the young man has perhaps been denied knowledge for someone else's benefit. Even the climax of the film does not conclusively demonstrate that Williams was completely free of complicity with his partner and his criminal associates. Thus, although Detective Williams represents the positive image of the father, that image has to be accepted by both Jeffrey and the viewer largely on faith.

Immediately after Jeffrey has been warned away from the investigation by her father, Sandy emerges from the darkness of her yard (the way the shot is presented she could as well be emerging from the darkness inside the ear) to give Jeffrey the information he needs to begin his own investigation of the case. Sandy partly represents the anima—pointing Jeffrey in the direction he must go in order to get in touch with his deepest feelings—but also she is the acceptable mother substitute. Although at least a couple of years younger than Jeffrey (he is in college; she's still in high school), Sandy is completely supportive and nurturing of the young man. She offers him commonsensical objections to his investigative plans, but in the end always goes along with them. She is appalled to discover—just after she and Jeffrey have told each other, "I love you"—that her lover has had a sexual relationship with Dorothy Vallens; but when he calls Sandy from the hospital (where Dorothy has been taken), reaffirms his love for her, and asks to be forgiven—she immediately says, "I forgive you, Jeffrey. . . . I love you." In no other part of the film is the wish-fulfillment aspect of dream more obvious than in the characterization of Sandy, who both makes possible Jeffrey's quasi–incestuous relationship with Dorothy Vallens and provides a safe alternative to it.

Just before Jeffrey enters Dorothy Vallens's apartment at night, Sandy says to him, "I don't know if you're a detective or a pervert." Although Jeffrey evades answering the question ("That's for me to know, and you to find out"), the viewer will probably have little difficulty arriving at the answer "a bit of each." He initially wanted to get into Dorothy's apartment merely because Sandy told him the woman was somehow involved with the incident of the ear; but after seeing Dorothy in the apartment (when he visited it disguised as an insecticide sprayer) and as singer at the night club, he undoubtedly has a second motive added to the first. When Dorothy finds him in her closet, she asks him what he wants, and he replies, "I didn't mean to do anything, except see you." This statement seems to indicate that his primary (indeed he says *only*) goal was voyeuristic. He intends to reassure her that he meant to do nothing to her other than look at her, but he also admits (to the viewer, if not as well to himself) that investigating the mystery of the severed ear was not looming large in his mind as he observed Dorothy in her underwear in the living room, then completely naked down the hall in the bathroom.

The script of the film describes Dorothy Vallens as "a very beautiful woman in her late thirties,"[4] thus someone literally old enough to be Jeffrey's mother. Isabella Rosselini doesn't look that old in the film, but Dorothy is linked in other ways with Jeffrey's mother. In the phone conversation Jeffrey overhears from inside her closet, she refers to herself as "Mommy," and Frank addresses her as such in his first visit to her apartment. When she appears naked and battered in Jeffrey's front lawn, Sandy's former boyfriend Mike asks sarcastically, "Who's that, huh? Is that your mother? Is that your mother, Jeffrey?" Jeffrey does not reply, but the two-fold answer clearly is, "Literally, no; symbolically, yes." Dorothy is Jeffrey's dream or fantasy mother with whom he commits incest. As such, she is an emotionally volatile woman, almost the exact opposite of his cool and self-contained real life mother. It might be said that she represents the hidden passionate self that Jeffrey suspects his mother conceals from him and the world at large.

Dorothy is also two familiar female types from *film noir* rolled into one. When she initially menaces Jeffrey with a carving knife, she seems cast as the *femme fatale*. Kneeling on the floor with her knife pointed directly at the young man's genitals and asking him to "come closer," she is perhaps the most blatant embodiment of the castrating female thus far seen in American film. But *femme fatale* is merely a role she has chosen to play for her own—and Jeffrey's—titillation. Underneath, she is the female victim, the damsel in dire distress. And her pose of menace, along with some of the things she says to Jeffrey—"Don't look at me. . . . Don't touch me, or I'll kill you"—is simply imitative of Frank's sadistic dallying with her.

Jeffrey learns of Dorothy's extreme vulnerability in the sequence which at least two critics (quite correctly in my view) have identified as a variant on Freud's "primal scene" in which a child views his parents having sexual intercourse.[5] Dorothy's tormenting and arousing of Jeffrey is interrupted by the arrival of Frank, who immediately takes the dominant position over her that she had assumed with the younger man. Through the blinds of the closet Jeffrey observes the perverse sexual scene between the two older people. What he and we the viewers see is much like a child's confused perspective on parental intercourse. The man and the woman identify each other as "Mommy" and "Daddy"— although at certain moments of intensity "Daddy" prefers to become "Baby": "Baby wants to fuck." Frank has to enhance his arousal by sniffing some sort of gas from an inhaler he claps over his nose and mouth as he simultaneously stares at Dorothy's crotch. (The script identifies the gas as helium,[6] but Dennis Hopper doesn't speak in the higher pitched voice that helium should give rise to.) When he engages in intercourse, Frank doesn't seem to lower his pants; and of course in an R-rated film we don't see his penis penetrate Dorothy's vagina. What we do see is the strap of her blue velvet robe placed fetishistically with one end in her mouth, the other in his as he reaches orgasm.

From an adult point of view the scene is totally perverse, but it also seems like a child's misconception of adult love making. ("What do Mommy and Daddy do in bed with each other?" "I dunno. Maybe they talk dirty. Maybe they put something in each other's mouths.") But what chiefly strikes both Jeffrey and the viewer about this scene is the violence and cruelty with which Frank dominates Dorothy in pursuit of his pleasure. As Freud has said apropos the "primal scene":

> If children at [an] early age witness sexual intercourse between adults . . . they inevitably regard the sexual act as a sort of ill-treatment or act of subjugation: they view it, that is, in a sadistic sense.[7]

The scene between Dorothy and Frank that Jeffrey has witnessed completely alters his perception of the woman: now she is no longer the beautiful and dangerous female, simultaneously arousing him and threatening him with castration, but the woman in distress, object of his pity as well as of his lust. Where she earlier tried to intimidate him, she now seeks Jeffrey's protection and—by addressing him with her husband's name—suggests he, like Frank, can play the role of Daddy to her Mommy: "Don, hold me, hold me. I'm scared." Now she tries to reverse their relationship from their first scene together, where she played the sadistic role, and invites him to hit her. "Feel me; hit me," she says; and after he fails to comply, she pounds her fist against the wall and repeats the second request (command?) three times. Jeffrey is not yet ready to play Frank's role with Dorothy and leaves the apartment after finding and examining the photograph of her son (with the propeller cap on) and husband and also her wedding certificate. Don is yet another substitute for Jeffrey's own father since he is forced into impotent submission to Frank's will just as Mr. Beaumont is helpless in his hospital bed. The boy who is wearing the propeller cap might be said to represent the young man's own lost childhood—the innocence he will perhaps lose once and for all when he admits to the presence within him of the sadistic sexual impulses that Frank manifests.

Jeffrey will yield to Dorothy's desires and hit her—thereby intensifying his sexual excitement—on his fourth visit to her apartment, but before we consider that scene we should first ponder the implications of the dream (within a dream) Jeffrey has after the first night-time visit. This dream offers no coherent narrative, merely a fragmented series of images.

It opens with a distorted face, that I find unrecognizable, although it seems to be male. It is replaced by a close-up in profile of Frank's face, his mouth opening as if in a savage cry. We cut to a flickering candle flame against a black background. When the flame goes out, Frank's voice says, "Now it's dark." The black screen is then replaced by Dorothy's face in tight close-up, with closed eyes and her bright red lips parting to say, "Hit me." As if in response to her request, there is a shot of Frank lashing out. Then Jeffrey wakes up in his bedroom at home. What is this series of images supposed to convey to Jeffrey or to the viewer?

They are obviously intended to affect one more on an emotional than an intellectual level, but a few speculations can be offered. The distorted face may of course be Frank's—struggling as it were to come into focus. But it could also be the face of Jeffrey's father or of Jeffrey himself, for I will argue in greater detail later that Frank could be considered a projection of darker qualities within either of them. Frank's spoken comment, accompanied by the black screen, repeats what he said when Dorothy turned off the brightest electric light in the apartment and lit a single candle to replace it prior to their sexual encounter. But the phrase is also quite appropriate to the criminal who represents the dark side of human nature (he will later repeat it just before he takes Jeffrey off to beat him into unconsciousness). The close-up of the candle flame also refers back to the sex scene between Frank and Dorothy; and the enlarged flame, accompanied by equally magnified sounds of burning, furthermore serves as a traditional metaphor for sexual passion. (Frank blows out the candle in Dorothy's apartment after he has achieved orgasm.) Through this group of images Jeffrey seems to be telling himself that if Dorothy wants someone to hit her she should turn to Frank: it's not the sort of thing Jeffrey can imagine himself doing.

But of course, when they are together a couple of nights later, he does hit her. She lures him into it when they are lying naked together on her bed. "Are you a bad boy?" she asks. "Do you want to do bad things? Anything? Anything?" The language—as in so much of the film—is simple, childlike. The perverse mother is tempting her little boy to do naughty things. When Jeffrey acts as if he doesn't understand what she is talking about, Dorothy gets specific about her own "bad" desires: "I want you to hurt me." Jeffrey, desperately clinging to his good boy persona, protests, "No, I don't want to hurt you; I told you I want to help you." But when she tries to kick him out of her bed, he impulsively slaps her—then, after a pause as if he is consciously choosing his next action, Jeffrey strikes her again—harder. And they proceed to have sexual intercourse in slow motion, with thunderous roaring noises on the sound track. Both the sound and the slow motion suggest that the sexual experience for each of them has been greatly intensified by the act of violence. The same idea is underlined by a recurrence of the close-up of the burning candle, followed by an even closer shot of just the flame after he strikes her. Dorothy has successfully introduced Jeffrey to the pleasures of badness.

The next sequence opens with Jeffrey holding the propeller cap of Dorothy's son Donny. Dorothy takes it from him and clasps it to her bosom, almost as if the hat were the missing child. Jeffrey has picked up the cap as if he were speculating upon—if not lamenting—his lost innocence. It was appropriate for Dorothy to take the cap from him, for in tempting him to hit her she has just removed some last measure of his innocence. But Dorothy yearns for her innocent child as she might for her own lost innocence. Frank has taken the child from her; did he also take her innocence by instilling or cultivating her taste for sado-masochistic sexuality? In this sequence, Dorothy abruptly says to Jeffrey, "You think I'm crazy, don't you? . . . I'm not crazy; I know the difference between right and wrong." To this statement Jeffrey can only respond, "That's good." But it's not so good if Dorothy knows the difference between right and wrong—and winds up supporting the cause of evil anyway. Her statement serves as a transition to the arrival of Frank Booth—Mr. Wrong, the personification of evil—who proceeds to dominate both Dorothy and Jeffrey in the scenes that immediately follow.

In the oedipal framework of the film Frank is the ideal candidate for parricide. Laura Mulvey characterizes him as "both the sadistic father of the primal scene, and a fearfully erotic father whose homosexual aggression threatens the hero child with sexual passivity and death."[8] Jeffrey would have to feel considerable guilt for desiring the death of his literal father—an apparently harmless middle-aged man, liberal enough to hire two blacks (one of them blind) as the staff in his hardware store. But Frank is a middle-aged man without a single redeeming characteristic. Criminal, killer, sadist, pervert—he is perhaps also the most foul-mouthed character in film history (rarely does a sentence pass his lips without containing the word "fuck" or some variant upon it). Scarcely anyone watching *Blue Velvet* would be likely to feel that Frank deserved less than the bullet in the middle of the forehead that Jeffrey fires in the film's climactic sequence. That's what makes him a perfect dream character. Twice in the film Frank appears wearing the so-called "well-dressed man" disguise with a wig and false mustache—although on neither occasion does there seem to be any necessity for him to wear such make-up. His use of this disguise I take to be the filmmaker's tip-off that *throughout* Frank is a character in disguise: he embodies the feared aspects of the father so blatantly exaggerated that he seems totally deserving of being murdered. Indeed parenticide in this film is made to seem not like murder but like righteous execution.

Frank's continual use of the explicative "fuck" stresses one of the most salient features of his personality: his aggressive sexuality. Lynch's script says that Frank possesses "a raw, mean sexuality,"[9] and the initial (primal) scene between him and Dorothy shows how inextricably interrelated aggression and sexual pleasure are for this man. His behavior with Dorothy seems to indicate that he cannot experience orgasm with a woman unless he acts violently toward her; and one suspects that all of his acts of violence toward others, female or male, are accompanied by some degree of sexual satisfaction. It is particularly interesting how Frank interprets the lyrics of the popular song "Love Letters" for Jeffrey:

> I'll send you a love letter. Straight from my heart, Fucker. You know what a love letter is? It's a bullet from a fuckin' gun, Fucker. You receive a love letter from me, you're fucked forever.

In Frank's vocabulary love and aggression are synonymous. A love letter, therefore, can be a bullet from a gun. Such a love letter would come "straight from [Frank's] heart" because acts of violence satisfy his deepest emotional desires. When he has intercourse with Dorothy, he brutalizes her and hurts her both physically and emotionally; so that it's not surprising that he could describe an act of murder in sexual terms: "fucked forever."

From the minute he discovers Jeffrey with Dorothy, Frank delights in exerting his dominance over the young man. He forces Jeffrey to go off in the car with him and his attendant thugs, brags to Ben (Dean Stockwell) that he can "make [the younger man] do anything I please," and approvingly permits Ben to punch the boy in the stomach. All of this, however, is merely preparatory to the second part of the car ride, which ends out by Meadow Lane. Before leaving from Ben's place, Frank announces, "Now it's dark. Let's fuck! I'll fuck anything that moves!" Although it is certainly possible that Frank does have sexual intercourse with Dorothy before the night is out, his statements are more metaphorical than literal. It is not literally dark at the exact moment when Frank says, "Now. . . ." He is still in a well-lighted room, and it has been dark outside for some hours prior to his announcement. What he seems to mean is that his mood is now properly (from his point of view) dark: he is psychologically ready for dark actions, ready to "fuck anything that moves"—either sexually or murderously.

Back in the car, by the simple method of sadistically pinching Dorothy's breasts right before the young man's eyes, Frank provokes Jeffrey into lashing out against him. When Jeffrey punches him in the mouth,

Frank is given the excuse to haul the boy out of the car and beat him savagely while he is held by the underling thugs. One thing that is interesting about the beating is that Frank treats it much like his sexual domination of Dorothy. As he had with Dorothy, he orders Jeffrey, "Don't you look at me. . . ." He sniffs the helium before the beating as before intercourse and wipes a piece of blue velvet across Jeffrey's mouth. Additionally he addresses Jeffrey as "Pretty, Pretty" and kisses him after smearing his own mouth with Dorothy's lipstick. Just before he actually starts pounding on him, Frank invites Jeffrey to feel his muscles—and presumably admire them. The whole lead-up to the thrashing of Jeffrey has overtones of a homosexual seduction. If sex must be violent for Frank, so violence has to be sexual. Not surprisingly the close-up of the flame with its amplified sound returns after the beating just as it had after Jeffrey's violent sexual encounter with Dorothy.

Just before Frank starts pinching Dorothy to incite a response from Jeffrey, he tells the younger man, "You're like me." And right before the beating starts, he quotes from the Roy Orbison song "In Dreams" that Ben had mimed in his apartment and that Frank has now ordered to be played on the car tape deck: "I walk with you. In dreams I talk to you. In dreams you're mine. . . . Forever in dreams." These lines are perhaps the most obvious clue to the central meaning of the film. Although Jeffrey finds it difficult to admit this to himself, he really is like Frank. Underneath he shares the same sexual and aggressive instincts as Frank, who is not merely the oedipal father but a personification of Jeffrey's own id. Just as all sons contain within them the potential to be the oedipal father, so in beholding Frank, Jeffrey is merely seeing his own latent instincts made manifest. And it is in dreams sometimes that instincts that we normally repress in waking life become unavoidably apparent to us—assault our awareness much as Frank assaults Jeffrey.

Although a viewer caught up the film may not notice it, the climax of the story deviates from probability even more than the remainder of the movie. Dorothy turns up stark naked on Jeffrey's lawn. What happened to her clothes? How did she get there? Did no one notice a naked woman walking down the street? Jeffrey discovers Dorothy's husband Don has been killed in her apartment (the strap of blue velvet in his mouth unambiguously identifies Frank as the killer)—why has he been brought there rather than being killed wherever Frank had been hiding him? Detective Gordon (in his yellow coat) is standing in the apartment with a bad head wound (blood from it has run down the side of his face and all the way down the front of his shirt), comatose, perhaps about to die. It seems likely that Frank shot him too, but why? Gordon was a valued criminal associate of his. And why does Frank return to the scene of his crimes (wearing the well-dressed man disguise) instead of just leaving his victims there? He does finish off Gordon while he is there, but this is something he certainly could have done before. A possible answer is that he came back for Dorothy (whom he had left there with no clothes on), but he never looks for her or even mentions her name after entering the apartment.

The only real answer to such questions is that these improbable cir-cumstances are set up to provide Jeffrey with the opportunity to shoot Frank and make the audience feel he is entirely justified in doing so. Once again there is a childlike (or perhaps childish) quality to the climactic sequence in the apartment. Jeffrey is like a small child hiding from an angry parent, who is threatening to punish him severely once he is found. And many a child has perhaps fantasized about having a weapon handy to blow away the wrathful adult at the moment of confrontation.

Although Jeffrey kills the oedipal father, he does not choose to con-tinue his sexual relationship with his surrogate mother Dorothy. It is significant that even though she turns up in his yard he does not take her into his house but puts her in the car and tells Sandy, "We've got to get her out of here." It seems clear that he doesn't want to bring his dream mother together with his real mother. He faces problems enough allowing the two objects of his sexual fantasies to confront each other. Although Dorothy acts overtly as if she is barely aware that Sandy is even there, it is clear that she is laying her claim to Jeffrey in the younger girl's presence. She asks Jeffrey to "hold" her, addresses him as her "secret love," admits in a confidential tone that "he put his seed in me," and in her most direct appeal cries to him, "I love you; love me!"— lines that evoke a totally anguished gasp from Sandy. When Jeffrey tells Sandy that he "should go" to the hospital with Dorothy, it would seem that the older woman has triumphed in her competition with the younger woman.

But after he gets Dorothy safely into the hands of the doctors at the hospital, Jeffrey calls Sandy to reaffirm his love for her, and the two of them are together at his family's house at the end of the movie while Dorothy is seen alone in a park with her young son Donny. Apparently, continuing his sexual relationship with Dorothy stuck Jeffrey as too incestuous—even though the warm and entirely supportive Sandy is really more of an ideal mother figure despite being a couple of years younger than her "son." (Charley Partanna's theory from *Prizzi's Honor* could apply as well to this film: Jeffrey wants and seems to get from Sandy what he wanted but didn't get from his real mother.) Yet if the film in its entirety is regarded as Jeffrey's dream—a dream generated by some permanently infantile substratum of his psyche—it is possible that he possesses Dorothy as well as Sandy at the end. He is with Dorothy in the form of her son Donny—the representation of Jeffrey's regained innocence. It is in certain ways more satisfactory to possess Dorothy as Donny than as Jeffrey, for the child is presumably as yet unaware of his mother's deep neuroses and psychosexual hang-ups. Unlike the audience the boy cannot see the look of anxiety that replaces the one of joy on his mother's face as she holds him in her arms while her version of the song "Blue Velvet" (an emblem of her tormented relationship with Frank) fades in on the soundtrack.

Blue Velvet at the end returns to the bright, cheerful images of its opening and even adds a robin—reminding Sandy of her dream in which "the world was dark" and would remain so until the robins, standing for "love," came back. This ending seems pure wish-fulfillment, suggesting the restoration of order, harmony, light—not merely in the lives of all the leading characters (Mr. Beaumont is shown apparently completely recovered from his stroke) but in the world at large as well. But of course most viewers can't respond to the end of the film that optimistically, because the robin has a big bug in its beak; and that probably reminds many of us of those insects fighting to the death down in the grass the day of Mr. Beaumont's attack—and not merely on that day but undoubtedly on this day, and every other day of the year as well. In the image of the robin about to devour its prey we are reminded that violence is at the very core of existence on this planet—in nature, in human society, in the psyche of the protagonist of this film, and in each and every member of the audience.

13

"Permanent Damage": Maternal Influence in *The Grifters*

IN *The Grifters* as in *Prizzi's Honor* the two major female characters are both fatal women—instead of one being a good girl to balance the evil woman as in several of the 1940s *noir* films. Although the role of innocence and goodness may have been relatively impotent in certain of the '40s films (Ann in *Out of the Past* may be considered a good example), at least a "positive" female role model (warm, supportive, nurturing) had a distinct presence in those movies. To be sure the "good woman" has a nominal presence in *The Grifters* in the form of Carol, the nurse. But Carol's role is not only distinctly reduced from what it was in Jim Thompson's 1963 novel on which the film is (in large part closely) based, her physical stature is also minimal. Both Annette Bening (Myra) and Anjelica Huston (Lilly), the actresses in the lead female roles, tower over Noelle Harling who plays Carol. She literally looks like a child when she stands next to them. Roy (John Cusack) is doubtlessly correct when he interprets his mother Lilly's motives for hiring Carol to "look in" on him during his post-operative recuperation: "She hired you for me to fuck. To keep me away from bad influences" (chiefly Myra). After Roy has flustered Carol by saying this to her, Lilly orders her, "Go wait in the hall. Don't go away." But Carol is last seen walking off quickly down the hall toward a retreating camera, and Lilly makes no attempt to find her after concluding the brief follow-up conversation with Roy. Carol simply disappears from the film because there is no place for innocence within it.

Carol's height is not the only sign of her childlike quality: she displays very little bosom under her starched white nurse's uniform. In contrast, Myra's breasts—which are clearly displayed in two nude scenes—are distinctly ample. Roy comments on them in his first scene with her, and she says she is going to "smother" him with them. Although Roy indicates this will be a pleasant way to die ("O death, where is thy sting?"), in the context of the film as a whole the symbolism of the scene is ominously prophetic. The maternal breast is not a source of nurture, something life-giving, but a weapon of destruction—it can deprive the male of breath and life. In the literal story-line Myra simply doesn't notice that Roy has been seriously injured (he was butted in the stomach with a billy club when a bartender detected him in a scam); instead of getting him medical assistance she hurls herself on top of him preliminary to vigorous physical activity that will certainly not slow up his internal bleeding. In the scene in the hospital with Carol and Lilly, Roy deliberately rejects the possibility of relationship with a girl who would be his nurse and look after his health. Whether consciously or not, he prefers relationship with a woman who offers him nothing beyond self-destructive sexual gratification.

The film's visual emphasis on Myra's breasts (which are usually just as prominent when she is clothed as when she is undraped since she normally wears tight sweaters) casts her symbolically in the role of mother—bad mother because the breasts are smothering rather than nurturing. But Roy has his real mother in the film, who tries to wean him away, so to speak, from the bad substitute mother. At first Lilly seems to reenter Roy's life (after eight years of separation) as a decidedly positive force. Unlike Myra, she quickly discerns that Roy is seriously ill, and she is fierce in her determination to save her son's life: when a doctor tells her that he doesn't think Roy is "going to make it," Lilly replies coldly, "My son is going to be all right. If not, I'll have you killed." And after a period in Intensive Care Roy does survive. Even Myra has to acknowledge, "Roy, your mom saved your life."

In this part of the film (and perhaps even almost to the end) Lilly is largely a sympathetic character. Perhaps the viewer like Roy may find her a little too insistent on receiving credit where it's due not only for saving Roy's life here in Los Angeles but for having brought him into the world in the first place. When Roy finally says to her grudgingly, "I guess I owe you my life," she replies rather smugly, "You always did." But she has acted effectively to save her son's life when no one else would have—certainly not Myra, who didn't even notice there was something seriously wrong with Roy, or Roy himself, who tried to deny he was severely injured because he apparently felt he should have been man enough to take such a blow and shrug it off. Because Roy in reality is not nearly so tough as he would like to think himself, the advice that Lilly gives him more than once in the film is also potentially life-giving: "Get off the grift, Roy. . . . You haven't the stomach for it."

There is even a sacrificial aspect to Lilly's saving of Roy's life—although it is not a sacrifice she had any conscious intention of making. Because Lilly spends long hours at the hospital until she is certain Roy is going to recover, she fails to arrive at the race track to place bets on the long shot Troubador to bring the odds down and reduce the possibility of a big payoff if the horse wins. (Bringing down the odds is Lilly's job for the gambling syndicate that employs her.) Lilly's car is still caught in slow-moving traffic as Troubador races to an upset victory. (Shots of the race are intercut with close-ups of Lilly nervously listening to it over the car radio—also close, low-angle shots of the fast moving horses with high angle long shots of the barely moving traffic.) Shortly thereafter Lilly's boss Bobo Justus (Pat Hingle) turns up to punish her for her transgression. When Lilly explains that she failed to get her bets down because she was worried about her son in the hospital, Bobo asks, "What the fuck are you doing with a son?" Then when he is convinced she actually has one, he mutters scornfully, "Motherhood"—as if the feelings that have obstructed her in the performance of her duty have to be acknowledged although he regards them as in no sense being deserving of respect. She has, however, apparently engaged his sympathies suffi-ciently that he has decided merely to hurt for her crime and not kill her.

The first thing Bobo does when he has her alone in his hotel room is punch her in her stomach dropping her to her knees. (The act obviously parallels the bartender's punishment to Roy for grifting in his tavern.) The next torment he has devised for her is psychological. Bobo orders Lilly to bring him a towel from the bathroom, then drops a bag full of oranges at her feet, and tells her to wrap them in the towel. He asks her if she knows what the oranges can be used for. She tells how if a person is beaten with the oranges in the towel, "big ugly bruises" are produced, but the person doesn't "really get hurt—not if you do it right." Bobo then asks, "And if you do it wrong?" Realizing what Bobo is implicitly threatening, Lilly says, "It can louse up your insides"; then she breaks down as she tries to sum up, "You can get p-p-p-p-p-," before she finally manages to get out the words "permanent damage." Bobo summarizes the effect of the beating less abstractly: "You never shit right again." Then he rises to his feet, advances from the desk where he was sitting, and tells Lilly to "bring [him] the towel." As she does, the camera tracks with the towel sagging full of oranges. Bobo takes the towel, twists the ends of it to get a better grip, and raises it high as if to strike Lilly with it. Then he simply empties the oranges out on the floor. The viewer, and perhaps Lilly as well, may think at this point that he isn't going to hurt her any more after all. But he immediately shoves her to the floor with his foot in her back and then brands her on the back of her right hand with his lighted cigar.

The whole sequence is fraught with sado-masochistic sexual perver-sion. Bobo is toying with Lilly all the way through in order to establish his absolute masculine dominance over her—which reaches its climax when he straddles her on the floor and thrusts the burning cigar into her hand. As with Kubrick's General Jack D. Ripper in *Dr. Strangelove*,

Bobo's big cigar seems an emblem of sexual potency, which the man in actuality may no longer possess. Bobo is quite a bit older than Lilly Pat Hingle, was sixty-seven when *The Grifters* was made; Anjelica Huston was thirty-nine), and he is also shorter than she is (especially in her high heels). But by terrifying her and bringing her down at his feet, he can assert his male superiority. Once that is established, he can be gracious and forgiving toward her. (He even returns the $10,000 she paid under the pretense that it was the winnings from her bets on Troubador.) In their final scene together on the balcony of his hotel suite Lilly is clearly still very wary of Bobo, but she strives to reinforce his benevolent mood by complimenting him on his suit: ". . . somehow it makes you look taller." Most of this scene is done in long shot showing the whole bodies of the actors and making Lilly appear even taller than Bobo than she does in other scenes.

Lilly's total submissiveness to Bobo is in sharp contrast to her aggressiveness with other men in the film—for instance, the one who tries to pick her up in a restaurant, whom she drops to the floor with a sharp blow from her elbow to his windpipe. Her lack of resistance to her brutal treatment from Bobo can perhaps be attributed to her acceptance of the authority structure of the criminal organization to which she belongs. Members who try to cross it wind up dead. But it is possible that her acceptance of this punishment is also for her a sort of validation of her commitment to her son Roy. In order to save his life she was not only willing to put out the money for his hospital bills, she was willing to endure physical pain and humiliating submission. In this sense the burn mark on her hand may represent a sort of stigmata, a sign of her sacrificial love for her son.

When Roy later notices the wound and asks about it, Lilly only explains it as "an accident." Because Roy doesn't know the burn mark is part of the price she paid to heal him, he thinks he can clear his obligation to Lilly by giving her $4000 to cover his hospital expenses. "I pay my debts," he announces to her self-righteously. (In Jim Thompson's 1963 novel Roy gave his mother $3000; the film, which is set in the present, fails to take into account the soaring inflation rate of hospital costs since the time of the book. Roy probably isn't even meeting his financial debt to Lilly let alone his personal one.) When she tells him, "Roy, take that money back; I don't want it," he simply refuses: "No." He won't accept the money back from her just as he wouldn't accept Carol from her—and perhaps the most important thing he rejects from her is her advice. "I guess you won't be getting a straight job either," Lilly remarks bitterly after Roy has indicated his unwillingness "to play it straight" with her. She regards his career as a grifter as potentially fatal to her son and is not reassured by his protestations that he can "walk away from it anytime."

The latter part of this conversation between Roy and Lilly is shot in alternating close-ups (usually over the shoulder of the other speaker). Roy's face is smooth and unblemished; in his white shirt he appears guileless and innocent. But toward the end of the sequence he withdraws his eyes from the camera and from Lilly's gaze—first by looking down at a newspaper, then by putting on black sunglasses. He clearly doesn't want Lilly to see into his true feelings any more than he wants to see into them himself. Lilly in the sequence wears a black dress, almost as if she is in mourning for the fatal course she sees her son's life set upon— or perhaps for the demise of their relationship. Lilly's facial expressions throughout the sequence are quite expressive in contrast to Roy's bland mask. She is clearly hurt by his refusal to let her pay for his hospitaliza- tion and very much worried about his future. In the final shot of the sequence the camera holds on her face as Roy gets off the bed opposite her and leaves her motel room. As he starts to leave, he passes directly in front of the camera, seemingly causing a dark shadow to pass quickly across Lilly's face. Her expression of anguished concern contrasts sharply with her final dismissive words about her son: "You little prick."

But the real contrast in the film is between Lilly's behavior toward Roy in the film up to this point and her behavior toward him at the end. The Lilly of the first three-quarters of the movie is essentially a caring and concerned mother, willing to make significant sacrifices for the welfare of her child. Lilly at the end of the film appears to be the mother from Hell. She steals her son's money, attempts to seduce him, and finally kills him. (Technically the latter act is not murder but man- slaughter, but that fact probably doesn't make it any less appalling to most viewers.) Is it really possible to regard Lilly at the end of the film as a dramatically logical extension of Lilly as she has appeared in the remainder of it? One possible answer is that Lilly in the first three- quarters of the movie is not truly the caring and concerned mother she appears to be: she is instead someone who is *trying* to be a caring and concerned mother. Paying for Roy's hospitalization is not a serious sacri- fice for her because at the time she has thousands of dollars stashed in the trunk of her car. Her punishment from Bobo for failing to get her bets down on Troubador is not an intentional sacrifice: she was trying to get to the track on time but was held up in traffic. At the end of the film when her own interests come into conflict with her son's, she chooses to act differently than she had when she didn't perceive such a conflict. But perhaps even more significantly Lilly's behavior toward Roy at the end of the film is strongly influenced by a third party: Myra Langtry.

In Jim Thompson's novel Roy realizes toward the end that he had been attracted to Moira because of her resemblance to Lilly: "*Moira, another older woman, who had in essence been Lilly*. . . ."[1] In the film the only notable similarities between Lilly and Myra are their height (particularly in contrast to Carol) and their bitchiness toward each other. There is scarce resemblance between them in terms of facial features, hair coloring, or manner of speech. (Lilly, even with Bobo, sounds like a mature woman; Myra tends fall into piping, teasing, little-girl tones.) But the two women do try to play the same kind of controlling role with regard to Roy Dillon: both strive to influence the future course of his life. Lilly wants Roy to get off grift and go straight so that he can avoid the inevitable crash that occurs in such a profession. Myra also wants Roy to give up the "short con" but only to join her in practicing the big cons she had formerly pulled off with Cole Langley (J. T. Walsh). Even Roy seems to realize toward the end of the film that Lilly's advice would be healthier for him to follow than Myra's.

Myra is a woman seeking an identity, and for part of the film she thinks Roy's assistance is essential to her finding it. She formed her sense of who she ought to be when she was working with Cole Langley; after Cole cracked up, she lost the role he had created for her. When she tries to recruit Roy for the part Cole had formerly played, she is straightforward about her motivation. She is trying to reclaim her past, to recapture the identity she once had: "I had ten good years with Cole, and I want them back." Myra never stops to consider whether those ten years with Cole were truly good, but a symbol planted in the scene that introduces her into the film suggests that in truth they were not.

Myra enters a jewelry store intending to sell a diamond bracelet, doubtless a remnant of her prosperous years with Cole. The jeweler regretfully informs her that even though the platinum setting is genuine, the diamonds are fake. He observes, "A fine setting and workmanship usually means precious stones. It always hurts me when I find they are not. I always hope I am mistaken." This speech has more than one set of latent meanings. After discovering that her bracelet is worth much less money than she had thought, Myra has just offered to sell the jeweler her last remaining asset: her body. His comment on the bracelet is a comment on her: he is disappointed to discover that she, despite her fine setting, is in essence merely a slut. But the bracelet also symbolizes her past life with Cole. She sees it as possessing great value, so much so that she wants to recreate it with Roy. But in reality the satisfactions of this life were as ersatz as the diamonds in the bracelet. Cole eventually went mad, but Myra clings to the illusion that their way of life was fulfilling rather than ultimately destructive.

Myra is fatally out of touch with reality. Her inability to realize that

Roy is seriously ill after he has received his blow to the stomach is consistent with her failure to perceive the sickness at the core of her existence with Cole. Myra does, though, perceive sickness at the core of Roy's relationship with his mother. When Roy turns down Myra's offer to take Cole's place with her in a major league con, she is bewildered until she decides what his true motivation is: "My God, it's your mother." Myra's intuitive leap ignores the practical reasons Roy has for declining her offer. She has admitted to him that Cole ended up in an asylum for the criminally insane. Even if Myra doesn't, the viewer has to acknowledge the validity of Roy's stated reason for not teaming up with her: ". . . you scare the hell out of me." He states she is the sort of woman whom "sooner or later the lightning hits. And I'm not gonna be around when it hits you." Her accusations that Roy is carrying on an incestuous relationship with his mother, therefore, can be taken as evasions of the truths Roy has spoken about her and the course of life she has chosen to follow. And Roy's final characterization of her is accurate: "Your mind is . . . filthy. . . ." Yet the very violence of Roy's reaction to her accusations indicates that he is resisting a measure of truth within them. If Myra's imputations of outright incest between Roy and Lilly are surely false (David Denby sees "a suggestion of past incestuous relations" between Roy and Lilly,[2] but I do not), her final line to him—"And you don't even know it"—seems more genuinely perceptive.

After she leaves Roy's apartment building, Myra goes after Lilly—and Lilly's money. Myra's motivations undoubtedly go beyond simple greed. She and Lilly have been at odds since their first meeting at the hospital where they exchanged snide remarks about each other's age (Myra to Lilly: "Now that I see you in the light, you're plenty old enough to be Roy's mother." Lilly to Myra: "Aren't we all?"). Myra now sees Lilly as directly her rival for Roy's commitment; it seems to her that it is Lilly who stands between her and her dream to relive the glory days with Cole, merely substituting Roy as her partner. She considers it perfectly appropriate, therefore, that she should attempt to remove Lilly from the scene once and for all and steal her money—perhaps to finance future big cons (she had asked Roy to contribute ten to fifteen thousand dollars for that purpose, but he had refused).

When Myra enters the office of the motel in Arizona to which she has followed Lilly, the desk clerk at first mistakes her for Lilly (both women are wearing black scarves): "I thought you were the other lady." After a brief pause Myra replies, "No, I'm me." In a sense this is the statement she is trying to make throughout this part of the film. She perceives that for Roy she has merely been a substitute for his true love—his mother. By killing Lilly she thinks she can demonstrate her superior importance as an individual. But the next scene with her in her motel room indicates that she truly lacks a firm sense of the individuality she is trying to assert. She stands in the middle of her room searching through a large ring of master keys for one likely to open the door locks at the motel. When she finds one she suddenly notices she is standing directly in front of a mirror. The camera moves slowly from showing her in profile to peering over her shoulder from behind, then adjusts its lens to bring her reflected image into sharp focus just as she sees herself. The next shot is only the reflected image with Myra looking uncertainly at herself as if wondering "Who is that woman?" Or perhaps she is wondering if she is capable of carrying out the crime she has planned. If the latter is the case, her concern is justified, for in attempting to murder Lilly, Myra does not succeed in affirming or establishing her identity, merely in losing it altogether.

When Roy comes to the morgue in Phoenix to identify his mother's corpse, both he and the camera look closely at the body's right hand which lacks the red burn that would identify Lilly. But he doesn't say, "That body can't be my mother," instead with his back to the camera he heaves a couple sighs of evident grief and then turns back to it, saying only the single word, "Mom." The curious slight smile on his face after he utters this word is either unnoticed by or uninterpretable to the FBI agent in the room with him. The viewer may have a little trouble with this smile as well. Does it express Roy's admiration for his mother's survival skills? Or his perception of the irony of Myra's fate: in death she is condemned to bear ever after the identity of a woman she hated?

Roy's exact attitude toward his mother throughout the film could be said to be every bit as ambiguous as that smile. He clearly attempts to resist what he regards as her attempt to take control of his life after she saves him from dying of internal bleeding. He rejects her "gift" of Carol and endeavors to reimburse her for his hospital expenses. He is trying to maintain the independence he thought he established by breaking away from Lilly in his teens. On the train back from La Jolla he tells Myra that Lilly has no influence over him: "I make my own decisions. . . . I don't care what she thinks. I left home when I was seventeen with nothin' but stuff I bought and paid for myself. Nothin' from Lilly." But in saying this he ignores what Lilly tried to remind of in the hospital: his life itself is a gift from her, and the only way he can ever be in the condition of having "nothin' from Lilly" is by giving up that life (or, as actually happens in the film, by having her take it back). But after Myra has accused him of having an incestuous relationship with his mother, Roy immediately picks up his phone and calls Lilly to ask if they can "just talk—you know like have a conversation." What is his motivation? Does he want to see her close up to find out if he truly does have incestuous feelings toward her? (Lilly seems to dress for this proposed meeting in a manner designed to encourage such feelings: she is wearing a short black cocktail dress with narrow straps that reveal her shoulders and fair measure of cleavage.) In any case this is the first instance in the film where Roy has made an attempt to reach out toward Lilly, and he is clearly disappointed to arrive at her motel that evening and find her gone (he kicks the balustrade opposite the closed door to her apartment). Roy possibly doesn't understand his own motives for seeking this meeting. After calling her, he asked himself rhetorically, "Who's a boy gonna talk to, if not his mother?" Then he gave a faint snicker and lowered his head, simultaneously raising his hand to his brow, as if amused and then dismayed by the inadequacy of his stated motivation for the interview.

When Roy does next see Lilly, he finds her stealing the money he has hidden in the frames of the clown pictures in his room—the proceeds of several years of successful grifting in the Los Angeles area. Lilly's motives for stealing from her own son probably go beyond simple greed or her need for a survival fund after she has been forced to abandon both her job with Bobo and the money in her car that she stole from him. Lilly has been informed over the phone that someone has "blown her out with Bobo," informed him about her car full of money. When she fled, she was followed by Myra, obviously intent on stealing the money after killing her. Lilly knows Myra as Roy's girlfriend. What would be more logical than for Lilly to conclude that Roy and Myra were plotting together to murder and rob her—that he had arranged their meeting for that night merely as a part of his scheme for setting her up for the kill? It would seem simple justice to her, therefore, to take Roy's money to establish herself up in a new life. To be sure, Lilly does not voice such suspicions to Roy when he catches her in his apartment, but to hurl accusations at him would be contrary to her strategies of playing on his sympathies and then, when that appeal doesn't work, his erotic feelings for her.

Lilly, having killed Myra, has in some sense merged her identity with the (slightly) younger woman. When she comes to Roy's apartment, Lilly is wearing the dress Myra was wearing when pursuing her, which is also the dress Myra wore the last time she visited Roy. When Mr. Simms, the apartment manager, sees her pass by in the lobby, he addresses her as "Miss Langtry." Finally, after all else has failed, she resorts to attempting to take Myra's role as Roy's lover. This extreme gambit is necessary because her encounter with her son has up to this point paralleled Roy's final confrontation with Myra, who, like Lilly, wanted his money (to finance a big con set up on the lavish scale established by her former partner and lover, Cole). Roy had given the same succinct answer to her proposal that he now gives to Lilly's intention to take his money: "No."

Tom Milne's analysis of the manifold implications of this brief utterance seems sound to me:

> Roy's terse "No!" resounds like a poetic distillation of the entire tragedy, simultaneously encompassing his nascent pity for his mother, his awareness that money offers her no avenue of escape, his unwillingness to give up his hard-earned cash, and his triumph at having finally avenged his unhappy childhood.[3]

Roy's triumph chiefly consists in his denying his mother what she professes most to need at this point in her life: "Roy, I need this money. I can't run without money. And if I can't run, I'm dead!" This denial probably seems appropriate to him because of his sense that she denied him what he most needed as a child: a mother's love. What she does offer to him later in this sequence—the illusion that he can satisfy his Oedipal desires for her—is not quite the same thing.

The quarrel between mother and son over the money is quite ironic. Roy is doubtlessly correct that Lilly would be better off not taking the money and starting a new life in a legitimate job totally free of any associations with the mob. But even though Roy professes that he is going to follow his own advice and get a legitimate job, he doesn't intend to give up his ill-gotten gains. Lilly tells Roy she "wanted out of the rackets for years" and "now [she] can make a clean break." Roy responds, "You've already made a break. I don't know how clean it is." While Roy is referring most directly to Lilly's having Myra's blood on her hands, the truth is that neither Lilly nor Roy can make a "clean break" so long as they are in possession of stolen money. Roy is upset that Lilly is stealing *his* money, but it properly belongs to all the people he conned to get it. In Jim Thompson's novel Roy Dillon has the offer of a legitimate and potentially well-paying job—sales manager at the firm he has been working at to provide a cover of legitimacy for his illegal activities—but Roy has no such offer in the film.[4] When Lilly shouts indignantly at Roy, "I've never had a legit job in my life!"—as if his suggestion that she get one is totally unreasonable—the viewer has to wonder if Roy is any better prepared to make such an adjustment.

The scene in which Lilly comes on sexually to her own son is shocking and offers vivid substantiation of her earlier statement to him—"You don't know what I'd do—you have no idea—to live." She begins her seduction by asking, "Roy, what if I wasn't really your mother? . . . You'd like that, wouldn't you? Sure you would." She advances toward the camera until she comes into tight close-up, and then the camera tracks with her—still in close-up—as she advances across the room toward Roy. In alternating shots Roy appears first in medium shots (the camera tracking toward him slowly as Lilly advances), then in a medium close-up until finally the characters share the same frame as they come close enough to kiss. Because Lilly for much of this sequence appears as a huge head moving inexorably toward her much smaller son, he appears especially vulnerable; it almost seems that Lilly is approaching with the intent to devour him. Roy is much like the prey hypnotized by the snake as he allows Lilly to initiate a kiss, to which he briefly responds with enthusiasm before pulling back from her.

If Lilly's sexual advance toward Roy is shocking, her next action and its consequences are utterly appalling. She lashes out at him with the attaché case she has filled with his money and shatters the glass he was raising to take a drink from, driving the shards from it into his neck, severing an artery, and causing him to bleed to death. I earlier characterized this killing as "manslaughter," but there is some evidence that could be interpreted as pointing to premeditated murder. Lilly is the one who suggests that she and Roy have something to drink. She selects the glasses for ice water from Roy's kitchen, and she urges the larger of the two glasses upon him ("Take whichever one you want," she says turning the tray so that the bigger glass is closest to his hand). But if Lilly had truly intended to kill Roy, this method would seem rather fluky (it would have been far more certain for her to pick up a knife in his kitchen). Lilly's reaction shots to the blood gushing out of Roy's neck also display both surprise and horror. It therefore seems more likely to me that Lilly was merely intending to disable Roy temporally by hitting him in the neck with the case as she had disabled the drunk in the restaurant with the blow from her elbow. I'd say her seductive routine with Roy was intended to set him up for a mugging, not for the kill.

But whatever her exact intention was, she drops to her knees over her dying son and gives great gasping cries of grief. Then she sobs the word "No!" six times. This process of grieving and denial is brief, though, for she shortly turns aside from the body and starts to gather up the scattered cash from the attache case (which flew open when she hit Roy). The sobs of grief, however, continue as the actions of self-preservation are performed. Lilly then goes into the kitchen to wash the blood off her hands. (We hear the sound of running water although we only see—in long shot through the kitchen door—her legs, hips, and lower back as she leans over the sink.) The last shot of this sequence begins with a close-up of the attaché case standing on the floor. Then Lilly's hand reaches down into the frame to pick up the case, and we see her legs step over Roy's corpse and stride quickly to the door and out into the hall. Lilly's prime sexual attribute throughout the film has been—not the maternal breast—but her long legs, their shapeliness enhanced by the high heels she habitually wears. Now these legs efficiently carry her away from the scene of her crime, their motion in a low-angle shot sharply in contrast to the next shot—a high-angle, full-body shot of the dead Roy absolutely inert on the floor of the apartment.

My reading of the end of the film is that Lilly simply gets away. Tom Milne seems to want to believe she has not gotten away cleanly: "Lilly may escape at the end, but a car, surely ominously, is following her."[5] That car appears less ominous to me than it does to Milne. As Lilly is driving away from Roy's apartment building, the camera focuses on an apparently empty car parked at the curb that Lilly's car soon passes. That shot may remind the viewer of the earlier shot when Lilly drove off from the motel in La Jolla and passed an apparently empty car, into the front seat of which Myra soon rose to set off in pursuit of Lilly. But here at the end of the film we do not see anyone rise into the driver's seat, and the car does not pull out after Lilly. The car Milne mentions simply turns out from a side street into the stream of traffic as Lilly's car passes the corner. I see no reason to assume that this car is behind Lilly's at the end of the film for any reason other than pure chance. The last action we see in the film is a man running across the street (in extreme long shot) as a break occurs in the flow of traffic. There is no reason to believe that this man has anything to do with Lilly either.

Lilly's behavior toward her son at the end of the film made Pauline Kael recall the line spoken by the actress's father John Huston as Noah Cross in *Chinatown*: "Most people never have to face that at the right time and right place, they're capable of anything."[6] Indeed most people would prefer to believe that there are certain things they wouldn't be capable of at any time or place. Or if it turns out that one is capable of them, after performing such an action one should be overwhelmed by guilt. When Lilly washes up in the kitchen, I'd like to believe she can no more get all the blood off her hands than could Lady Macbeth. But the film actually offers little hope that Lilly will suffer psychological punishment any more than legal punishment. (Myra Langtry will be regarded as Roy's killer since Simms identified Lilly as such when she entered the building.) The moral perspective of *The Grifters* is even more bleak than that of *Chinatown*. Jake Gittes at least believed in justice even if he couldn't achieve it. Lilly Dillon merely believes you do what you have to in order to insure survival—and accept the scars that come along with it. The film expresses what may be the male's ultimate fear: that the nurturing woman ultimately cares more for her welfare than for his.

14

"We Don't Live in That Kind of World, Thelma": Triumph and Tragedy in *Thelma & Louise*

THELMA & *Louise* differs in several respects from every other film I've discussed thus far—and perhaps from the vast majority of all American popular films. As Carol J. Glover has remarked, "Precious few American films have had women at the center and men on the periphery. . . ."[1] And far fewer of those films center their plots on crime and violent death. To be sure, one can argue, as William Johnson does, that the female characters dominate *The Grifters*: ". . . neither Myra nor Lilly is subordinate: both are strong and resourceful. Roy is the least aggressive and most cautious of the trio . . . ; to some extent, he is the sex object over which the other two fight."[2] But Roy nevertheless is a central character in the film, and the audience at the end is far more likely to pity him as a victim than to exult in Lilly's survival. The films that present the fatal woman as a major character do not represent a woman's perspective but rather male fears of loss of dominance and control through yielding to a woman's will. Virtually all men in the real world have considerable experience in their lives of such loss of control and power—as boys when they obey their mothers, as men when they do not what they want to do but what their girlfriends and wives wish them to do. The controlling women of *film noir* and its variants dramatize the male sense that such yielding to female will deprives one of manhood; it is fatal to the ideal of "self-sufficient phallic potency" that Frank Krutnik saw portrayed by Sam Spade in *The Maltese Falcon*.[3] If Krutnik is correct in stating that "patriarchal culture relies upon the maintenance of a gender-structured disequilibrium,"[4] then the controlling female is perceived as a threat not merely to the individual male but to the culture as well.

This point is well-illustrated in the conclusion of *Thelma & Louise* when a veritable army of law enforcement officers stands poised with a massive array of weaponry to blow the two women to pieces unless they capitulate to male authority. The actual crimes the women have committed (manslaughter, armed robbery, kidnapping of a law enforcement officer, property destruction) are less important than what these crimes represent: female resistance to, indeed defiance of, male desire and male control. In the end Thelma (Geena Davis) and Louise (Susan Sarandon) are treated less as criminals than as revolutionaries who must be destroyed lest they foment rebellion among others in their oppressed class. The film itself may be regarded as subversive because, to me at least, it suggests that female violence is a legitimate response to the inherent injustices of the patriarchal culture. The tragedy of the film is not that Louise's earlier experience of this injustice (when she was raped in Texas and nothing was apparently done to punish her assailant) causes her to kill a man bent on performing the same outrage on her best friend, but that the belief of both women in their inability to gain true justice in a male dominated world ultimately leads them to kill themselves.

The deaths of the characters (which we merely anticipate at the very end of the film since it concludes with a freeze-frame of their car poised in mid-air over the Grand Canyon) create a particularly strong sense of tragic waste because the two women have undergone such conspicuous (and in my view positive) growth and development in the course of the film. At the beginning both Thelma and Louise are fixed in essentially limiting roles. Thelma, who was married at eighteen to a man she had been going with since the age of fourteen, is still a child. Louise in contrast seems to be a thoroughly responsible adult, but her role has its limiting and self-destructive aspects as well.

Thelma's childishness is stressed in her opening phone conversation with Louise. "Don't be a child," Louise tells her when Thelma says she has not yet asked Darryl's permission to go off with her for the weekend. Although Thelma doesn't respond to Louise's rhetorical question about Darryl—"Is he your husband or your father?"—it is apparent from their first scene together that Darryl behaves toward her as if he is her father: "Don't holler like that," he commands as if to a small child: "Haven't I told you I can't stand it when you're hollerin'?" The irony of Darryl's treatment of Thelma is that she realizes, as she later tells J.D., that Darryl is childish himself, in fact "prides himself on being infantile." Yet she lets him play the role of heavy father toward her without disputing his right to do so. When Darryl is putting the finishing touches on his hair (presumably in front of a mirror the camera stands in for), Thelma tentatively utters, "Hon," as if about to begin her request for permission to go off with Louise for the weekend. But when he responds with an irritated "What!" she asks him instead what he wants for dinner. She never does ask his permission; instead, like an irresponsible child she simply runs off with Louise without telling him, justifying her behavior to Louise by complaining, "He never lets me do one goddamn thing that's any fun."

Additional instances of Thelma's immaturity abound in the early parts of the film. There is her style of packing: she simply throws things willy-nilly into a big suitcase, at one point dumping in an entire drawer full of disarrayed clothes. (In contrast Louise neatly packs items of apparel still in polyethylene bags from the cleaner's.) She brings a lantern and a pistol along with her for the trip because of childish fears of "psycho killers, bears, snakes" (the kind of menace that the pistol will actually be used against is not anticipated by her). In the car, again like a small child, she puts her feet up on the dashboard. (Louise chides her with a harsh "Thelma!"—probably concerned that she is revealing too much of her long bare legs to men in passing cars.) At one point Thelma poses in the car mirror, pretending to smoke an unlit cigarette. She says she's "smokin' . . . I'm Louise"—exactly like a small child associating maturity with one of the conspicuous bad habits of an adult. Finally, again like a small child she begs Louise "stop somewhere for a minute" instead of driving straight through to their destination. "I never get to do stuff like this," she says in a whiny tone.

Although she has implicitly criticized Darryl for assuming the role of father to Thelma, Louise clearly falls easily into the corresponding role of Thelma's mother—a role more acceptable to the younger woman because Louise is an affectionate and indulgent parent in contrast to the authoritarian and repressive Darryl. Louise's behavior in contrast to Thelma's is conspicuously adult, but it also displays a measure of the hypocrisy that can be regarded as a characteristic negative aspect of adulthood. In the restaurant Louise criticizes two teenaged girls for smoking: "Ruins your sex drive," she warns them. But then she immediately lights up a cigarette for herself when she gets back behind the counter. The instant contrast between her advice and her behavior at first merely seems to be a stock comic device, but the joke perhaps contains a more serious level of meaning. Louise would just as soon ruin her sex drive because in the past it perhaps got her into the situation in Texas where she was raped, and now it has placed her in a relationship with Jimmy that probably seems to her to be going nowhere. Before leaving on her trip with Thelma, Louise tries to call Jimmy from her apartment; his answering machine replies, "I'm not here right now." She reacts by turning his picture face down, as if to suggest her judgment that he is rarely if ever "here right now" for her. Louise, unlike Thelma, has striven to make her life tidy and orderly. The last shot of her apartment displays her immaculately clean kitchen sink. She wears her hair tightly drawn up at the back and further wears a scarf in her convertible lest her hairdo become disarrayed in the breeze. Thelma's hair is loose and flowing, and she allows it to blow freely in the wind. Their hair in a way seems to sum up the two women's characters. Thelma is open, spontaneous, but vulnerable. Louise has tried to make herself tight and controlled to protect herself from forces that would threaten her emotional equilibrium. The incident at the Silver Bullet demonstrates where their chosen patterns of behavior are capable of leading—when a male catalyst is added.

At the bar Thelma's behavior is not exactly more mature but does represent a more advanced age level than her previous childish actions. With Harlan she behaves like an irresponsible adolescent—as if once she is free of Darryl's control, she goes back to behaving the way she did before they were married. She is repeating her past in another way, by once again making a bad choice of male partner. Thelma doubtlessly has no conscious awareness of repeating the past; Louise is dimly aware of that possibility when she first enters the saloon. She tells Thelma, "I haven't seen a place like this since I left Texas." Then out in the parking lot she sees again something she last saw in Texas: a rape about to take place—but with Thelma in the position she was in back then. When she forestalls the rape, Louise for the most part still seems to be tightly in control. With the exception of a couple of vernacular expressions Louise is almost school-marmish in the way she lectures Harlan on his misconduct: when he explains what he was doing by saying, "We're just havin' a little fun," Louise comments, "Looks like you got a real fucked-up idea of fun," and later explains, "When a woman's cryin' like that, she isn't having any fun." She even continues her educational efforts after Harlan is dead: "You watch your mouth, Buddy," she advises his corpse slumped against the rear bumper of a car.

But even if what Louise says during this sequence is perfectly rational, her shooting of Harlan would certainly seem to be completely irrational. She has already prevented the rape; all she and Thelma have to do is drive away from the scene to escape further threat from Harlan. Why does Louise snap and pull the trigger when he declares, "I said, suck my cock"? The film offers no firm basis for answering this question. It is possible that Harlan is repeating something her own rapist said to her back in Texas. Even if that is not the case, certainly in killing Harlan she is symbolically killing the man who brutalized her in the past. Perhaps the exact words Harlan speaks are not important—it is his male arrogance that goads Louise into shooting. His comments—"suck my cock" is preceded by "Bitch, I shoulda gone ahead and fucked her"—indicate to Louise that her efforts at education have failed: Harlan is incapable of *feeling* there was anything wrong with what he was trying to do to Thelma. Perhaps what Louise is trying to kill is the male conception that women are merely objects to be used for their pleasure and that a man need feel no obligation to show any concern for a woman's feelings.

After they drive off from the scene of the shooting, the relationship between Thelma and Louise resumes the course it followed before— with Louise playing mother to Thelma's child. When they stop at the side of the road, Louise notices Thelma's face is bloody, so she pulls out her own scarf to clean up the younger woman's face. Before that she has also played a maternal role in trying to educate Thelma about the workings of the world: she says there's no point in telling the police Harlan was shot because he was trying to rape Thelma. Too many people saw them dancing cheek-to-cheek; everyone would assume Thelma was leading him on and deserved what she got from him. When Louise sums up, "We don't live in that kind of world, Thelma," she means they don't live in the kind of world that believes in women's testimonies about rape (or in general) honors their feelings. Her sweeping generalization is undoubtedly based on her own experience with the rape in Texas. Although shaken by her experience Thelma seems essentially unchanged by it. She does not question Louise's judgment as an adult might, she simply accepts it. As they are driving along the highway, when Louise asks how much money she has, Thelma allows a twenty-dollar bill to fly out of her hand off into the landscape, diminishing her contribution to their funds from $61 to $41. When they stop at a motel, Louise suggests that Thelma go out to the pool and take a swim, "while I figure out what to do." Again Thelma voices no objection to being sent out to play while Mommy determines their destiny.

In the next section of the film, which culminates in her armed robbery of the convenience store, Thelma makes significant strides toward maturity. But a scene in a truck-stop cafe closely following the shooting at the Silver Bullet provides a necessary preliminary step for her later growth. Sitting across the table from Louise, Thelma ironically complains, "This is some vacation. I sure am havin' a good time; this is real fun." Louise bitterly responds, "If you weren't concerned with havin' so much fun, we wouldn't be here right now." Thelma first wonders aloud what Louise's statement is supposed to mean and then is unable to avoid the correct interpretation: "So this is all my fault, is it?" The initial expression on Louise's face in the reaction shot seems to answer this question in the affirmative, then the following close-up of Thelma shows her dawning recognition of the justice of that interpretation. She does not then maturely accept her responsibility and apologize to Louise for having placed her in the situation that led to the shooting; instead she gets up from the table, knocking her coffee cup and saucer to the floor, and announces she is going to the bathroom. It is ambiguous whether

her muttered "sorry" is directed toward Louise or the waitress who has to pick up the broken crockery. Thelma's going off to hide in the bathroom is once again reminiscent of the behavior of a little girl or teenager. Before she gets to the bathroom, though, she attempts to call home. (We hear the phone ringing in the empty house, and the camera tracks in on the microwave oven where Thelma has left Darryl's dinner and a note of explanation.) Thelma's motives for calling are uncertain; but it seems to be a conservative, and perhaps still childish, impulse: a reaching out to patriarchal authority as represented by her husband in hopes it will be able provide a solution to her dilemma. Louise reaches out in much the same way when she attempts to call Jimmy (and once again gets his answering machine). Both women repeatedly learn and ultimately accept in the course of the film that men cannot provide a true answer to their problems.

But the following section of the movie—the journey to and sojourn in Oklahoma City—marks the high point of their hopes as they are centered in men. Thelma's hope, however, is no longer reposited in Darryl after she calls him at home from a pay phone at a roadside store. Although he complains about her not being at home and orders her to return that same day, his true indifference to her is evidenced by his missing part of what she is saying to him because he is more interested a fumble occurring in the football game he is watching on his large-screen television. Irritated by his commands to her, Thelma finally paraphrases the line Louise had spoken to her at the beginning of the film: "Darryl, you're my husband, not my father." Darryl, showing more perceptiveness than he does at any other point in the movie, correctly identifies the source of this observation: "That Louise is nothing but a bad influence." But then he goes on to issue a series of vague threats to Thelma, to which she responds by telling him to him to "fuck" himself—and hanging up. When Louise asks her back in the car how the conversation had gone, Thelma ironically says the things he should have said to her, ending in "Honey, I love you." Then she abruptly asks, "So, how long before we're in goddamn Mexico?"—indicating that all her former reservations about committing herself to flight with Louise have been obliterated by the phone call to Darryl.

After Thelma turns away from Darryl, though, she is tempted to replace him as the man in her life by the hitchhiker J.D. (Brad Pitt). She initially compares Darryl unfavorably to J.D., telling Louise the young man has a "cute butt"—especially in contrast to her husband's: "You could park a car in the shadow of his ass." When Louise finally does consent to allowing J.D. to ride with them, Thelma freely criticizes Darryl in front of him, leading J.D. presently to offer the following character assessment: "If you don't mind my saying so, he sounds like a

real asshole." Thelma clearly doesn't mind, and later doesn't mind invit-
ing J.D. into her motel room and then allowing him to make love to
her, even after he has admitted to being an armed robber who is currently
violating parole. In the morning, after apparently having had the first
orgasm(s?) of her life Thelma is transformed: "I finally understand what
all the fuss is about now." She doesn't indicate to Louise that she has
made any plans concerning a future life with J.D., but she apparently
trusts her lover enough to have left him alone in her motel room with
the envelope of money ($6700) Jimmy has brought to Louise to finance
their escape to Mexico. Thelma thereby learns another important lesson: just because a man can satisfy you physically doesn't mean that he
is satisfactory in other important respects.

Jimmy (Michael Madsen), in contrast to J.D., would seem to be a
suitable, caring, and concerned lover. When Louise called him the
morning after the killing of Harlan, she asked him directly, "Do you
love me?" He hesitated a bit and took another puff on his cigarette
before responding with "Yeah." This delay made Louise unwilling to
pursue the topic any further, but by the time he meets her at the motel
in Oklahoma City Jimmy seems to have decided to make a firm commitment. He not only brings her the $6700 but an engagement ring. Louise
is not only surprised by the ring but plainly reluctant to accept it: "Why
now?" she asks. Jimmy's response is revealing of men's attitudes toward
women: "I thought that's what you wanted." A serious commitment to
a woman—like marriage—is something men offer only because they
think women desire it. (Just as the plainclothes detective advises Darryl
to be gentle with Thelma if she calls, "like you really miss her. Women
love that shit.") Jimmy was not willing to propose to Louise while they
were going together, but now that he perceives the danger of losing her
altogether he makes a last-ditch attempt to bind her to him. It's not
surprising that Louise is reluctant to accept the ring. She tells Jimmy,
"I do love you," but also says, "I think it's time to let go." (While she
does accept the ring when Jimmy presses it upon her the following
morning in the motel restaurant, she ultimately trades it along with all
the rest of her jewelry for an old man's cowboy hat in the final stages
of her flight with Thelma.) In their last conversation in the restaurant
Louise professes amazement at Jimmy's new found ability to "say all the
right stuff," including the following: "I'm not gonna tell anybody anything, and I'm not gonna say that I even saw ya." The only problem is
that he doesn't keep this promise any longer than it takes investigator
Hal Slocumbe (Harvey Keitel) to find him when Jimmy returns home.

Louise undoubtedly comes to suspect Jimmy's betrayal of his promise
(that may be at least one of the reasons she gives his ring away), but
Thelma learns of J.D.'s betrayal immediately when she and Louise return

to her room to find both J.D. and the money missing. Thelma's reaction to the theft is unexpected. Her first response is predictably childish: "I never been lucky, not one time." But then she simply apologizes to Louise and advises her, "Just don't you worry about it." At this point in the film the two women's previous roles reverse: Thelma becomes the mother, gathering up her belongings from the room as Louise sits crying on the floor. Finally she grabs her distraught child by the hand and drags her off to the car. At the beginning of the next sequence with the two women in the car their role reversal is even more complete: Thelma is not only in the driver's seat of the Thunderbird but lights up a cigarette and takes a puff on it. This action, though, is merely preliminary to Thelma's attempt to restore Louise to her normal behavior. First, she promptly hands the cigarette to Louise; then after returning from her robbery of the convenience store, she makes Louise get back behind the wheel for their getaway. Louise can be and is restored to her normal behavior, but after successful execution of the armed robbery Thelma can never go back to her role of irresponsible child again.

We see the robbery only on the convenience store's video tape, but Thelma is clearly poised and recites J.D.'s lines almost as suavely as he had performed them for her in the motel room. She even improvises a few lines and asks the clerk to put in with the money a few of the miniature bottles of Wild Turkey that she favors. The tape of the crime fully supports Thelma's contention to Louise: "It was like I'd been doing it all my life." Later she is equally cool and poised (and polite) when she disarms the highway patrolman and forces him into the trunk of his patrol car. (Here it is Louise's behavior that is more childish: instructed by Thelma to shoot the radio, she first shoots the built-in car radio and has to be further instructed to shoot the police radio.) As the women drive away from the patrol car—Thelma reloading her revolver and Louise putting a clip in the patrolman's automatic—Thelma says, "I just feel I got a knack for this shit," and Louise has to agree: "I believe you do." From the beginning of the film up until about the middle Louise had been the dominant partner in the relationship between the two women; she was more mature and gave Thelma both instruction and guidance. After the robbery the women essentially become equals— with Thelma frequently taking initiative when Louise is unable to do so.

The equality in relationship between Thelma and Louise is accompanied by significant changes in their appearance. At the outset of their trip Louise wore pants and had her hair tightly pulled back in a bun. Thelma wore a loose long dress and her hair was down and flowing. Louise's appearance suggested an almost mannish sense of control while Thelma looked girlish and uninhibited. Toward the end of the film both women are wearing pants; Thelma has her hair drawn back much the same as Louise's, and perhaps equally significant both women conceal their hair under hats. Louise wears the cowboy hat she bartered from the old man; Thelma has on the truck driver's cap she scooped up from the ground after she and Louise blew up his gasoline truck. Their apparel at the end of the film diminishes their feminine attributes (while waiting in the car outside the convenience store Louise started to restore her make-up, then threw her lipstick away instead). We still of course know that Thelma and Louise are women, but they have chosen to discard the appearances designed to appeal to the male sex as if to state un-equivocally that they are not sex objects but human beings.

Thelma in particular achieves levels of insight toward the end of the film that we never would have anticipated from her at the beginning. When she remembers the expression on Harlan's face as Louise shot him, the reason why Louise shot suddenly comes to her: "It happened to you didn't it? . . . In Texas." Although Louise says she's "not talking about it," her reaction clearly indicates that Thelma is correct in her belief that her friend was raped in Texas. Later Thelma comes to terms with her own feelings toward Harlan: "I'm not sorry that son of a bitch is dead: I'm just sorry it was you that did it, not me." Just as Louise's shooting of Harlan was probably also a symbolic punishment of the man who raped her years before, Thelma's rage toward Harlan is fueled by years of grievances toward Darryl. Since she has apparently not had an orgasm with Darryl in all the years of their marriage, sex with him may have often seemed like rape. With the highway patrolman, Thelma states that her aggressive treatment of him is rooted in her marriage: ". . . if you was ever to meet my husband, you'd understand why." When the officer whines to her that he has a wife and kids, Thelma instructs him to be kind to his wife: "My husband wasn't sweet to me; look how I turned out."

For both women, men in the film tend to blur together. The truck driver is simply another version of Harlan the sexual exploiter. Thelma paraphrases a sexist remark of his virtually in Harlan's actual last words: "Does that mean 'suck my dick'?" Both women then fire on his truck, ultimately blowing it up and punishing his sexual harassment of them with loss of property rather than loss of life. Any member of the audience who does not share the attitudes of Harlan and the truck driver probably feels that both men get what they deserve. But the pervasive distrust and hostility the two women come to feel toward all men is ultimately fatal to them. They are unable to trust Hal Slocumbe who seems genu-inely sympathetic toward their plight and concerned for their welfare. To be sure, Slocumbe is not entirely free of sexism: he repeatedly refers to Thelma and Louise as "girls" not "women" ("Don't let them shoot those girls"). And Louise may very well be correct in assuming that his sympathy—even if sincere—will not carry over into the predominantly male judicial system that will try them for their 'crimes.' Still I have to question the wisdom of their decision to drive off the edge of the cliff at the end of the film.

If the decision of Louise and Thelma to take their own lives strikes me personally as misguided, I have to acknowledge that for the two characters and for certain critics of the film it is profoundly satisfying emotionally. Kathleen Murphy, for instance, describes the ending of the film in these terms: "As these splendid creatures choose—rather than accept—their fate, they kiss, mouth to mouth, clasp hands, and head into even higher country, celebrating that rarity in American fiction, a 'holy' marriage of females, transcending gender and even common humanity."[5] The impression of transcendence at the end of the film of course is created almost entirely by the freeze frame—with the car suspended in midair seemingly defying gravity. Psychologically, at this moment, Thelma and Louise have achieved a supreme high. Thelma proposes the final action in these words: "Let's not get caught. . . . Let's keep goin'." For Thelma and Louise driving off the edge of the precipice is a final act of defiance, an ultimate refusal to yield to male authority. They wish to "keep goin'," and more importantly they want to go together. Moreover, both the kiss and the handclasp seem to signify their desire to die together as lovers.

There is a certain amount of critical controversy over the question of whether Thelma and Louise should be regarded as lesbians. In an interview the screenplay writer, Callie Khouri, seems to give support for both sides of the issue: she states emphatically, "I didn't want there to be any question that Thelma and Louise loved each other," but she goes on to profess to have been annoyed when she heard someone say "that Thelma and Louise have a latent lesbian relationship."[6] The film definitely gives the impression that the final kiss is the only overt sexual contact that has taken place between them. But some of Thelma's irresponsible behavior in the first half of the movie could be explained as a masking response to her latent sexual attraction to Louise. Her flirting with Harlan can of course also be explained as Thelma's attempt to pay Darryl back for his philandering (that she must suspect even she has no direct knowledge of it). But consider also that she is going away with Louise for the weekend and even announces to her at the outset of the trip, "I've never been out of town with another girl." Flirting with Harlan may be her way of demonstrating to Louise (and herself) that her (Thelma's) desires are strictly heterosexual and Louise, therefore, shouldn't consider "pulling any funny stuff" over their weekend together. (I don't believe Thelma is consciously aware of any her motives in this regard, but I still consider them a possible strong directing force for her behavior.) Flirting with Harlan, however, leads only to disaster, and that disaster bonds Thelma much more tightly to Louise than she has ever been before. When Louise announces that she is going to Mexico and asks Thelma what she plans to do, Thelma nervously responds, "I don't know what you're asking." She does know that Louise is implicitly asking her to go along with her to Mexico, but she doesn't know what kind of relationship she would be committing herself to if she went along.

As Alice Cross notes, it seems rather incredible that Thelma after being "brutally assaulted and nearly raped" the night before would invite a man she barely knew into her motel room.[7] But this action also needs to be seen in the context of her relationship with Louise. When J.D. arrives at Thelma's door, Louise has already gone off to Jimmy's room, leaving Thelma both jealous and lonely. By succumbing to the suave J.D., Thelma is giving heterosexuality one more try after the disillusionments of her marriage and the assault by Harlan. Her behavior in the restaurant the next morning demonstrates that it is important to Thelma not merely that she has had a satisfying sexual experience with J.D. but that Louise know about it. Leaving the money behind with a self-proclaimed professional robber is not a careless but a deliberate (albeit probably unconscious) act. Thelma partly wants to test J.D., to find out if his commitment to her is stronger than the temptation to pick up easy money. More importantly, she secretly *wants* to lose Louise's money. If she goes on to Mexico with Louise and the entire trip is financed by Louise's savings, Thelma will be in an even greater degree of dependency in the relationship than she was before. Losing the money enables Thelma to step into the role of breadwinner, to gain Louise's respect and to reestablish their relationship on a level of equality. After the convenience store robbery, Thelma has ceased to be the child (her abandonment of the tiny bottles of Wild Turkey for a pint size bottle in the latter part of the film is a sort of visual symbol of this change); now both women are adults together.

Finally, they are also lovers. After Louise's longest phone conversation with Hal Slocombe, Thelma is upset and says to Louise, "You aren't gonna give up on me, are ya?" She fears that Louise may be going to "make a deal with that guy"—a deal that would break up their relationship. She is even more afraid that Louise's relationship with another guy, Jimmy, will come between them. She tries to ascertain the depth of Louise's commitment to her old lover by saying, "In a way you've got something to go back for—Jimmy." Thelma makes this speech in long shot with her back to the camera. After Louise calmly but emphatically replies, "Jimmy's not an option," the film cuts to a giant close-up of Thelma as she delivers her next lines: "Somethin's crossed over in me, and I can't go back. I mean . . . I mean I just couldn't live." Then in an equally large close-up, Louise says, "I know. I know what you mean." Thelma delivers the greater part of her lines in this exchange without making eye contact with her friend, but Louise in delivering her lines makes direct eye contact with Thelma, who retains it in her reaction shot. The seriousness with which the characters speak and their eye contact imply that they are saying more than is strictly expressed by their words. What Louise "knows" is that Thelma is really saying, "I just couldn't live" *without you*. What Thelma's words "mean" is a declaration of love.

No overt declaration of love on the part of either character immediately follows this exchange (Louise breaks off the seriousness of the conversation by making a flip comment about the Geraldo show), but the encounter with the truck driver that shortly follows seems to imply the two women are symbolically burning (blowing up) all the bridges that formerly connected them with men. The closest they come to a verbal expression of love is Thelma's comment to Louise just before they reach the canyon: "You're a good friend." But the kiss and the handclasp at the end are clear nonverbal statements of love. By driving off the rim of the canyon the women seem to be saying that, given the nature of society and their own backgrounds, the only way they can consummate their love is through dying together. As the Thunderbird speeds toward the rim, a picture that Louise had taken of both of them at the start of the trip flies out of the car; their former superficial selves have been discarded as their new, deeper selves head toward union in death.

The ending of the film deserves thorough consideration. Thelma proposes the idea of driving off the edge of the cliff in these words: "Let's not get caught. . . . Let's keep goin'." Thelma and Louise do not seem to realize that they are going to die, to cease to exist as the individuals they have become. They see driving into the canyon as a way of avoiding capture (and forced submission to the patriarchal society) and a way of sustaining their relationship (going on together). The film also allows the viewer to deny the deaths of the characters by ending on a freeze frame of the car in mid-air followed by a montage of brief shots from earlier sequences in the film (the last one of Louise giving her driver's license to the highway patrolman suggests that by sailing off into the canyon the two women have successfully evaded the oppressive force of the law). But if one stretches one's imagination beyond the freeze frame, it's impossible not to envision Thelma and Louise having second thoughts on the way down. Romantic delusion sends Thelma and Louise over the edge of the cliff, and film technique invites the viewers to share that delusion—but some of us resist that invitation.

The film leaves the Thunderbird and the two characters hanging in mid-air, but as Janet Abrams pointed out in her review, the film also leaves "plenty of issues suspended in mid-air."[8] One reason Thelma and Louise choose to die is that neither of them believes there is any possibility of their being treated justly (let alone compassionately) by the legal system. Thelma at first seems reluctant to accept Louise's dictum, "We don't live in that kind of world . . . ," but toward the end of the film she calmly accepts the logic of both Louise's killing of Harlan and their flight after the event: "they [legal authorities, the patriarchy] would have made out like I asked for it." But there is really no reason why the viewer should accept the reasoning of the two women. Even in Arkansas a good criminal lawyer might be able to mount a successful defense for Louise in the killing of Harlan. And certainly Thelma and Louise would seem to stand a better chance with the court system than with the floor of the Grand Canyon.[9] Although they are wearing pants at the end of the film and have engaged successfully in 'masculine' activities like armed robbery, property destruction, and high-speed car chases, Thelma and Louise in their final decisive act are stereotypical women in that they are motivated by emotion rather than reason. The emotions that cloud their reason are love (which deludes them into thinking that killing themselves is a way of remaining together) and despair (which convinces them they have absolutely nothing to hope for from men or the patriarchal structure of society—the mere presence of Hal in the film indicates that this assumption is not entirely true). For the viewer who doesn't share the women's final delusions, the dominant emotion created by the ending of the film is a sense of tragic waste. Both women have learned so much about themselves in the course of the film and have developed capacities for action far beyond what they or society would have previously expected of them that it is a great pity they fling away all they have gained in a final dramatic gesture—no matter how satisfying it may have seemed at the time.

Notes

Introduction

1. Mary Anne Doane, *Femmes Fatales: Feminism, Film Theory, Psychoanalysis* (New York and London: Routledge, 1991), 2.

2. Frank Krutnik, *In a Lonely Street:* Film Noir, *Genre, Masculinity* (London and New York: Routledge, 1991), 42.

3. Ibid., 96.

4. Laura Mulvey, *Visual and Other Pleasures* (Bloomington: Indiana University Press, 1989), 198.

Chapter 1. *La Belle Dame Sans Merci* and the Neurotic Knight: Characterization in *The Maltese Falcon*

1. Stanley J. Solomon, *The Film Idea* (New York: Harcourt, 1972), 214.

2. Ibid., 220.

3. Stanley J. Solomon, *Beyond Formula: American Film Genres* (New York: Harcourt, 1976), 211.

4. Thomas Schatz, *Hollywood Genres: Formulas, Filmmaking, and the Studio System* (New York: Random House, 1981), 128.

5. Ibid.

6. Ibid., 129.

7. Sinda Gregory, *Private Investigations: The Novels of Dashiell Hammett* (Carbondale: Southern Illinois University Press, 1985), 96.

8. Schatz, *Hollywood Genres*, 128.

9. Solomon, *Beyond Formula*, 218.

10. Bernard J. Paris, "Third Force Psychology and the Study of Literature, Biography, Criticism, and Culture," *The Literary Review* 24 (1981): 193.

11. Dashiell Hammett, *The Maltese Falcon* (1929, 1930; New York: Vintage, 1972), 29.

12. All dialogue quotations are taken from John Huston, *The Maltese Falcon*, ed. Richard J. Anobile (New York: Avon, 1974).

13. Solomon, *The Film Idea*, 218.

14. Julie Kirgo, "*The Maltese Falcon* (1941)," *Film Noir*, ed. Alain Silver and Elizabeth Ward (Woodstock, N.Y.: Overlook Press, 1979), 182.

15. Janey Place, "Women in Film Noir," *Women in* Film Noir, ed. E. Ann Kaplan (London: British Film Institute, 1986), 35.

16. Solomon, *The Film Idea*, 219.

17. Lawrence Benequist, "Function and Index in Huston's *The Maltese Falcon*," *Film Criticism* 6 (1982): 47.

18. Krutnik, *In a Lonely Street*, 96.

19. Virginia Wright Wexman, "Kinesics and Film Acting: Humphrey Bogart in *The Maltese Falcon* and *The Big Sleep*," *The Journal of Popular Film and Television* 7 (1978): 48–49.

CHAPTER 2. SOMETHING LOOSE IN THE HEART: WILDER'S *DOUBLE INDEMNITY*

1. Schatz, *Hollywood Genres*, 128.
2. Pauline Kael, *Kiss Kiss Bang Bang* (Boston: Little, Brown, 1968), 305.
3. James M. Cain, *Double Indemnity* (1941), in *Cain X 3* (New York: Alfred A. Knopf, 1969), 378.
4. Billy Wilder and Raymond Chandler, *Double Indemnity* (1943; Hollywood, Calif.: Script City, n.d.), A-16.
5. John Allyn, "*Double Indemnity*: A Policy the Paid Off," *Literature/Film Quarterly* 6 (1978): 120.
6. Clair Johnston, "*Double Indemnity*," in *Women in Film Noir*, ed. E. Ann Kaplan (London: British Film Institute, 1986), 101.
7. Ibid., 105–6.
8. Wilder and Chandler, *Double Indemnity*, A-10.
9. Brian Gallagher, "'I Love You, Too': Sexual Warfare & Homeroticism in Billy Wilder's *Double Indemnity*," *Literature/Film Quarterly* 15 (1987): 242.
10. Cain, *Double Indemnity*, 440–41.
11. Wilder and Chandler, *Double Indemnity*, D-127.
12. Ruth Prigozy, "*Double Indemnity*: Billy Wilder's *Crime and Punishment*," *Literature/Film Quarterly* 12 (1984): 168.
13. Richard Schickel's description of Walter Neff's death scene is probably accurate in conveying the effect the filmmaker sought: "At least he dies in the right arms [those of Keyes] . . . within the relationship he should not have spurned, within a circle of light, contrasting vividly with the darkness that has closed more and more tightly around him since his first meeting with Phyllis"—*Double Indemnity* (London: British Film Institute, 1992), 64.

CHAPTER 3. A DIVE INTO THE BLACK POOL: EDWARD DMYTRYK'S *MURDER, MY SWEET*

1. Robin Wood, *Howard Hawks* (London: British Film Institute, 1983), 169.
2. Edward Dmytryk, *It's a Hell of a Life But Not a Bad Living* (New York: Times Books, 1978), 60.
3. Alain Silver and Elizabeth Ward, eds., *Film Noir* (Woodstock, N.Y.: Overlook, 1979), 192, 92.
4. To be sure, the detective is just as ineffectual in Chandler's novel, where in his own apartment he allows Velma/Helen to shoot Malloy five times in the stomach and then escape unmolested; in that scene he would have been shot himself if Mrs. Grayle had not already used all her bullets on Moose before turning the gun on Marlowe—Raymond Chandler, *Farewell, My Lovely*, (1940; New York: Vintage Books, 1976), 240.
5. Dmytryk, *It's a Hell of a Life But Not a Bad Living*, 61.

6. Ibid., 59.

7. John Paxton, *Murder, My Sweet* (Hollywood, Calif.: Script City, n.d.), 127.

CHAPTER 4. LOVE IN THE DARK: HOWARD HAWKS'S FILM VERSION OF *THE BIG SLEEP*

1. Raymond Chandler, *The Big Sleep* (1939; New York: Vintage Books, 1982), 216.

2. Gerald Mast, *Howard Hawks, Storyteller* (New York: Oxford University Press, 1982), 269.

3. Chandler, *The Big Sleep,* 214.

4. Mast, *Howard Hawks, Storyteller,* 270.

5. Chandler, *The Big Sleep,* 10.

6. Donald C. Willis, *The Films of Howard Hawks* (Metuchen, N.J.: Scarecrow Press, 1975), 119.

7. Chandler, *The Big Sleep,* 153.

8. Ibid., 140.

9. James Paris, Julie Kirgo, Alain Silver, "*The Big Sleep* (1946)," in *Film Noir,* 34.

10. Annette Kuhn, *The Power of the Image: Essays on Representation and Sexuality* (London: Routledge and Kegan Paul, 1985), 91–92.

11. Joseph McBride, *Hawks on Hawks* (Berkeley: University of California Press, 1982), 105.

12. David Thomson, "At the Acme Book Shop," *Sight and Sound* 50.2 (1981): 125.

CHAPTER 5. *OUT OF THE PAST:* THE PRIVATE EYE AS TRAGIC HERO

1. Tom Flinn, "*Out of the Past,*" *Velvet Light Trap* 10 (1973): 43.

2. George Turner, "*Out of the Past,*" *American Cinematographer* 65 (1984): 33.

3. Aristotle, *Poetics, XII, Aristotle's Theory of Poetry and Fine Art,* 4th ed. translated by S. N. Butcher (London: Macmillan, 1907), 45.

4. Tom Flinn, "*Out of the Past,*" 39.

5. Michael Walsh, "*Out of the Past:* The History of the Subject," *Enclitic* 5–6 (1981–1982): 10.

6. Ibid., 15.

7. Krutnik, *In a Lonely Street,* 110.

8. Daniel Mainwaring, "Screenwriter Daniel Mainwaring Discusses *Out of the Past,*" *Velvet Light Trap* 10 (1973): 45.

CHAPTER 6. "WITH YOU AROUND, MA, NOTHIN' CAN STOP ME": THE TANGLED EMOTIONS OF CODY JARRETT

1. Ivan Goff and Ben Roberts, *White Heat,* edited by Patrick McGilligan (Madison: University of Wisconsin Press, 1984), 15.

2. Jack Shadoian, *Dreams and Dead Ends: The American Gangster/Crime Film* (Cambridge: MIT Press, 1977), 197.

3. Goff and Roberts, *White Heat,* 30–31.

4. Shadoian, *Dreams and Dead Ends,* 200.

5. Ibid., 199.

6. Thomas Clark, "*White Heat:* The Old and the New," *Wide Angle* 1:1 (1979): 60.

7. Krutnik, *In a Lonely Street,* 200.

8. Shadoian, *Dreams and Dead Ends,* 207.

9. Many viewers of the film (I for one) may be disappointed that the killer of Cody's Ma gets off with minimal punishment at the end of the film. In the last shot in which she appears Verna is in the custody of the police, but they have no more knowledge than Cody of the murder she has committed; hence, she will probably serve only short prison sentence as Cody's accomplice. In the screenplay more strict justice was done: Verna was killed (perhaps accidentally) in hale of shots directed by Cody toward the Treasury agents—Ivan Goff and Ben Roberts, *White Heat,* 190.

10. Tom Conley, "Apocalyse Yesterday," *Enclitic* 1–2 (1981–1982): 141.

11. Patrick McGilligan, *Cagney: The Actor as Auteur* (San Diego: A. S. Barnes, 1982), 200.

12. The screenplay makes Cody Jarrett's death wish somewhat more explicit than the film does. Cody tells Pardo/Fallon that when he was talking to his mother out in the woods, ". . . it was like I was dead. too. And it was kind of a good feelin'"—Ivan Goff and Ben Roberts, *White Heat,* 169.

CHAPTER 7. A DREAMER AND HIS DREAM: ANOTHER WAY OF LOOKING AT HITCHCOCK'S *VERTIGO*

1. Robin Wood, *Hitchcock's Films* (New York: A. S. Barnes, 1977), 77.

2. Warren Sonbert, "Alfred Hitchcock: Master of Morality," *Film Culture* 41 (1966): 35.

3. Wood, *Hitchcock's Films,* 79.

4. Ibid.

5. François Truffaut, *Hitchcock* (New York: Simon and Schuster, 1967), 186.

6. Robin Wood, "Male Desire, Male Anxiety: The Essential Hitchcock," *A Hitchcock Reader,* ed. Marshall Deutelbaum and Leland Pogue (Ames: Iowa State University Press), 228.

7. Ibid., 222.

8. Sigmund Freud, "On Dreams," *The Freud Reader,* ed. Peter Gay (New York: W. W. Norton, 1989), 171.

9. For another interpretation of the figure in black, see William Rothman, "*Vertigo:* The Unknown Woman in Hitchcock," *Images in Our Souls: Cavell, Psychoanalysis, and Cinema,* ed. Joseph H. Smith and William Kerrigan (Baltimore: Johns Hopkins University Press, 1987), 77–78.

10. Lesley Brill, *The Hitchcock Romance: Love and Irony in Hitchcock's Films* (Princeton: Princeton University Press, 1988), 202.

11. de Lauretis, *Alice Doesn't,* 154.

12. Ibid.; and Truffaut, *Hitchcock,* 184,186.

13. Stephen F. Bauer, M.D., Leon Balter, M.D., and Winslow Hunt, M.D., "The Detective Film as Myth: *The Maltese Falcon* and Sam Spade," *American Imago* 35 (1978): 282.

14. Sigmund Freud, *Civilization and its Discontents,* in *The Freud Reader,* 745.

CHAPTER 8. A REVENGER'S TRAGEDY: JOHN BOORMAN'S *POINT BLANK*

1. James Michael Martin, "*Point Blank,*" *Film Quarterly* 21.4 (1968): 40.

2. Michel Ciment, *John Boorman,* trans. Gilbert Adair (London: Faber and Faber, 1986), 79.

3. Stephen Farber, "The Outlaws," *Sight and Sound* 37.4 (1968): 173.

4. Stephen Farber, "The Writer in American Films," *Film Quarterly* 21.4 (1968): 6.

5. Shadoian, *Dreams and Dead Ends*, 318–19.

6. Martin, "*Point Blank*," 42.

7. Shadoian, *Dreams and Dead Ends*, 312.

8. Stephen Farber, "The Writer II: An Interview with Alexander Jacobs," *Film Quarterly* 22.2 (1968–1969): 2–3.

9. Ibid., 3.

10. T. J. Ross, "*Point Blank*: A Stalker on the City," *Film Heritage* 5.1 (1969): 25.

11. Martin, "*Point Blank*," 41.

12. Farber, "The Writer II," 5–6.

13. John Lindsay Brown, "Islands of the Mind," *Sight and Sound* 39.1 (1969–1970): 21. à

14. Farber, "The Writer II," 7.

15. Farber, "The Writer in American Films," 6.

CHAPTER 9. "THE WORST PART": SCORSESE'S *MEAN STREETS*

1. Martin Scorsese, Mardik Martin, and Ethan Edwards, *Mean Streets* (*Season of the Witch*) (Hollywood, Calif.: Script City, n.d.), 111–12.

2. F. Anthony Macklin, "'It's a Personal Thing for Me': An Interview With Martin Scorsese," *Film Heritage* 10.3 (1975): 26.

3. *The Random House College Dictionary*, rev. ed.(New York: Random House, 1982).

4. Michael Bliss, *Michael Scorsese and Michael Cimino* (Metuchen, N.J.: The Scarecrow Press, 1985), 73.

5. Pauline Kael, *Reeling* (Boston: Little, Brown, 1976), 171.

6. Scorsese, Martin, and Edwards, *Mean Streets*, 110–12.

7. Mary Pat Kelly, *Martin Scorsese: The First Decade* (Pleasantville, N.Y.: Redgrave, 1980), 18.

8. Ibid.

9. Macklin, "'It's a Personal Thing for Me," 26.

10. Ibid.

CHAPTER 10. "THE INJUSTICE OF IT ALL": POLANSKI'S REVISION OF THE PRIVATE EYE GENRE IN *CHINATOWN*

1. Virginia Wright Wexman, *Roman Polanski* (Boston: Twayne, 1985), 94–95.

2. Roman Polanski, *Roman by Polanski* (New York: William Morrow, 1984), 348.

3. John G. Cawelti, "*Chinatown* and Generic Transformation in Recent American Films," *Film Genre Reader*, ed. Barry Keith Grant (Austin: University of Texas Press, 1986), 186.

4. Polanski, *Roman by Polanski*, 351.

5. Robert Towne, *Chinatown* (third draft) (Hollywood, Calif.: Script City, n.d.), 128.

6. Ibid.

7. John Simon, *Reverse Angle: A Decade of American Films* (New York: Clarkson N. Potter, 1982), 156.

8. Polanski, *Roman by Polanski*, 348.

9. Towne, *Chinatown* (third draft), 145.

10. Ibid.

11. Ibid., 141.

12. Barbara Leaming, *Polanski, A Biography: The Filmmaker as Voyeur* (New York: Simon and Schuster, 1981), 142.

13. R. Barton Palmer, "*Chinatown* and the Detective Story," *Literature/Film Quarterly* 5.2 (1977): 117.

14. Polanski, *Roman by Polanski*, 350.

15. Ibid., 14–15.

16. Ibid., 58.

17. Barbara Linderman, "Oedipus in Chinatown," *Enclitic* 5–6 (1981–1982): 202.

CHAPTER 11. EATING THEIR CHILDREN: THE HONOR OF THE PRIZZIS

1. Richard Condon, *Prizzi's Honor* (New York: Coward, McGann & Geoghegan, 1982), 115.

2. Ibid., 314–15.

3. Pauline Kael, *State of the Art* (New York: Dutton, 1985), 377.

4. Ibid., 378.

5. Lawrence Grobel, *The Hustons* (New York: Charles Scribner's Sons, 1989), 761.

6. Richard Condon and Janet Roach, *Prizzi's Honor* (Hollywood, Calif.: Script City, 1984), 66.

7. Pauline Kael, *State of the Art*, 376.

8. Terence Raftery, "House Odds," *Sight and Sound* 54.4 (1985): 255.

9. Grobel, *The Hustons*, 752.

CHAPTER 12. "NOW IT'S DARK": THE CHILD'S DREAM IN DAVID LYNCH'S *BLUE VELVET*

1. For example, see Steve Jenkins, "*Blue Velvet*," *Monthly Film Bulletin* 54 (1987): 100 and Betsy Berry, "Forever in My Dreams: Generic Conventions and the Subversive Imagination in *Blue Velvet*," *Literature/Film Quarterly* 16.2 (1988): 88.

2. Tracy Biga, "*Blue Velvet*," *Film Quarterly* 4.1 (1987): 45.

3. Ron Magid, "*Blue Velvet*—Small Town Horror Tale," *American Cinematographer*, November 1986: 83.

4. David Lynch, *Blue Velvet* (third draft) (Hollywood, Calif.: Script City, n.d.), 28.

5. Biga, "*Blue Velvet*," 45; Pauline Kael, "The Current Cinema: Out There and In Here," *The New Yorker*, 22 September 1986: 100.

6. Lynch, *Blue Velvet*, 43.

7. Sigmund Freud, "Three Essays on the Theory of Sexuality," in *The Freud Reader*, 271.

8. Mulvey, *Visual and Other Pleasures*, 198.

9. Lynch, *Blue Velvet*, 42.

CHAPTER 13. "PERMANENT DAMAGE": MATERNAL INFLUENCE IN *THE GRIFTERS*

1. Jim Thompson, *The Grifters*, (1963; New York: Vintage Crime, 1990), 188.

2. David Denby, "Pros and Cons," *New York*, 10 December 1990: 84.

3. Tom Milne, "The Grifters," Monthly Film Bulletin, February 1991: 32.

4. Such an offer is made to Roy in the screenplay, but he declines it—Donald Westlake, The Grifters (Hollywood, Calif.: Script City, n.d.), 61. 91.

5. Milne, "The Grifters," 32.

6. Pauline Kael, Movie Love: Complete Reviews 1988–1991 (New York: Plume, 1991), 286.

Chapter 14. "We Don't Live in That Kind of World, Thelma": Triumph and Tragedy in *Thelma & Louise*

1. Leo Braudy, Peter N. Chumo II, Carol J. Glover, Harvey R. Greenberg, Brian Henderson, Albert Johnson, Marsha Kinder, and Linda Williams, "The Many Faces of Thelma & Louise," Film Quarterly 45.2 (1991–1992): 21.

2. Albert Johnson, "The Grifters," Film Quarterly 45.1 (1991): 36.

3. Krutnik, In a Lonely Street, 95.

4. Ibid., 75.

5. Kathleen Murphy, "Only Angels Have Wings," Film Comment July-August 1991: 29.

6. Kari J. Winter, "On Being an Outlaw: A Conversation with Callie Khouri," Hurricane Alice 8.4 (1992): 6.

7. Toni Kamins, introd.; Cynthia Lucia, introd.; Pat Dowell, Elayne Rapping, Alice Cross, Sarah Schulman, and Roy Gundmann, "Should We Go Along for the Ride? A Critical Symposium on Thelma & Louise," Cineaste 8.4 (1992): 33.

8. Janet Abrams, "Thelma & Louise," Sight and Sound, July 1991: 56.

9. Pat Dowell says that Thelma and Louise in the film are not really at the edge of the Grand Canyon—"it's actually Dead Horse Point in Utah"—but no one in the film corrects the women's identification of the setting. See Toni Kamins et al, "Should We Go Along for the Ride?," 29.

Selected Bibliography

Abrams, Janet. *"Thelma & Louise."* *Sight and Sound,* July 1991: 55–56.

Allyn, John. *"Double Indemnity:* A Policy that Paid Off." *Literature/Film Quarterly* 6 (1978): 116–24.

Aristotle. *Poetics, XII, Aristotle's Theory of Poetry and Fine Art.* 4th ed. Translated by S.N. Butcher. London: Macmillan, 1907.

Bauer, Stephen F., M.D., Leon Balter, M.D., and Winslow Hunt, M.D. "The Detective Film as Myth: *The Maltese Falcon* and Sam Spade." *American Imago* 35 (1978): 275–96.

Benaquist, Lawrence. "Function and Index in Huston's *The Maltese Falcon." Film Criticism* 6 (1982): 45–50.

Berry, Betsy. "Forever in My Dreams: Generic Conventions and the Subversive Imagination in *Blue Velvet." Literature/Film Quarterly* 16.2 (1988): 82–89.

Biga, Tracy. *"Blue Velvet." Film Quarterly* 41.1 (1987): 44–49.

Bliss, Michael. *Martin Scorsese and Michael Cimino.* Metuchen, N.J.: The Scarecrow Press, 1985.

Braudy, Leo, Peter N. Chumo II, Carol J. Clover, Harvey R. Greenberg, Brian Henderson, Albert Johnson, Marsha Kinder, Linda Williams. "The Many Faces of *Thelma & Louise." Film Quarterly* 45.2 (1991–1992): 20–31.

Brill, Lesley. *The Hitchcock Romance: Love and Irony in Hitchcock's Films.* Princeton: Princeton University Press, 1988.

Brown, Jon Lindsay. "Islands of the Mind." *Sight and Sound* 39.1 (1969–1970): 20–23.

Cain, James M. *Double Indemnity,* (1941). In *Cain X 3.* New York: Alfred A. Knopf, 1969.

Cawelti, John G. *"Chinatown* and Generic Transformation in Recent American Film." In *Film Genre Reader,* edited by Barry Keith Grant. Austin: University of Texas Press, 1986.

Chandler, Raymond. *The Big Sleep.* 1939; New York: Vintage, 1976.

Ciment, Michel. *John Boorman.* Translated by Gilbert Adair. London: Faber and Faber, 1986.

Clark, Thomas. *"White Heat:* The Old and the New." *Wide Angle* 1:1 (1979): 60–65.

Condon, Richard. *Prizzi's Honor.* New York: Coward, McGann & Geoghegan, 1982.

Condon, Richard, and Janet Roach. *Prizzi's Honor.* Hollywood, Calif.: Script City, 1984.

Conley, Tom. "Apocalypse Yesterday." *Enclitic* 1–2 (1981–1982): 137–46.

de Lauretis, Teresa. *Alice Doesn't.* Bloomington: Indiana University Press, 1984.

"Denby, David. "Pros and Cons." *New York,* 10 December 1990, 84, 88.

Dmytryk, Edward. *It's a Hell of a Life But Not a Bad Living.* New York: Times Books, 1978.

Doane, Mary Ann. *Femmes Fatales: Feminism, Film Theory, Psychoanalysis.* New York and London: Routledge, 1991.

Farber, Stephen. "The Outlaws." *Sight and Sound* 37.4 (1968): 170–76.

———. "The Writer in American Films." *Film Quarterly* 21.4 (1968): 2–13.

———. "The Writer II: An Interview with Alexander Jacob." *Film Quarterly* 22.2 (1968–1969): 2–14.

Flinn, Tom. *"Out of the Past." Velvet Light Trap* 10 (1973): 38–43.

Freud, Sigmund. *The Freud Reader.* Edited by Peter Gay. New York: W. W. Norton, 1989.

Gallagher, Brian. "'I Love you, Too': Sexual Warfare & Homoeroticism in Billy Wilder's *Double Indemnity." Literature/Film Quarterly* 15 (1987): 237–46.

Goff, Ivan, and Ben Roberts. *White Heat.* Edited with introduction by Patrick McGilligan. Madison: University of Wisconsin Press, 1984.

Gregory, Sinda. *Private Investigations: The Novels of Dashiell Hammett.* Carbondale: Southern Illinois University Press, 1985.

Grobel, Lawrence. *The Hustons.* New York: Charles Scribner's Sons, 1989.

Hammett, Dashiell. *The Maltese Falcon.* 1929, 1930; New York: Vintage, 1972.

Jenkins, Steve. *"Blue Velvet." Monthly Film Bulletin* 54 (1987): 99–100.

Johnson, Albert. *"The Grifters." Film Quarterly* 45.1 (1991): 33–37.

Johnston, Claire. *"Double Indemnity."* In *Women in* Film Noir, edited by E. Ann Kaplan. London: British Film Institute, 1986.

Kael, Pauline. "The Current Cinema: Out There and In Here." *The New Yorker,* 22 September 1986: 99–103.

———. *Kiss Kiss Bang Bang.* Boston: Little, Brown, 1968.

———. *Movie Love: Complete Reviews 1988–1991.* New York: Plume, 1991

———. *Reeling.* Boston: Little, Brown, 1976.

———. *State of the Art.* New York: Dutton, 1985.

Kamins, Toni, introd.; Cynthia Lucia, introd.; Pat Dowell, Elayne Rapping, Alice Cross, Sarah Schulman, Ray Gundmann. "Should We Go Along for the Ride? A Critical Symposium on *Thelma & Louise." Cineaste* 18.4 (1991): 28–36.

Kelly, Mary Pat. *Martin Scorsese: The First Decade.* Pleasantville, N.Y.: Redgrave, 1980.

Kirgo, Julie. "*The Maltese Falcon* (1941)." In *Film Noir,* edited by Alain Silver and Elizabeth Ward. Woodstock, N.Y.: Overlook, 1979.

Krutnik, Frank. *In a Lonely Street: Film Noir, Genre, Masculinity.* London and New York: Routledge and Kegan Paul, 1991.

Kuhn, Annette. *The Power of the Image: Essays on Representation and Sexuality.* London: Routledge and Kegan Paul, 1985.

Leaming, Barbara. *Polanski, A Biography: The Filmmaker as Voyeur.* New York: Simon and Schuster, 1981.

Linderman, Barbara. "Oedipus in Chinatown." *Enclitic* 5–6 (1981–1982): 190–203.

Lynch, David. *Blue Velvet* (third draft). Hollywood, Calif.: Script City, n.d.

Macklin, F. Anthony. "'It's a Personal Thing for Me': An Interview With Martin Scorsese." *Film Heritage* 10.3 (1975): 13–28, 36.

Magid, Ron. "*Blue Velvet*—Small Town Horror Tale." *American Cinematographer,* November 1986: 60–74.

Mainwaring, Daniel. "Screenwriter Daniel Mainwaring Discusses *Out of the Past.*" *Velvet Light Trap* 10 (1973): 44–55.

Martin, James Michael. "*Point Blank.*" *Film Quarterly* 21.4 (1968): 40–43.

Mast, Gerald. *Howard Hawks, Storyteller.* New York: Oxford University Press, 1982.

McBride, Joseph. *Hawks on Hawks.* Berkeley: University of California Press, 1982.

McGilligan, Patrick. *Cagney: The Actor as Auteur.* San Diego: A.S. Barnes, 1982.

Milne, Tom. "*The Grifters.*" *Monthly Film Bulletin,* February 1991: 31–32.

Mulvey, Laura. *Visual and Other Pleasures.* Bloomington: Indiana University Press, 1989.

Murphy, Kathleen. "Only Angels Have Wings." *Film Comment,* July-Aug. 1991: 26–29.

Palmer, R. Barton. "*Chinatown* and the Detective Story." *Literature/Film Quarterly* 5.2 (1977): 112–17.

Paris, James, Julie Klrgo, and Alain Silver. "*The Big Sleep* (1946)." In *Film Noir,* edited by Alain Silver and Elizabeth Ward. Woodstock, N.Y.: Overlook, 1979.

Paris, Bernard J. "Third Force Psychology and the Study of Literature, Biography, Criticism, and Culture." *The Literary Review* 24 (1981): 181–221.

Paxton, John. *Murder, My Sweet.* 1944; Hollywood, Calif.: Script City, n.d.

Place, Janey. "Women in *Film Noir.*" In *Women in* Film Noir, edited by E. Ann Kaplan. London: British Film Institute, 1986.

Polanski, Roman. *Roman by Polanski.* New York: William Morrow, 1984.

Prigozy, Ruth. "*Double Indemnity:* Billy Wilder's *Crime and Punishment.*" *Literature/Film Quarterly* 12 (1984): 160–70.

Raftery, Terence. "House Odds." *Sight and Sound* 54.4 (1985): 255–57.

Ross, T. J. "*Point Blank:* A Stalker on the City." *Film Heritage* 5.1 (1969): 21–26.

Rothman, William. "*Vertigo:* The Unknown Woman in Hitchcock." In *Images in Our Souls: Cavell, Psychoanalysis, and Cinema,* edited by Joseph H. Smith and William Kerrigan. Baltimore: Johns Hopkins University Press, 1987.

Schatz, Thomas. *Hollywood Genres: Formulas, Filmmaking, and the Studio System.* New York: Random House, 1981.

Schickel, Richard. *Double Indemnity.* London: British Film Institute, 1992.

Scorsese, Martin, Mardik Martin, and Ethan Edwards. *Mean Streets (Season of the Witch).* Hollywood, Calif.: Script City, n.d.

Shadoian, Jack. *Dreams and Dead Ends: The American Gangster/Crime Film.* Cambridge, Mass.: MIT Press, 1977.

Simon, John. *Reverse Angle: A Decade of American Films.* New York: Clarkson N. Potter, 1982.

Solomon, Stanley J. *Beyond Formula: American Film Genres.* New York: Harcourt, 1976.

———. *The Film Idea.* New York: Harcourt, 1972.

Sonbert, Warren. "Alfred Hitchcock: Master of Morality." *Film Culture* 41 (1966): 35–38.

Stark, Richard. *Point Blank! (The Hunter).* Greenwich, Conn.: Fawcett, 1962.

Thomson, David. "At the Acme Book Shop." *Sight and Sound* 50.2 (1981): 122–25.

Towne, Robert. *Chinatown* (third draft). Hollywood, Calif.: Script City, n.d.

Truffaut, Francois. *Hitchcock.* New York: Simon and Schuster, 1967.

Turner, George. "*Out of the Past.*" *American Cinematographer* 65.3 (1984): 32–36.

Walsh, Michael. "Out of the Past: The History of the Subject." *Enclitic* 5–6 (1981–1982): 6–16.

Westlake, Donald. *The Grifters*. Based on the novel by Jim Thompson. Hollywood, Calif.: Script City, n.d.

Wexman, Virginia Wright. "Kinesics and Film Acting: Humphrey Bogart in *The Maltese Falcon* and *The Big Sleep*." *The Journal of Popular Culture Film and Television* 7 (1978): 42–55.

————. *Roman Polanski*. Boston: Twayne, 1985.

Wilder, Billy, and Raymond Chandler. *Double Indemnity*. 1943; Hollywood, Calif.: Script City, n.d.

Willis, Donald C. *The Films of Howard Hawks*. Metuchen, N.J.: The Scarecrow Press, 1975.

Winter, Kari J. "On Being an Outlaw: A Conversation With Callie Khouri." *Hurricane Alice* 8.4 (1992): 6–8.

Wood, Robin. *Hitchcock's Films*. New York: A. S. Barnes, 1977.

————. *Howard Hawks*. London: British Film Institute, 1983.

————. "Male Anxiety: The Essential Hitchcock." In *A Hitchcock Reader*, edited by Marshall Deutelbaum and Leland Pogue. Ames: Iowa State University Press, 1986.

Index